BLACK'S NEW TESTAMENT COMMENTARIES

GENERAL EDITOR: HENRY CHADWICK, D.D.

THE PASTORAL EPISTLES

I TIMOTHY   II TIMOTHY   TITUS

BLACK'S NEW TESTAMENT COMMENTARIES

THE GOSPEL ACCORDING TO ST. MATTHEW
Floyd V. Filson

THE GOSPEL ACCORDING TO ST. MARK
Sherman E. Johnson

THE GOSPEL ACCORDING TO ST. LUKE
A. R. C. Leaney

THE GOSPEL ACCORDING TO ST. JOHN
J. N. Sanders and B. A. Mastin

THE ACTS OF THE APOSTLES
C. S. C. Williams

THE EPISTLE TO THE ROMANS
C. K. Barrett

THE FIRST EPISTLE TO THE CORINTHIANS
C. K. Barrett

THE SECOND EPISTLE TO THE CORINTHIANS
C. K. Barrett

THE EPISTLE TO THE PHILIPPIANS
F. W. Beare

THE FIRST AND SECOND EPISTLES TO THE
THESSALONIANS
Ernest Best

THE PASTORAL EPISTLES
Timothy I & II, and Titus
J. N. D. Kelly

THE EPISTLE TO THE HEBREWS
H. W. Montefiore

THE EPISTLES OF PETER AND OF JUDE
J. N. D. Kelly

THE JOHANNINE EPISTLES
J. L. Houlden

THE REVELATION OF ST. JOHN THE DIVINE
G. B. Caird

COMPANION VOL. I
THE BIRTH OF THE NEW TESTAMENT
C. F. D. Moule

A COMMENTARY ON
THE PASTORAL EPISTLES

I TIMOTHY   II TIMOTHY   TITUS

J. N. D. KELLY, D.D., F.B.A.

PRINCIPAL OF ST. EDMUND HALL, OXFORD

ADAM & CHARLES BLACK
LONDON

FIRST PUBLISHED 1963
REPRINTED 1972, 1976
A. & C. BLACK LIMITED
35 BEDFORD ROW, LONDON WCI

ISBN 0 7136 1366 1

PRINTED IN GREAT BRITAIN BY
REDWOOD BURN LIMITED
TROWBRIDGE & ESHER

CONTENTS

PREFACE   vii

INTRODUCTION   1

    1. THE PERSONALITIES   1

    2. THE CRITICAL PROBLEM   3

    3. THE BIOGRAPHICAL SETTING   6

    4. THE FALSE TEACHERS   10

    5. THE MINISTRY   13

    6. THEOLOGICAL ATMOSPHERE   16

    7. LANGUAGE AND STYLE   21

    8. TWO PRELIMINARY CONCLUSIONS   27

    9. THE QUESTION OF AUTHORSHIP   30

    10. DATE AND MUTUAL RELATIONS   34

    SELECT BIBLIOGRAPHY   37

THE FIRST EPISTLE TO TIMOTHY: TRANSLATION
AND COMMENTARY   39

THE SECOND EPISTLE TO TIMOTHY: TRANSLATION
AND COMMENTARY   153

THE EPISTLE TO TITUS: TRANSLATION AND
COMMENTARY   225

INDEX   260

PREFACE

Anyone working on a commentary on the Pastorals must become increasingly conscious of the debt he owes his predecessors. In my case this is particularly great to the classic exegetes of patristic and Reformation times, whose exposition remains as stimulating as ever, and, among their modern successors, to W. Lock, E. F. Scott, J. Jeremias, M. Dibelius and C. Spicq, who have gone over the ground with such erudition and insight that they have left little for others to glean. To my regret I have not been able to use Dr. C. K. Barrett's admirable short edition, which only appeared when this book was in page-proof.

Inevitably the problem of authorship looms large in the following pages, but I have tried to prevent it from overshadowing the letters themselves. Whether written by Paul or an inspired disciple (the most convinced adherent of either view must, if he is open-minded, admit the strength of the opposite case), they certainly do not match the too common description of them as mere manuals of bourgeois piety and static orthodoxy. They are full of splendid statements of Christian truth and inspiring calls to Christian witness; and they provide incomparable glimpses into the conditions and tensions of church life at a period for which other evidence, on any reasonable theory of dating, is almost completely lacking. As such they deserve to be studied with the closest and most devout attention by Christian people today.

It only remains to inform the reader that, like other editors in this series, I have made my own translation of the original, and to thank the numerous friends who have given me help and encouragement. Among these I should particularly like to mention Professor F. F. Bruce, who kindly read and commented on the Introduction, the Reverend D. Guthrie, who offered valuable suggestions, and Mrs. Etta Gullick, in whose Somerset house the book was begun and in part typed out and who prepared the Index.

Ascension Day, 1963.

ABBREVIATIONS

al.	*Aliter*, i.e. 'otherwise'.
AV	Authorized, or King James, Version of the Bible.
LXX	Septuagint (Greek version of the Old Testament).
m	Marginal note.
Moffatt	*The Bible, A New Translation* by J. Moffatt.
MS(S)	Manuscript(s).
NEB	The New English Bible (New Testament).
N.T.	New Testament.
O.T.	Old Testament.
PG	*Patrologia Graeca*, ed. J. Migne.
PL	*Patrologia Latina*, ed. J. Migne.
RSV	Revised Standard Version of the Bible.
RV	Revised Version of the Bible.
Vulgate	The Vulgate, or Latin, version of the Bible.

Other commentaries have usually been cited by their authors'
names.

INTRODUCTION

1. THE PERSONALITIES

THESE three letters, which form a distinct group in the Pauline corpus, claim to be dispatches of the great Apostle to two of his most trusted lieutenants. They have been given the title 'Pastoral' since early in the eighteenth century because they are addressed to chief pastors and are largely concerned with their duties.

Timothy is one of the best known minor characters of the New Testament. The son of a heathen father and a converted Jewish mother, he first joined Paul's entourage at Lystra, in Lycaonia, at the beginning of the latter's second missionary tour. He was already a Christian of some standing, having probably been converted by Paul when he preached in the locality a year or two previously. The Apostle evidently took to him and persuaded him to accompany him, but first circumcised him as a concession to Jewish susceptibilities (Acts xvi. 1-3). Henceforth he was Paul's constant companion and intimate friend, collaborating with him in several of his letters (1 and 2 Thess., 2 Cor., Phil., Col., and Phm.) and being entrusted with important missions, e.g. to Thessalonica (1 Thess. iii. 2) and Corinth (1 Cor. iv. 17). The Apostle regarded him as his 'fellow-worker', his 'beloved and faithful child in the Lord' (Rom. xvi. 21; 1 Cor. iv. 17). When he was setting out on his last journey to Jerusalem, Timothy was in the party (Acts xx. 4), and he was at his side during his Roman imprisonment. Indeed Paul drew especial comfort from his presence and planned sending him on a mission to the Philippian church (Phil. ii. 19-24).

Our information about Titus is scantier, but he too seems to have been a convert of Paul's and to have enjoyed his fullest confidence. A pagan by birth, he escorted his master on his second journey to Jerusalem, where an attempt, most likely unsuccessful, was made to have him circumcised (Gal. ii. 1-5). Later, when relations with the Corinthian church were at breaking-point, he went there as the Apostle's personal envoy,

1

carrying the harsh letter which was virtually an ultimatum. He seems to have managed the awkward situation skilfully, restoring the community to loyalty and obedience, and after reporting to Paul in Macedonia he was sent back to Corinth to deliver 2 Corinthians and to complete the collection there (2 Cor. vii. 6-16; viii. 6; xii. 17 f.). If he did not stand quite so close to the Apostle as Timothy, he must have been a stronger character, and his service to him started earlier and covered an even longer span.

According to the picture set out in the letters, Timothy and Titus are now apostolic delegates in temporary charge of the churches of Ephesus and Crete respectively. Timothy at any rate is still relatively young (1 Tim. iv. 12; 2 Tim. ii. 22), perhaps in his middle or late thirties, and we get the impression that he is a timorous, sensitive man, whose morale needs bracing. 1 Timothy represents him as presiding over the Ephesian congregation; Paul has left him there, or at any rate has requested him to stay on there, and plans to visit him before long. In the meantime he encourages him to re-establish the sound tradition of Christian teaching in the face of divisive heretical tendencies and, with that objective in view, to organize the ministry and the daily life of the congregation on a proper basis. The letter to Titus, which is similar in occasion and aim, implies that Paul and his correspondent have previously carried out a joint mission in Crete. The Apostle himself has now gone to Greece, intending to spend the winter at the Adriatic town of Nicopolis; Titus has been left behind with the task of setting up a properly ordered ministry in all the towns of the island, and also of putting a stop to the false teaching which is widespread. His assignment seems to be envisaged as of shorter duration, since Paul looks forward to his joining him at Nicopolis.

Both these letters, while addressed to individuals, are plainly intended (if they are real letters) to be read out to the assembled congregation as well. This comes out especially in the greetings at the end, which are in the plural. The tone of 2 Timothy is much more personal, although it too ends with a plural greeting. It has the appearance of being the latest of the three in date, since it represents the Apostle as in close confinement in Rome, chained like a criminal and expecting his execution in the predictable future. Timothy, it seems, is still at Ephesus, and the false teachers are still a menace with their demoralizing influence; Paul puts him on his guard against them. But much of the letter consists of the Apostle's personal admonitions to his disciple to carry out his ministry steadfastly whatever suffering it entails. He longs for his presence, and urges him to come to him before winter sets in.

2. THE CRITICAL PROBLEM

If taken at their face value, the Pastorals thus have a special interest and importance. As letters they differ from the majority of the Paulines, being written to individuals rather than churches, and from Philemon since their character is in varying degrees official, not exclusively personal. They lift the curtain revealingly from aspects of the Apostle's activities which are largely ignored in the rest of his correspondence. They show us something of his relations with his more intimate, responsible colleagues, and illustrate his concern for administrative arrangements, his approach to practical problems, and the new emphases in his later theology. They also supply fascinating glimpses of the Church's life and organization, and of the doctrinal distortions with which it had to wrestle, in the sixties of the first century. So far as Paul himself is concerned, it goes without saying that their evidence for his movements and attitude in his later years is immeasurably precious.

It is as such that the Pastorals were treasured by Christians from the earliest times down to the nineteenth century. Their attestation in the sub-apostolic age and the early second century has been claimed to be as good as that of any of the Paulines except Romans and 1 Corinthians. Several passages in 1 Clement (c. 95), and still more convincingly several in the Ignatian letters (c. 110), seem to echo passages in them so closely that only excessive caution refuses to admit direct dependence. In the latter case the relationship is so close that the counter-theory has been advanced that the author of the Pastorals was himself the copier. On the other hand, it is practically certain, and few have doubted, that Polycarp of Smyrna knew them and quoted them in his well-known letter to the Philippians (at latest c. 135).

From the middle of the second century their position is assured, and they are cited as unquestionably Pauline by Irenaeus, Tertullian, the Muratorian Canon, and Clement of Alexandria. It is true that the heretic Marcion (*c.* 140) did not include them in his mutilated New Testament canon, but the reason is much more likely to have been his dislike of their anti-heretical tone and of their esteem for the Old Testament than that they did not yet belong to the Pauline corpus. The recently discovered *Gospel of Truth*, plausibly ascribed to Valentinus (*c.* 150), also makes no reference to them, although quoting every other book of the New Testament. This again is not surprising; the Gnostics generally, according to Clement and Jerome, repudiated them, and their anti-Gnostic strain supplies a sufficient explanation.

The one really puzzling fact is that the Pastorals do not feature in the Chester Beatty Papyrus (P 46), the earliest Pauline codex (early third century). This has been explained in various ways. As Philemon is also missing, it is possible that the collection in the Papyrus covered only letters addressed to churches. Again, it cannot be ruled out that the complete codex contained the letters. As it stands, the last seven leaves are lacking, and although the space they would have provided seems too short for the Pastorals, there are signs that the copyist was crowding more and more words into each page as he drew near the end. Alternatively, he may conceivably have added three or four more pages to the book. In any case the inference that they did not belong to the Pauline corpus known in Egypt in the early third century is unwarranted, for we have already noted Clement's familiarity with them.

Unfortunately it can by no means be taken for granted today that the letters really come from the Apostle. Since the first decades of the nineteenth century a barrage of criticism has been directed against accepting the claim which they themselves put forward. It is glaringly inconsistent, critics have argued, not only with our information about Paul's life and movements, but with the psychology, the theological spirit, and the very style of the Pastorals, not to mention the heresies and the developed church organization they portray. Many have found these arguments irresistible, and while the traditional view still has sup-

4

porters, the prevailing opinion is that the letters as they stand derive from the sub-apostolic age, perhaps even the middle of the second century, having been composed by some Pauline enthusiast who desired to combat the errorists and brace the Church of his own day with the weight of the Apostle's authority. The utmost that some are willing to concede is that a few genuine Pauline fragments, mostly of a personal character, may have been incorporated in the otherwise pseudonymous text.

This is clearly an issue of overriding importance; our judgment of the value of the letters as well as our understanding of their message must depend on whether the voice speaking through them is Paul's or that of an inspired disciple. Nor can it be settled by simply pointing to the plain statement in their opening paragraphs, supported by direct and indirect references elsewhere, that it is Paul's. Pseudonymity, or the practice of publishing one's own works under the name of some revered personage of the past, was fashionable in both Jewish and Christian circles about the beginning of our era. A large proportion of Jewish writings, both in the Bible and outside it, produced between 250 B.C. and A.D. 200 bear the names of Enoch, Daniel, the patriarchs, and others. Early Christian books like the *Didache* and the apocryphal Gospels and Acts claim to come from apostles and personages like Nicodemus, and there is ground for supposing that certain books of the New Testament itself, such as 2 Peter, Jude, and James, are also pseudonymous. The modern reader who feels an initial shock at what he takes to be fraud should reflect that the attitude, approach, and literary standards of that age were altogether different from those accepted today. The author who attributed his own work to an apostle was probably sincerely convinced that it faithfully reproduced the great man's teaching and point of view. It is also likely that, in the first and early second century at any rate, Christians had little or no interest in the personality of the human agent who wrote their sacred books. The Spirit who had spoken through the apostles was still active in prophetic men, and when they put pen to paper it was he who was the real author of their productions. It was therefore legitimate to attribute all such writings (apart, of course, from compositions which were by their very nature personal) to one or other of the apostles, who had been the mouthpieces of the Spirit and whose disciples the actual authors, humanly speaking, were.

In the following sections we shall be chiefly concerned, in the first instance at any rate, with the critical problem. This might at first sight appear a rather one-sided approach, and liable to give at best a partial impression of the letters. As the problem is posed, however, the discussion will inevitably range over all their key-aspects, and the reader should thus be enabled to see them in perspective and form a comprehensive view of their contents and character.

3. THE BIOGRAPHICAL SETTING

The references to Paul and his activities in the letters are clearly of prime importance. From them we may reasonably expect to form a picture of the situation in which the Pastorals were written, and so perhaps to obtain a clue to their origin. There is general agreement that they cannot be fitted into the Apostle's career as it can be reconstructed from Acts and the acknowledged Paulines, i.e. down to his Roman imprisonment recorded in Acts xxviii.

In 1 Timothy the key passage is i. 3, which reveals that when journeying to Macedonia Paul requested Timothy to stay in Ephesus because of the troubles there. If we assume, with most commentators, that he had himself set out from Ephesus, it is difficult to interpret his trip as a temporary move to the Greek mainland during his three years' residence in the city (Acts xix). We nowhere hear of such a move, and if he had undertaken one it must have been very brief and would not have necessitated arming Timothy with plenipotentiary authority. Still less can it be identified with his final departure from Ephesus mentioned in Acts xx. 1. We know that on that occasion he sent Timothy on ahead, while his own destination was Corinth and, ultimately, Jerusalem; there is no hint of the plans to revisit Ephesus referred to in 1 Tim. iii. 14 and iv. 13. On the other hand, if we assumed that his starting-point was somewhere else than Ephesus, we are left with his much earlier visit to Macedonia in the course of his second missionary tour (Acts xvi. 9 ff.). At that date, however, the Ephesian church was at

6

best embryonic, and was certainly not the going concern depicted in 1 Timothy.

Titus presents similar difficulties, for it presupposes a fairly recent, extensive evangelistic effort by Paul and his young colleague in Crete. His only known visit to the island is the one described in Acts xxvii, when the ship conveying him to Rome sailed along the coast. Its sole stop, however, was a temporary one at Fair Havens, which can scarcely have given him a chance for missionary activity. Further, he spent the following winter at Malta, not Nicopolis (Tit. iii. 12). It has been suggested that he might have crossed over to the island either from Corinth or from Ephesus during his prolonged stays at those places. The former possibility, however, is ruled out by the fact that Tit. iii. 13 represents Apollos as an active Christian worker, whereas he was not converted until after Paul had left Corinth, and the latter is hard to reconcile (among other things) with Titus's involvement in the period in question with the affairs of the Corinthian church. In addition, it is scarcely conceivable that, for all its gaps, Acts could have omitted any mention of such a large-scale, important piece of missionary work.

According to 2 Timothy, Paul is in close confinement, almost certainly at Rome (i. 17), and despite the successful outcome of the preliminary investigation he knows that his fate is sealed (iv. 6; 18). He wants Timothy, who is probably still at Ephesus, to come to him, picking up Mark on the way. We might be tempted to infer that this is the Roman captivity of Acts xxviii, were it not that Timothy and Mark were then in Rome with the Apostle (Col. i. 1; iv. 10; Phm. 24). Further, the references to the cloak left at Troas, to Erastus remaining at Corinth, and to Trophimus lying ill at Miletus (iv. 13; 20) suggest that Paul has been in Asia Minor recently, whereas we know that he came from Caesarea to Rome by way of Crete and Malta and had not been in Asia Minor in the three preceding years. His two years' imprisonment at Caesarea itself (Acts xxiii-xxvi) has therefore been proposed as an alternative. In favour of this is the fact that Paul's itinerary before reaching Caesarea took him through Corinth, Troas, and Miletus. On the other hand, since according to Acts xxi. 29; xx. 4 both Trophimus and Timothy were with their master in Jerusalem, it is hard to see how the one could

7

have been left ill at Miletus and to explain the presence of the other at Ephesus. The mention of Demas, too, creates difficulties; in 2 Tim. iv. 10 he is reported to have abandoned Paul, but we shortly afterwards (on this time scheme) find him in Rome as one of his helpers (Col. iv. 14; Phm. 24). Most important of all, however, is the unambiguous pointer of i. 17 to Rome as the place where the letter was written.

Facts like these make it impossible to find a place for the Pastorals in Paul's known life. This is generally admitted, but widely differing conclusions have been drawn. One which springs readily to mind, especially if Paul's death is assumed to have taken place shortly after the events described in Acts xxviii, is that the situations portrayed, with their various incidents and personal allusions, have been artificially contrived, being either pure inventions or adaptations of actual scenes in the Apostle's career. For confirmation its supporters point to certain contradictions, as they consider them, in the letters themselves. They find it odd, for example, that in 1 Timothy Paul should go to the trouble of writing out detailed instructions and advice for a disciple whom he has just left and is proposing to revisit shortly. Again, while 2 Timothy professes to be written from Rome, the personal and local names mentioned in iv. 10-20 are suspiciously reminiscent (as has already been hinted) of Paul's last journey to Caesarea and of his trial there. For this reason some would argue that the author intended this letter to evoke Paul's Caesarean imprisonment. His mention of Rome at i. 17 is variously explained as an interpolation or an egregious blunder.

This is the line taken by critics who are inclined to doubt the Pauline authorship. It is also adopted, with the necessary modifications, by supporters of the 'fragments hypothesis'. These agree that the general picture of the Apostle's movements is artificial, but claim that the letters incorporate certain authentically Pauline elements whose date and place of composition can, in most cases, be plausibly identified. The alleged inner contradictions will be discussed in the Commentary, and the validity of the 'fragments hypothesis' will come in for examination in a later section of this Introduction. At this stage it will only be observed that, if the letters are really non-Pauline, it is surprising that the author has not made a more convincing job of his pseudo-historical framework. As on this assumption he was acquainted with Acts and the ten Paulines, we should have expected him to represent his letters as originating in readily recognizable situations of the Apostle's life. As it is, the background he has supplied is either one which is entirely imaginary, as in the case of Titus, or one which can only be reconciled with Acts on the theory of inexplicable errors on his part, as in the case of 2 Timothy.

The explanation advanced by conservative critics stands in marked contrast with these theories. According to them, the Pastorals, like the situations they presuppose, belong to the period of Paul's life subsequent to Acts xxviii. 31, and there is therefore no need to be disturbed by the difficulty of fitting them into his career prior to that. They thus reject the widespread modern view that his Roman captivity ended with his execution, arguing that its relative mildness and the nature of the charges brought against him make this most unlikely. There is no suggestion in Acts that it did; properly read, Paul's speech at Miletus (Acts xx. 22-25), which is often taken as implying it, merely gave expression to his expectation at the time. We know that the proconsul Festus was satisfied of his innocence (Acts xxvi. 31 f.), and the report he sent to Rome must have been favourable. The Apostle himself clearly anticipated seeing his friends soon (Phil. i. 25 f.; ii. 24; Phm. 22). His martyrdom cannot in any case be placed earlier than A.D. 64, the year of the outbreak of Nero's pogrom (Eusebius puts it in 67), and it is difficult to see how his house arrest could have lasted so long. It is therefore extremely likely that he was released; and if he was, we are entitled to infer that he resumed his evangelistic work until it was cut short by a second, and this time final, imprisonment in the capital. Such a course of events, however, would clearly allow ample room for the writing of the Pastorals as well as for the activities implied in them.

So far as their account of the closing phase of Paul's life is concerned, the conservatives have made out a very strong case. The question of the authorship of the letters is, of course, logically separate and can be left on one side for the moment. But it is worth pointing out that, whether authentic or pseudonymous, they themselves should probably be taken as the best possible evidence that the Apostle survived his two years' captivity. In the ancient Church it was generally accepted (e.g. Eusebius, *Hist. eccl.* ii. 22) that he had been acquitted and had undertaken a further ministry of preaching before being finally arrested and put to death. There is no need to assume that this tradition merely reflects the contemporary exegesis of 2 Timothy. As early as 95 we find Clement of Rome stating (1 *Clem.* v. 7) that Paul had travelled 'to the limit of the west', which in a Roman writer could only mean Spain; and less than a hundred years later another Roman document, the Muratorian Canon, explicitly declares that he went there from Rome. It is uncritical to dismiss this as a legendary gloss on Rom. xv. 24 and 28, where the Apostle expresses his firm intention of visiting Spain. Clement at any rate was writing at most thirty years after his death, in a church which had full access to the facts and in which people who had known him well were probably still alive to check statements about him. For these reasons the theory of a second Roman imprisonment seems firmly grounded. But if it in fact took place, the alleged difficulty of finding a place for the Pastorals in Paul's career at once vanishes.

4. THE FALSE TEACHERS

In all three letters the writer is greatly preoccupied with heretics, as he considers them, who hawk round a message distinct from, and opposed to, the true gospel, sow strife and dissension, and lead morally questionable lives. He reverts again and again to the theme, impressing on Timothy and Titus (whether these are real persons or characters in his fiction) the urgency of taking counter-measures with every means at their disposal. What is this 'heterodoxy' (1 Tim. i. 3) which he so much dreads, and which has already brought about the spiritual downfall of men like Hymenaeus and Alexander (*ib.* i. 19 f.)? Whatever theory of authorship is adopted, it is reasonable to assume that a concrete type of teaching, or at any rate attitude to Christianity, is envisaged, and even if, as is highly likely (especially if the situations implied are in any sense historical), it took somewhat different forms in Ephesus and Crete, its broad pattern seems to have been much the same at both centres. Despite much obscurity of detail, the following picture, admittedly incomplete and tantalizingly vague, can be pieced together; a fuller discussion will be found in the notes.

The most obvious characteristic of the heresy is its combination of Jewish and Gnostic ingredients. On the one hand, its exponents profess to be 'teachers of the law' (1 Tim. i. 7), although according to the writer they do not know how to make a proper use of it; in Crete a group of them are actually called 'those of the circumcision' (Tit. i. 10). They engage in disputes about the law (*ib*. iii. 9), and are much taken up with 'fables and genealogies' (1 Tim. i. 4), for which a Jewish background is likely since we hear of 'Jewish fables' in Tit. i. 14. On the other hand, they were not Judaizers of the kind Paul had to combat in his earlier ministry. Theirs was an ascetic doctrine involving, for example, renunciation of marriage and abstinence from certain kinds of food, possibly also from wine (1 Tim. iv. 3; v. 23). As a corrective the writer makes a point of defining strictly the limits within which bodily self-discipline may properly be practised (*ib*. iv. 8). Since he also goes out of his way to emphasize the goodness of all God's creation (*ib*. iv. 3-5), there can be little doubt that the people he was criticizing disparaged the material order. Their spiritualizing of the resurrection, which amounted to denying that the body participated in salvation (2 Tim. ii. 18), was of a piece with this dualism. So was their boast to be possessors of a higher, esoteric *gnōsis* (1 Tim. vi. 20), which the writer dismisses as not real knowledge at all, but simply perfervid disputatiousness (*ib*. vi. 4). It is possible, although on the whole unlikely, that they also practised magic (2 Tim. iii. 8; 13).

Because of its Gnostic colouring, many identify the false teaching with the fully developed Gnosticism with which the Church came to grips in the middle of the second century. They find support in the 'fables and genealogies' of 1 Tim. i. 4 (cf. Tit. i. 14; iii. 9), taking the latter term as a reference to the families of aeons which thinkers like Valentinus interposed between God and the world. The unlikelihood of this interpretation will be shown in the Commentary (see pp. 44 f.). In general there is nothing in the sparse, vague hints we are given to indicate that the doctrine attacked had the elaboration or coherence of the great Gnostic systems. As we have seen, it had a markedly Jewish strain, and its exponents were still within the church. Even more implausible is the theory that it was Marcionism. Those who hold this detect in 'the counter-affirmations of what is falsely called knowledge' (1 Tim. vi. 20) an allusion to the *Antitheses* of Marcion (†c. 160), and interpret the writer's concern for the Old Testament (*ib.* iv. 13; 2 Tim. iii. 15 f.) as prompted by Marcion's disparagement of it. But, quite apart from the absence of any organized treatment of the specific tenets of Marcionism in the letters, (*a*) Marcion was not strictly a Gnostic, whereas the heretics had palpable Gnostic leanings; (*b*) it is difficult to see how he, with his literalist approach, could have countenanced 'fables'; and (*c*) the errorists were clearly attached to the law, for which he had no use.

It is in fact unrealistic to look to the well-known Gnostic, or near-Gnostic, systems of the second century for light on the teaching which provoked the Pastorals. Everything suggests that it was something much more elementary; and it is significant that much of the writer's polemic is directed, not so much against any specific doctrine, as against the general contentious-ness and loose living it encouraged. It is perhaps best defined as a Gnosticizing form of Jewish Christianity. This is in itself illuminating, for it is nowadays recognized that Judaism, and particularly sectarian Judaism, provided a fertile soil in which Gnosticism flourished freely. But it also has a significant bearing on the date of the letters. It is apparent that as early as Galatians Paul had found himself up against would-be Christians who combined Gnostic ideas about the world rulers with strict ad-hesion to the Mosaic law. It is the syncretistic Christianity of the Colossian heretics, however, with its *gnōsis*, ascetic regulations, and Jewish legalism, which, in spite of striking differences, supplies us with the most instructive parallel. If anything, it seems to have been more advanced and more destructive of basic Christian truth than the heresy of the Pastorals. But this only serves to emphasize that there is no need, unless we are driven by compelling evidence to the contrary, to look outside the first century, or indeed the span of Paul's life, for such an amalgam of Jewish and Gnostic traits in the Levant.

5. THE MINISTRY

The references in the Pastorals to church organization and the ministry have a special, though inevitably tantalizing, interest. The acknowledged Paulines do not treat the subject directly, although they contain a number of allusions to clergy and other officials as opposed to pneumatics. The reason for this need not be, as is sometimes assumed, that Paul lacked interest in the efficient government of his communities; it is a sufficient explanation that the situations which prompted these letters did not call for such treatment. If the position is different in the Pastorals, this is the result of their author's conviction that, in the special crisis threatening the churches for which he was responsible, the ministry must be one of his chief weapons for combating error and defending the true faith.

So Timothy and Titus are represented as standing at the head of their respective communities; they are apostolic delegates, and the former at any rate has been ordained by Paul himself (2 Tim. i. 6). They have full authority to organize the church, discipline offenders, and in general promote the Christian cause. Under them, and apparently appointed by them, we hear of overseers (or bishops) and elders (or presbyters). At Ephesus, but not, apparently, in Crete, there are also deacons and, in all probability, deaconesses, and provision is made at Ephesus for an order of widows with strict rules of membership. The Ephesian deacons are clearly subordinate officials; they collaborate with their superiors in administrative and pastoral work, without, it seems, having any responsibility for teaching or hospitality. The overseers and elders are represented as presiding over the community, and they receive regular stipends. Since the qualities demanded of both are similar and the two titles seem interchangeable (Tit. i. 5-7), it is highly likely that the offices are identical, or at least overlap. The only argument against this is the fact that 'the overseer' is always used in the singular, while elders are usually spoken of in the plural; but it is fairly certain that the singular is to be taken generically (see note on 1 Tim. iii. 2). The overseers or elders have been ordained by the laying-on of hands (*ib*. v. 22), possibly (but see note on *ib*. iv. 14) form a college with power to ordain, and seem to contain an inner group who, in addition to general oversight, preach and teach (*ib.* v. 17).

It has been suggested that these arrangements find their aptest parallel in Ignatius of Antioch's description of the churches of Asia Minor about 110. According to this, each church had its 'monarchical' bishop, its senate of presbyters, and a group of deacons closely attached to the bishop's person. Who on this interpretation represents the bishop in the Pastorals? If he is taken to be the overseer of 1 Tim. iii. 2 and Tit. i. 7, the objections have to be faced (*a*) that the singular in these texts is probably generic, and (*b*) that there is no hint elsewhere in the letters that any single local official possessed the overriding authority and prestige of the Ignatian bishop. It is indeed hard to see how such a one-man episcopate could have functioned where apostolic delegates armed with the powers of a Timothy or a Titus were installed. In view of this it has been proposed that the passages which mention 'the overseer' may be interpolations reflecting a later stage in the evolution of the office; but this is a desperate expedient without textual warrant. Other scholars, recognizing these difficulties, have boldly identified Timothy and Titus as monarchical bishops, arguing that they are such in all but name. The impression left, however, is that they are the Apostle's personal emissaries, with an *ad hoc*, temporary mandate. Further, had the author intended to represent them as bishops, he would surely have avoided using the title in dealing with the other officials. What in any case the Ignatian letters reveal is a closely articulated hierarchy, with the functions of each order and their relation to each other clearly defined. Of this there is not a breath in the Pastorals, the whole atmosphere of which is much simpler and less sophisticated and indicative of a rather earlier stage in the growth of the ministry.

Is it a stage which is congruous with the degree and type of organization achieved in Paul's lifetime? It cannot nowadays be denied that, for all the respect paid to prophets and other Spirit-moved individuals, there were always officials of a more practical, functional kind in his churches. He frequently mentions them, speaking, for example, of 'those who labour among you and are over you and admonish you in the Lord' (1 Thess.

v. 12), and of 'persons who lend assistance and exercise rule' (1 Cor. xii. 28). In Phil. i. 1 he actually designates them by the names used in the Pastorals, 'overseers and deacons'. It is often objected that, while this is true, the fact that the letters speak of elders as well is a sure indication of a post-Pauline date. The Apostle himself, it is argued, nowhere mentions these by name in his acknowledged letters, and the first reliable testimony to them, apart from Acts, comes from the sub-apostolic age (e.g. Jas. v. 14; 1 Pet. v. 1 f.; 2 Jn. 1). Against this, however, we have unmistakable references in Acts to Paul's appointing elders in Asia Minor (xiv. 23) and summoning the Ephesian elders (xx. 17). A common explanation of these passages is that Luke must have adapted his terminology to what had become current practice when he wrote, but this involves (a) brushing aside what looks like eye-witness testimony, and (b) assuming a much later date for the composition of Acts than, in the opinion of many present-day scholars, seems plausible. No importance should certainly be attached to Paul's silence in earlier letters, since in them he only refers to church officials *en passant*; we should never, for example, have known that he knew overseers and deacons by those names were it not for the fortuitous allusion in Phil. i. 1. As a matter of fact, every Jewish community, in Palestine and the Dispersion alike, had a board of elders at its head, and it is therefore extremely likely that Paul would as a matter of course encourage the appointment of such boards in the churches for which he was responsible.

Our picture of the organization of Paul's churches is admittedly incomplete. There is nothing in it, however, which requires us to place the Pastorals outside his lifetime on the ground that the administrative arrangements they presuppose are more advanced than anything he could have known. We should in any case remember that the Church's institutions were developing rapidly at this time. There are indeed other pointers to an early date, such as the ambiguity in the meaning of 'elder', the lack of precision in regard to the duties of overseers and deacons respectively, the lack of a technical name for deaconesses, and the occasional hints that prophets have been active in recent memory. As regards the first of these, it is remarkable that the Ephesian church seems to be only at the stage of feeling its way towards a clear distinction between the board of elders charged with general supervision and the executive officials of the community (see note on 1 Tim. v. 17). The existence of an order of widows, it is true, has been hailed as demanding a post-Pauline date, and the passage in question certainly contains the earliest explicit mention of such an order. Acts, however, provides evidence that from the beginning widows were treated as an important element in the Christian congregations and were formally organized as a group. In any case the detailed character of the writer's instructions (1 Tim. v. 3-16) may be an indication that the institution was a novel one at Ephesus.

6. THEOLOGICAL ATMOSPHERE

From the theological point of view the Pastorals present a curiously ambiguous aspect. On the one hand, they contain numerous passages which, at first sight at any rate, seem faithfully to reflect the Apostle's characteristic ideas, attitude, and spirit. On the other hand, every reader is conscious of certain marked differences of theological tone, perhaps also of theology, when he turns to them from the acknowledged letters. There is no dispute about this general impression; controversy arises when it is asked how far-reaching and fundamental the theological differences are, and what conclusions are to be drawn from them. In this section we shall glance at a selection of the data, referring the reader to the Commentary for a discussion of particular points.

Let us start with the echoes, if such they are, of Paul's authentic teaching. This can surely be overheard in the author's heartfelt acknowledgement of the revelation of God's mercy in Jesus Christ and his own experience of it as a sinner and blasphemer (1 Tim. i. 12-17; Tit. iii. 3-7), in his clear affirmation that justification has nothing to do with man's deserts but depends wholly on God's grace (2 Tim. i. 9; Tit. iii. 5), and in his confession of Christ as the new man, the redeemer who gave himself a ransom for sinners (1 Tim. ii. 5 f.: cf. i. 15). To these can be added his description of eternal life as both the goal to which Christians are called and as something they can enjoy here and now (*ib.* vi. 12: cf. 2 Tim. i. 1; Tit. i. 2; iii. 7), and of faith in Christ as the means of attaining it (1 Tim. i. 16). His conviction, too, that God called us by his grace before the world was made (2 Tim. i. 9 f.; Tit. ii. 11) is in line with Paul's teaching, and his attitude to such matters as second marriages (1 Tim. iii. 2; 12; v. 9), slaves (*ib.* vi. 1), and the state (*ib.* ii. 1 ff.; Tit. iii. 1) is of a piece with the Apostle's. The same applies to his belief that his personal sufferings will be beneficial to the elect (2 Tim. ii. 10), as also to his remarks about the gentle consideration due to erring brothers (*ib.* ii. 25). It is noticeable that the characteristically Pauline formula 'in Christ' occurs seven times in 2 Timothy and twice in 1 Timothy.

So much, in brief summary, for the Pauline strain in the letters; its prominence is all the more striking since they are largely taken up with non-doctrinal matters. Now for their divergences from what is ordinarily taken to be Paul's teaching. First, we should notice a feature which strikes every reader of the Pastorals, their strong bias in favour of orthodoxy, and their exaggerated concern for the transmission of correct doctrine and loyalty to the inherited faith. For example, the writer harps on 'sound teaching' and has a predilection for the expression 'the knowledge of the truth' (1 Tim. ii. 4; etc.), where 'the truth' stands for orthodox belief in Christ. Evidently he conceives of the Church's faith as a formulated body of truths which must at all costs be preserved intact and which stands in sharp antithesis to every heretical system. In harmony with this is his reliance on creed-like formulae (e.g. 1 Tim. vi. 12 f.; 2 Tim. ii. 8; iv. 1). So, too, is his emphasis on the Church and his description of it as 'the pillar and buttress of the truth' (1 Tim. iii. 15), and his assumption that its officers form a succession of trustees charged with safeguarding and handing down the authorized doctrine (e.g. 2 Tim. ii. 2).

Secondly, the Pastorals as a whole, it is argued, evince what has been called a bourgeois attitude to Christianity, heavily weighted in favour of practical morality and conventional ethics. The virtues stressed are those of a settled, established community, and we hear much of moderation, self-control, and sober deportment. The religious ideal is epitomized for the writer in the Hellenistic term *eusebeia*, i.e. 'piety' or 'godliness', which is foreign to Paul's vocabulary and thinking, and he is repeatedly calling for 'good works' in a way which has no parallel in the acknowledged Paulines.

Thirdly, when we turn to specific theological points, it is noticeable that several of Paul's favourite doctrines, or doctrinal emphases, are absent from the Pastorals. The cross, for example, no longer holds the central position he normally accords it, and nothing is said about the conflict between the flesh and the spirit. Whereas 'Paul's religion was Spirit-filled to the last degree' (B. S. Easton), the Holy Spirit here receives only per-functory mention, while the idea of the believer's mystical union with Christ is (it is alleged) scarcely present at all. What is even more significant, the author, it is claimed, has misunderstood, and as a result has misrepresented, several key-doctrines in the Apostle's theology. Thus in 1 Tim. i. 7 ff. he seems to confuse the law of Moses with law in general, thinking of it merely as a check on evil-doers. Again, his conception of God is not, as was Paul's, that of the loving Father, but is coloured by Jewish and Hellenistic ideas of remoteness and unapproachable majesty (e.g. *ib*. i. 17; vi. 15 f.). Christ is for him the 'mediator', a term used by Paul only of Moses (Gal. iii. 19), while his description of him as 'Saviour' (2 Tim. i. 10; Tit. ii. 13; iii. 6) and his references to his 'manifestation' recall the Hellenistic cultus rather than the Apostle's idiom and thought. By 'faith', too, it is asserted, he means, not abiding trust in Christ or self-committal to him, in the Pauline sense, but either one Christian virtue among the others (2 Tim. ii. 22; iii. 10; Tit. ii. 2) or the accepted belief of the Church objectively understood (1 Tim. iv. 1; 6; vi. 21; Tit. i. 4). Grace, similarly, is not the transforming power it is for Paul, but a helping hand which allows for co-operation on man's part (e.g. Tit. ii. 11 f.).

The reaction of scholars to these seemingly contradictory phenomena has varied greatly. Many, giving full weight to the features just enumerated (and others like them) which seem either strange to Paul or frankly un-Pauline, see in them an insuperable obstacle to authenticity. Taken in conjunction with the general tone of the letters, they point conclusively, in their view, to a period after the Apostle's lifetime, when the creative phase of Christian theology was past and institutionalism was settling in. Put together in circles where Paul was highly esteemed, the Pastorals represent a sincere attempt to give fresh currency to what was believed to be his teaching and to get it accepted as the touchstone of orthodoxy. A difficulty which these critics have to face is the presence, side by side with these traits, of so much convincingly Pauline material. The 'fragments hypothesis', it should be observed, provides no loophole of escape, for none of the passages in question is among the verses it accepts as genuine. The explanation usually advanced is that, since the author is a devout Paulinist who has soaked himself in his master's letters and striven to reproduce their ideas and very language, it is scarcely surprising if he has on occasion come very near success. Even so, it is part of their case that a sharp ear can detect an un-Pauline note here and there in the very passages which are hailed as authentically Pauline.

This reasoning, however, has not convinced everyone. In the opinion of other scholars the Pauline traits are inescapable, and remain the key to the origin of the letters. They freely acknowledge, of course, their prosaic tone and more institutional atmosphere, as well as their theological idiosyncrasy. But, in the first place, these differences seem to them no more than we should expect, having regard to their special purpose, the relatively late date when they were written, and Paul's altered circumstances. For example, since the correspondence is directed against dangerous doctrinal errors, it is only natural that it should lay special stress on orthodoxy and the carefully preserved deposit of doctrine. While this emphasis is admittedly exceptional, a concern for the apostolic tradition is visible in the acknowledged letters, and it is also recognized today that these abound in citations from, or at least echoes of, semi-stereotyped credal formulae. The absence of reference to doctrines prominent in other letters should not surprise us, since the Pastorals only touch on doctrinal matters incidentally. In any case Paul was not called upon to develop every aspect of his teaching in every letter, and (to take but one example) he mentions the Holy Spirit only once in Colossians, only once in 2 Thessalonians, and not at all in Philemon. Again, certain doctrinal novelties in the Pastorals may have been suggested to him by the changed environment of his later years. Thus he may well have derived the Hellenistic religious terms in which he speaks of God and Christ from the imperial cult, of which he must have become increasingly aware, and the language of which he was already beginning to exploit for his own purposes in Phil. iii. 20.

In the second place, these scholars argue that the discrepancies have in any case been greatly exaggerated. For example, the attitude to the law implied in 1 Tim. i. 7 ff. is seen, on careful exegesis, to be fully in accord with the Pauline position as revealed elsewhere. Again, in calling for good works in *ib.* ii. 10; v. 10; 25; etc. (a demand which fits in naturally with his practical aim), the author is not thinking of works enjoined by the Mosaic law but of the visible fruits of the Christian's life of faith, and there are parallels to this in Paul (e.g. Rom. ii. 7; 2 Cor. ix. 8; Gal. v. 6; 2 Thess. ii. 17). If he only designates God 'Father' in his opening greetings, we should remember that the title occurs very rarely in the body of Romans (vi. 4; viii. 15; xv. 6) and 1 Corinthians (viii. 6; xv. 24), despite their greater length and more solidly theological content; while the suggestion that he is oppressed by a sense of God's remoteness is untenable in view of his portrayal of him as a Saviour who desires the salvation of all men (1 Tim. ii. 4) and whose guiding motive is goodness and loving-kindness (Tit. iii. 4). The idea of mystical union with Christ may, in view of the character of the letters, be somewhat in the background, but it is clearly presupposed in at least some of the uses of the formula 'in Christ' (e.g. 1 Tim. i. 14; 2 Tim. i. 9; 13). In the same way the admittedly peculiar treatment of faith in the Pastorals can be largely explained as springing from their preoccupation with what is generally binding upon Christians rather than with personal religion. Even so, we should notice that in his acknowledged letters Paul occasionally gives the word the objective sense of 'the faith' (e.g. Phil. i. 27; Col. ii. 7), while he frequently treats it as a virtue alongside other Christian virtues (e.g. 1 Cor. xiii. 13; 2 Cor. viii. 7; Gal. v. 22; 1 Thess. i. 3). Nor is it true that the characteristic Pauline meaning is entirely absent from the Pastorals, for it can surely be detected in such passages as 1 Tim. i. 16; iii. 13; 2 Tim. iii. 15.

A factor to be borne in mind, in attempting to assess the theological character of the Pastorals, is the strongly Jewish, not to say rabbinical, background of several important passages (e.g. 1 Tim. i. 9 f.; ii. 13-15; iv. 14). This should help to set the Hellenistic traits, on which attention is often exclusively focussed, in proper perspective. The discussion of these and other issues will be continued, with greater detail and over a wider range, in the Commentary. But the illustrations already given indicate that the theological gulf between the Pastorals and the other letters may well be narrower and less significant than is often claimed. It must be admitted that, when all is said and done, a number of peculiarities remain, both in general theological tone and in specific points of doctrinal expression. But it may be pertinently asked whether these are not more likely to be due to the Apostle himself, whose theology never became stereotyped and who was prepared to adapt his thinking to his changing environment, or perhaps to his secretary, than to an imitator steeped in his thought, whom we should expect to have been careful to avoid anything for which there was not a clear precedent in his master's teaching.

7. Language and Style

We must now turn to the language and style of the Pastorals, about which there has been intense discussion since the beginning of the nineteenth century. There is general agreement, on the one hand, that the letters abound in clauses, sentences, even short paragraphs, with an unmistakably Pauline ring, and that their formal structure is also thoroughly Pauline. Their length, for example, like the majority of the Apostle's letters, greatly exceeds the average length of contemporary letters, which worked out at less than ninety words; and their opening and closing formulae are not only closely in line with Paul's, which differed markedly from current practice, but also fit in neatly with the progressive development which these were undergoing (see pp. 39-41). On the other hand, these agreements are offset by at least equally striking differences. Not only is the vocabulary of the letters full of surprises, but their author lacks the Apostle's vigour and variety; he writes smooth, often monotonous sentences, instead of piling up parentheses and anacolutha in the struggle to bring his thoughts to birth. Some go so far as to assert that they can detect a definitely second-century flavour in his writing. It is obvious that, if correctly interpreted, these latter phenomena have an important bearing on the question of authorship, and they have in fact been used as a trump card by those who feel unable to assign the letters to Paul.

First, it is undeniable that in vocabulary the Pastorals stand in a class by themselves in the Pauline corpus. Every keen-sighted reader is vaguely conscious of this, and any doubts he may feel should be set at rest when the data are scientifically analysed. The pioneer in this field was P. N. Harrison, who sought to demonstrate, among other things, (a) that the pro-portion of 'hapax legomena' (i.e. words not to be found else-where, either in the N.T. or in the other Paulines) is inordinately high in the Pastorals as compared with the acknowledged Paulines, (b) that a host of characteristically Pauline expressions are lacking from them, while a number of common words are used with a different meaning than in the other letters, and (c) that the Pastorals have a predilection for certain expressions and word-forms which Paul does not employ elsewhere. Ex-amples of these last are the adjectives 'self-controlled' (Gk. *sōphrōn*) and 'pious' (Gk. *eusebēs*), along with their related nouns and verbs, the use of *epiphaneia* ('manifestation') and *charin echō* ('I thank') for Paul's normal *parousia* and *eucharistō*, and the formula 'It is a trustworthy saying'. Harrison made the further point that a considerable number of the 'hapaxes' of the Pastorals occur in the Apostolic Fathers and the Apologists, which suggested to him that their vogue was in the early second rather than the first century.

Harrison's statistics have been sharply challenged, most suc-cessfully on the ground that his criterion throughout was the defective one of the average of words per page. Even so, the critics of his method have not been able to shake his theses that the vocabulary of the Pastorals is (a) homogeneous, and (b) markedly different from that of the acknowledged Paulines. More recent work, carried out with the aid of up-to-date statistical techniques, has only served to set these conclusions in a clearer and more convincing light. As regards the former, it has been shown that if the words peculiar to each of the Pastorals and the words common to all three are studied in relation to the total vocabulary, the result is a strikingly uniform pattern of distribution, and one peculiar to the Pastorals. As regards the latter, it has been demonstrated, by considering the ratio of total vocabulary to passage length (in terms of number of words) and also by straightforward statistics, (*a*) that the Pastorals deploy a much richer and more varied vocabulary than the other Paulines, and (*b*) that the character of this vocabulary, as shown by the author's choice of individual words and types of words, diverges strikingly from Paul's normal usage. Exact statistics also confirm that the Pastorals are more sparing in Septuagint words, and more lavish in Hellenistic words, than the other letters.

When we turn to style proper, we are confronted by broadly similar phenomena. Most students, for example, have noticed the correct and formal diction of the Pastorals. They show little or none of the dialectical tension, and few if any of the signs of pent-up thought breaking the very framework of language, which normally distinguish the Apostle; the writer seems content for the most part with assertion and exhortation. In general the style of the Pastorals, like their vocabulary, betrays a far closer affinity with that of the educated Hellenistic world and of the popular diatribe than the acknowledged letters. If these seem relatively subjective considerations, it is possible to point to objective and calculable factors, such as the striking absence of a host of particles, prepositions, and pronouns which feature in the acknowledged Paulines. Again, in such things as his use of the definite article the writer differs noticeably from the Apostle, since he avoids such constructions favoured by the latter as the definite article with the infinitive, with the nominative in place of the vocative, with the numeral, with an adverb, and with a whole sentence. He also has no examples of the Pauline use of the adverb or conjunction *hōs* (='as', 'how', 'so that', 'when', etc.) with a participle, an adverb, or *an*. An interesting by-product of these stylistic deviations, as also of the altered vocabulary, is the fact that the average length of a word in the Pastorals is 5·50 letters (5·58 in 1 Tim., 5·26 in 2 Tim., and 5·66 in Tit.), whereas it is 4·82 letters in the Paulines generally.

When illustrated with a wealth of detail, these phenomena

make an impressive showing, and the critics of Pauline authorship have not been slow to exploit them. The weakest and most
speculative of their conclusions is that the Pastorals must be
assigned to the second century, and there can be no doubt that
on this issue at any rate they have gone beyond the evidence. In
general it must be wellnigh impossible, having regard to the
paucity of literature, and particularly Christian literature, available, to be absolutely sure that this or that word or usage smacks
of, say, 125 rather than 65. More particularly, the claim that a
high proportion of the 'hapax legomena' are to be found in the
Apostolic Fathers and the Apologists has proved a boomerang.
First, it has been shown that almost exactly the same proportion
of the 'hapaxes' to be found, for example, in such an undoubted
epistle as 1 Corinthians occur in these very same writers.
Secondly, the proportion in question, 93 out of 175 (going by
Harrison's figures), hardly suggests, even if taken at its face
value, that the author's vocabulary was distinctively second-
century. Thirdly, and more devastatingly, it has been pointed
out that almost all the 'hapaxes' in the Pastorals (on this estimate, 153 out of 175) were in use by Greek writers prior to
A.D. 50. There is clearly nothing in the vocabulary alone which
demands a second-century date for the letters.

What then of the critics' main conclusion, viz. that the discrepancies between the Pastorals and the other letters are inconsistent with the former being the work of Paul? Conservative
students have often tried to challenge it by arguing that, if the
statistical approach is to be successful, the body of material to
be examined must be far more extensive than all three Pastorals
taken together. Nowadays this plea has been robbed of its force
by the development of techniques whose results are absolutely
trustworthy. The homogeneity of the Pastorals with one another
and their dishomogeneity with the other Paulines must be
regarded as an established fact. While this must be freely
admitted, however, it cannot be too strongly urged that the
inference that the Apostle cannot therefore be their author does
not necessarily follow. Two lines of argument may be advanced
in support of this.

First, while difference of authorship is clearly one possible
explanation of the stylistic divergences between two sets of

writings, it is by no means the only one that is possible, and the critic is only warranted in concentrating exclusively on it if much of the other evidence converges in the same direction. If important considerations favour identity of authorship, he is bound to inquire if there are not other explanations which might account for the discrepancies. In the present case, where there are definite pointers to Pauline authorship, several such may be suggested. For example, the Pastorals are an altogether different *genre* of epistle from the rest of the Pauline corpus; they deal with an entirely fresh situation and treat of subjects, like church organization and the qualities desirable in ministers, which Paul had not handled directly before. Because of this we should antecedently expect a different atmosphere, linguistically and otherwise, in the Pastorals. Again, the fact that Paul had been living for several years in the west, facing new forms of pagan worship and propaganda, and probably conversing in Latin a good deal, may also have had an impact on his vocabulary and style. In confirmation it may be pointed out that, if the language of the Pastorals is closer to cultivated Hellenistic Greek than the *koinē* he usually employed, his style was already veering in this direction when he wrote Philippians. Finally, on the assumption that the Pastorals are his work, the Apostle was a much older man when they were penned. This might well account, among other things, for their flatness of style and lack of fire. It might also explain, in some degree at any rate, their relatively larger vocabulary, since *a priori* considerations and observation suggest that a writer's vocabulary increases with age and enlarged experience.

The second line of argument is more far-reaching, and cuts deeper. The question must be asked whether the whole linguistic approach does not suffer from a radical defect through taking for granted that the Apostle was personally responsible for every sentence and word in his letters. It is absolutely certain that he used the services of a secretary for some of them, and it is highly probable that he made use of one for all, including Philemon (cf. 19). Clear pointers to this are the reference to Tertius in Rom. xvi. 22 and his explicit statement in the closing paragraphs of several letters (1 Cor. xvi. 21; Gal. vi. 11; Col. iv. 18; 2 Thess. iii. 17) that he is inserting a farewell line or two in his own hand. In any case we know that, owing to the intractability of ancient writing materials and the resulting slowness of penmanship, it was exceedingly rare in antiquity for letters of the length of Paul's to be written out by the sender himself. This is generally admitted, but the common assumptión almost always is that the Apostle dictated his letters in the word-by-word fashion conventional today. Modern research, however, has rendered this extremely doubtful. There is reason to suppose that, again because of the materials available, dictation was a much slower, more laborious process than it is nowadays, and that it was therefore customary, instead of dictating word by word, to allow a trusted amanuensis a much freer hand in the composition of a letter. In the case of 2 Timothy, it has been pointed out, if Paul is the author and the historical situation is as it is represented, the likelihood of extensive secretarial assistance is doubly strong. He certainly cannot have written it out, or even drafted it in detail, himself, for according to the text he was a prisoner in chains; and the other two letters, which are stylistically of a piece with it, must have originated in the same way.

These are weighty considerations, and it is surprising that they have had little or no influence in this country. Continental scholars have been much readier to take account of them and to admit that they place the linguistic and stylistic differences between the Pastorals and the other Paulines in an entirely new light. It is important to be clear about the exact point at issue, especially as supporters of the 'secretary hypothesis' have often overstated their case. It is highly unlikely, in view of the very individual style of the acknowledged Paulines, with their outbursts of personal feeling and characteristic argumentation, that the secretary charged with writing them out was ever given an entirely free hand. The amanuensis who drafted the Pastorals may, for special reasons, have been allowed a greater measure of responsibility, but again it cannot have been complete freedom, for they are packed with expressions, turns of phrase, ideas, and sequences of thought which are strikingly reminiscent of the other letters. If we assume, as we surely must (in these as in all the Pauline letters), the cooperation of a secretary, we must also infer that he was in fairly continuous touch with the Apostle, possibly being from time to time supervised and supplied with hints and suggestions by him. The point is that, once it is conceded that the process was not one of word-by-word dictation and that the secretary enjoyed even a minimum of initiative and responsibility in drafting the letters, it becomes fruitless to engage in minutely meticulous comparisons of stylistic, or even theological, niceties. If Paul was using a new secretary when he prepared the Pastorals (a plausible supposition if Timothy was the secretary who helped him with the immediately preceding letters), there is ample scope for all the divergences of vocabulary, linguistic tone, style, and even doctrinal emphasis, on which critical attention has so eagerly fastened. We are even entitled to conjecture, in the light of the hints the letters themselves supply, that this new secretary may have been a Hellenistic Jewish Christian, a man skilled in rabbinical lore and at the same time a master of the higher *koinē*.

8. TWO PRELIMINARY CONCLUSIONS

The foregoing sections give an outline sketch of what has been, and continues to be, an immensely intricate debate. It is now time to draw the threads together and attempt to pronounce a verdict. As a first instalment two preliminary conclusions may be set down, the acceptance of which should help to narrow the issues.

First of all, then, irrespective of any decision about authorship, it should be clear that, from whatever angle they are considered, the Pastorals are much more likely to have been written in the first century, or at any rate before, say, 110, than at some date well into the second century. Several scholars have recently tried to locate them between 130 and 160 (or even 180); some would set them in the context of the Church's counter-attack on Marcionism. The improbability of the latter suggestion has already been touched on, and will be dealt with further in the Commentary. Any very late date, however, is difficult to reconcile with Irenaeus's frequent citation of the letters as the work of Paul in the eighties of the second century, not to mention the virtual certainty of Polycarp's use of them *c.* 135 at the latest. It could only be accepted if there were absolutely overwhelming considerations in its favour, and none such is forthcoming. It

27

does not do to argue that Marcion cannot have known the letters since he did not include them in his canon, for our authority on the subject, Tertullian, explicitly states that he rejected them. On the other hand, there is nothing distinctively second-century in their tone or language, and we have seen that the heresies denounced are still within the church and appear to have nothing in common with the elaborate Gnostic systems which were rearing their heads in the middle of the second century. Other traits like the disparaging portrait of Timothy, the apparent ignorance of Acts and the Johannine literature, and the hints that the Spirit is still visibly active, militate against a relatively late date. The clinching argument, however, is supplied by the church order they envisage, for most people are satisfied that it is pre-Ignatian. It is significant that the advocates of a very late date are uneasily conscious of this particular difficulty. They are sometimes driven to plead either that Ignatius's letters are spurious or that the church order they seem to describe, so far from being already established in Asia Minor *c*. 110, was merely an ideal polity which a minority group was agitating to get accepted.

Secondly, whoever wrote them, the letters seem to be the work of a single author; there is no sufficient reason for doubting their integrity. From time to time reference has been made to the 'fragments hypothesis', which has enjoyed a considerable vogue since the middle of last century. According to this the Pastorals were as a whole composed by a devout Paulinist, but by a stroke of luck this man had access to fragments of genuine letters of the Apostle to Timothy and Titus; these he worked into the pseudonymous epistles he was preparing in order to give them an enhanced air of authenticity. Surprisingly enough, supporters of the theory do not hail as Pauline any of the doctrinal passages listed in §6, but confine their attention almost exclusively to the personal and local references in 2 Timothy and Titus. They also differ widely among themselves about the fragments they identify as Pauline and the situations in the Apostle's career to which they assign them. As an example we may cite P. N. Harrison's most recent analysis,[1] which is prob-

---

[1] See *Expository Times*, lxvii, 1955, 80. In his *The Problem of the Pastoral Epistles* (1921) he identified five fragments, but gave a slightly different account of them.

ably the most authoritative in this country. He recognizes the following three sections as Pauline: (1) Tit. iii. 12-15, which he takes to have been written to Titus from Macedonia several months after 2 Cor. x-xiii (the severe letter) and before 2 Cor. i-ix; (2) 2 Tim. iv. 9-15, 20, 21a, 22b, which he suggests were written at Nicopolis after Titus had moved on; and (3) 2 Tim. i. 16-18, iii. 10 f., iv. 1, 2a, 5b-8, 11-19, which he describes as Paul's 'last letter', written from Rome after the preliminary hearing of his case in or about 62.

The attractions of the 'fragments hypothesis' are obvious. Opponents of Pauline authorship have always been embarrassed by the personalia, which are so lifelike and so characteristic of Paul, but which most people agree are most unlikely to have been invented by an imitator, however inspired. The whole theory, however, is a tissue of improbabilities, and it is impossible to find an exact parallel in ancient literature. However ingeniously they are pieced together, the fragments do not read like real letters; and if they are portions of larger wholes, what has happened to the rest of these? It is, of course, easy, with our scanty knowledge of Paul's movements, to propose moments in his career into which they can be more or less plausibly fitted— especially if one feels free to invent situations of which there is no historical evidence; but it is all pure guesswork, and the variety of guesses advanced casts doubt on the whole idea. In any case, what reason have we for detaching them from their present setting? It cannot be seriously maintained that they clash stylistically with their context, and in subject-matter they cohere naturally with it. Other questions, not altogether niggling, may be asked, such as how such banal scraps of correspondence, if they ever existed, came to be preserved, what induced the writer to combine his fragments in such a laborious and hotchpotch way (e.g. Harrison's third fragment is divided up over three chapters), why he did not insert any at all into 1 Timothy, and whether the procedure envisaged is psychologically attributable to a Christian of the first or early second century. Finally, his action poses an awkward dilemma. If the fragments were already known to be Pauline, their reappearance in these letters must have occasioned surprise; if they were not so known (a supposition which prompts the intriguing query how then he alone managed to get hold of them), he must have been sanguine to assume that people would immediately greet them as guarantees of authenticity.

9. THE QUESTION OF AUTHORSHIP

If these two conclusions can be regarded as reasonably assured, it is perhaps optimistic to expect agreement to be reached equally easily about the main critical issue. Certainly the problem of the Pastorals remains one of the most obstinate in the New Testament; one is sometimes tempted to infer that the golden key to its solution has yet to be discovered. Nevertheless there are signs that in more than one field of New Testament studies present-day scholars are not altogether happy with all the verdicts which critical orthodoxy recently regarded as established. To a large extent this is due to their enhanced appreciation of the complexity of the apostolic age, as well as of the tantalizingly fragmentary character of our knowledge of it. Far more, it is evident, was happening then, in the development of ideas and institutions as well as in the interplay of forces of which we often have no inkling, than appears on the surface; in particular, our ignorance of the conditions under which the earliest Christian writings were produced is profound. Paradoxically a by-product of this scepticism is a greater readiness to look again, not necessarily favourably, but more sympathetically, at traditional positions once held to be outmoded.

So far as the Pastorals are concerned, the time for such a reappraisal seems overdue. Three lines of thought, in the present editor's view, deserve to be stressed as making this clear. First, to judge by our examination of the features commonly alleged to be incompatible with Pauline authorship, the strength of the anti-Pauline case has surely been greatly exaggerated. The critics' arguments vary considerably in strength, and the weakest are undoubtedly those based on an analysis of the heresies denounced and of the church organization presupposed. However stringently the evidence is interpreted, these are not really inconsistent with a date in the Apostle's lifetime; and if this is held to have extended into the middle sixties, the difficulty, if difficulty there is, of fitting them in disappears entirely. The

argument from the theological atmosphere and doctrinal idio-
syncrasies of the letters looks at first sight more formidable, but
here again, if the conservative rejoinder set out in §6 has any
force at all, the critics seem to have overplayed their hand. Not
only are the discrepancies fewer than they claim, but several of
the more important are found on inspection to represent develop-
ments of ideas already present in the earlier correspondence;
and it is in any case hazardous to confine the Apostle's thought
within a predetermined mould, without allowing for the impact
of changing times and circumstances. The argument from style
and vocabulary, which many used to find overwhelming, can
also be charged with neglecting the all-important biographical
factor; but it completely collapses, as we have seen, if account is
taken, as it obviously must be, of the assistance which Paul
derived from his secretaries in drafting his letters. It is scarcely
surprising that the importance attached to it in critical circles
has visibly diminished in recent years.

Secondly, even a moderate degree of dissatisfaction with the
anti-Pauline case encourages one to carry the attack into the
critics' country. In this connexion it is worth observing that
the theory of pseudonymity is itself exposed to far-reaching
objections of its own. For one thing, no adequate explanation
has ever been produced why there should be three letters rather
than one, or at most two, seeing that they go over much the
same ground. It has been proposed that the three should be
regarded as a single communication whose threefold form is a
literary artifice, or alternatively that the determined writer may
have decided that his broadside would be all the more effective
if delivered in three successive salvoes; but neither of these pro-
cedures seems natural or likely. Again, only those who have tried
the experiment can appreciate how difficult it is to apply the
theory consistently in practice. In all its forms the assumption
is that the author, using the guise of the Apostle, is giving advice
to church officials contemporary with himself, but his selection
of apostolic delegates like Timothy and Titus, who had no exact
counterparts in the later first or early second century Church,
reduces the appositeness of his message. This is still further
obscured by the wealth of personal detail with which the leading
characters are represented. As an illustration we may cite 2 Tim.

i. 5, which makes excellent sense if understood as addressed by Paul to Timothy, but which, according to one typical exponent of the theory (F. D. Gealy), 'is best interpreted as showing the writer's great confidence and joy in third-generation Christian ministers, and the security he feels in the case of those who in the home have been rooted and grounded in the received (Pauline) form of Christianity. New converts are not to be trusted too far: they bring too many alien ideas and attitudes with them.' The only comment needed is that the original recipients of the letter must have been quick-witted to discern these recondite innuendoes behind the plain and simple meaning of the text. Equally improbable exegetical sleight is called for wherever the personal and historical allusions cannot readily be explained as artificial *mise en scène*.

This brings us face to face, thirdly, with an aspect of the Pastorals which has not been treated directly so far, but which is of crucial importance in determining their origin. Considered in themselves, they do not read like fictions, but give a very convincing impression of being real letters. In part this is created by the personalia which they contain and on which the 'fragments hypothesis' relies—detailed information about the Apostle and his fellow-workers, and instructions, often trivial, to the addressees. It is reinforced by the deeply moving passages, most prominent in 2 Timothy but present in the other letters too, in which Paul seems to be speaking out of his profound religious experience or giving utterance to deep personal emotion. It gains support, too, from the occasional glimpses which are supplied of local conditions and happenings in Ephesus and Crete. Examples of these are the mention of the downfall of Hymenaeus and Alexander (1 Tim. i. 20), the dark references to 'certain persons' who cause trouble (*ib.* i. 3; 6; 18; vi. 10; 21), and the hints that the heresy had a markedly Jewish colouring at Crete while the church organization there was more embryonic.

It is obvious that features like these provide a powerful argument for authenticity, and are particularly embarrassing to any theory of pseudonymity. It will not do to brush them aside, as some attempt to do, with the plea that anyone who was clever enough to devise fictitious epistles must have been equally able to invent a convincingly life-like setting for them. In theory he doubtless could; but the question is, in the first place, whether our supposed pseudonymous author of the first, or early second, century would be likely to possess the sure psychological touch and consummate artistry to introduce, for example, the noble farewell charge contained in 2 Tim. iv. 6 ff., and then to append to it the entirely human, disjointed string of requests, complaints, and personal recollections which fill the following paragraph. In the second place, it may be doubted whether the procedure suggested can be squared with the motives and mental attitude which, if we interpreted them correctly on pp. 5 f., lay behind the early Christian practice of pseudonymity. It is one thing to publish under the name of Paul or some other apostle a treatise, whether in the form of a letter or of something else, which the author sincerely believes to express the great man's teaching, or which he even believes to have been disclosed to him by the self-same Spirit which used the great man as his mouthpiece. It is quite another thing to fabricate for it a detailed framework of concrete personal allusions, reminiscences, and messages, not to mention outbursts of intensely personal feeling, which one knows to be pure fiction but which one puts together with the object of creating an air of verisimilitude.

As has already been remarked, this aspect of the letters is of far-reaching importance. If critics do not always do it justice, one of the main reasons, it may be suspected, is the unshakable conviction which most of them share that the imprisonment recorded in Acts xxviii marked the final chapter in the Apostle's career. On this there is a real divergence among scholars, and in view of the total lack of contemporary evidence this is perhaps inevitable. This very lack of evidence, however, should be a warning against dogmatism, since it implies that anything like certainty is out of the question. The present editor has tried to show (cf. §3) that, apart altogether from the literary problem, if due weight is given to tradition (which in a matter like this should be at its most trustworthy) as well as to the implications of the Pastorals themselves, the strong likelihood is that a further period of missionary activity, followed by a second and final imprisonment in the capital, awaited Paul after the events described in Acts. It is significant that two such scholars as

Harnack and Lietzmann, neither of whom was disposed to accept the Pastorals as Pauline, were both satisfied that the probabilities pointed in this direction.

The cumulative effect of these arguments is impressive. Taken in conjunction with the early external testimony to the letters, the relatively primitive situation they presuppose, and the mass of convincingly Pauline material they embody, it tips the scales perceptibly, in the judgment of the present editor, in favour of the traditional theory of authorship. Other views of course remain possible, since different scholars are likely to judge the evidence differently, and no more than a probable conclusion can in the nature of the case be expected; but he would claim a high degree of probability for this verdict. It is a more debatable question whether the Apostle should be conceived as being personally responsible for every word and phrase in the Pastorals. It is possible to argue that he was, but, if the discussion in §7 was soundly based, it seems much more likely that in composing these last letters he relied extensively— much more extensively, probably, than in his earlier ones—on the cooperation of a secretary. Nevertheless they remain, in substance and spirit as in occasion, his work, and the present-day Christian is justified in assuming that they enshrine his authentic message.

10. Date and Mutual Relations

If we are satisfied that the Pastorals derive from Paul, having been written by him either directly or through a trusted secretary following his instructions, we must place their composition in the shadowy period between his release from his first Roman imprisonment and his execution. As is well known, great uncertainty surrounds the absolute chronology of his life. According to one widely accepted scheme his original arrival in Rome should be dated in the spring of 59, which would give the spring of 61 for his release. According to another possible scheme these two events belong to 61 and 63 respectively. The years and precise circumstances of his death are even more obscure, the only reliable datum being that it took place in Nero's reign (54–68). Many moderns, assuming that he must have been one of the victims of the anti-Christian outburst following on the burning of Rome, point confidently to 64, while Eusebius in his fourth-century *Chronicon* gives 67. Anything like certainty is out of the question, for the fury let loose by Nero's cynical attempt to find scapegoats is not likely to have been confined to the capital or to have spent itself in a few months. It is clear, however, that on almost any calculation we are left with a gap of at least two or three years between our terminal dates.

Unfortunately almost complete darkness enshrouds the Apostle's movements at this time. Indeed, apart from the tradition of his journey to Spain, the only information at our disposal is what can be gleaned from the Pastorals themselves, and this is meagre enough. That 1 Timothy was written in Macedonia, i.e. the north-eastern part of the Greek mainland, emerges from 1 Tim. i. 3. A sojourn there is fully in accord with what we should expect, for the church of Philippi, to which he was so affectionately attached, was situated in Macedonia. His language does not necessarily imply that he had gone there direct from Ephesus, and some have argued that he may well have reached it from the west, having perhaps set out for Spain immediately after his release. This supposition is perfectly possible, as will be shown in the Commentary, but is on the whole less acceptable. As regards Titus, all we can gather from it is that the Apostle must have carried out an extensive missionary tour of Crete during these years, and that when he drafted the letter he was planning to spend the winter at Nicopolis (presumably the town of that name in Epirus). 2 Timothy alone gives really explicit information, for it represents him as a captive (for the second time, as we believe) in the capital at the time of writing, while the clear impression left by 2 Tim. iv. 13 ff. is that Troas, Miletus, and Corinth were the places he visited most recently before his arrest.

These scattered data make a disappointing harvest. It would be wonderfully satisfying if we could weave them together into a coherent scheme which would enable us to follow the Apostle on his journeys over Europe and Asia Minor and assign his three letters to determinate, reasonably well-supported dates, places, and situations. Scholars have produced a number of ingenious reconstructions, but the material they have to work with is so fragmentary and so bafflingly hard to piece together that no reliance can be placed on any of them. It must be remembered that we probably have several years to play with, and also that we have no means of ascertaining whether Paul set off for Spain immediately after his release, as is widely surmised, or whether he made first of all for Asia Minor, which the captivity epistles seem to represent as his intention. The only assured results are, first, that he was in Macedonia when he wrote 1 Timothy, and, secondly, that 2 Timothy, dispatched as it was from his Roman gaol, must be the latest of the three letters. Its composition may be plausibly assigned to either 63 or 65/6, depending on the chronological scheme adopted. We have no certainty at all either where Paul was when he wrote Titus or whether it preceded or followed 1 Timothy. The two-membered greeting at i. 4, contrasting with the three-membered formulae of the other two letters, has suggested to some, and what they conceive to be the more primitive state of the ministry implied to others, that it must be the earliest of the group, while still others have argued that it must be later than 1 Timothy either on the ground that it appears to be a résumé, almost a doublet, of it, or on the basis of their reconstruction of Paul's movements. All these theories are interesting but unconvincing; if we are honest, we must confess that, while these personal references are always likely to intrigue and fascinate us, they give us almost nothing firm to grip hold of. If a guess may be hazarded, it seems probable, in view of the fact that 1 Timothy and Titus go over much the same ground in very similar language, that these two letters at any rate were written fairly close to each other.

SELECT BIBLIOGRAPHY

CLASSICAL COMMENTARIES

Much valuable exegesis can still be found in John Chrysostom's 34 Homilies on the Pastorals (PG, lxii), and in the commentaries of Theodore of Mopsuestia (ed. H. B. Swete), Ambrosiaster (PL, xvii), Jerome (PL, xxvi: on Titus only), Pelagius (PL, xxx: also ed. A. Souter), J. Calvin, Guillaume Van Est (Estius), Dom Calmet, and J. A. Bengel.

EDITIONS

C. K. Barrett, *The Pastoral Epistles* (New Clarendon Bible. Oxford, 1963).

J. H. Bernard, *The Pastoral Epistles* (Cambridge Greek Testament. Cambridge, 1899).

M. Dibelius, *Die Pastoralbriefe* (Handbuch zum Neuen Testament. 3rd ed., revised by H. Conzelmann. Tübingen, 1955).

B. S. Easton, *The Pastoral Epistles* (London, 1948).

F. D. Gealy, *The First and Second Epistles to Timothy and The Epistle to Titus* (The Interpreter's Bible, 11. New York, 1955).

D. Guthrie, *The Pastoral Epistles* (London, 1957).

J. Jeremias, *Die Briefe an Timotheus und Titus* (Das Neue Testament Deutsch. 6th ed., Göttingen, 1953).

W. Lock, *A Critical and Exegetical Commentary on the Pastoral Epistles* (The International Critical Commentary. Edinburgh, 1924).

R. St. John Parry, *The Pastoral Epistles* (Cambridge, 1920).

E. F. Scott, *The Pastoral Epistles* (The Moffatt New Testament Commentary. London, 1936).

E. K. Simpson, *The Pastoral Epistles* (London, 1954).

C. Spicq, *Saint Paul: les Épîtres pastorales* (Études Bibliques. 3rd ed., Paris, 1947).

STUDIES, ETC.

K. Aland, 'The Problem of Anonymity and Pseudonymity in Christian Literature of the First Two Centuries' (*Journal of Theological Studies*, NS. xii, 1961).

H. von Campenhausen, 'Polykarp von Smyrna und die Pastoralbriefe' (*Sitzungsberichte der Heidelberger Akademie*, 1951); *Kirchliches*

Amt und geistliche Vollmacht in den ersten drei Jahrhunderten (Tübingen, 1953).

D. Daube, 'The Laying on of Hands' (*The New Testament and Rabbinic Judaism*, London, 1956).

K. Grayston and G. Herdan, 'The Authorship of the Pastorals in the Light of Linguistic Statistics' (*New Testament Studies*, vi, 1959).

D. Guthrie, *The Pastoral Epistles and the Mind of Paul* (London, 1956); 'The Development of the Idea of Canonical Pseudepigrapha in New Testament Criticism' (*Vox Evangelica*, i, London, 1962).

A. T. Hanson, *Studies in the Pastoral Epistles* (London, 1968).

P. N. Harrison, *The Problem of the Pastoral Epistles* (London, 1921); 'The Authorship of the Pastoral Epistles' (*Expository Times*, lxvii, 1955).

R. J. Karris, 'The Background and Significance of the Polemic of the Pastoral Epistles' (*Journal of Biblical Literature* xcii, 1973).

G. Kittel, 'Die γενεαλογίαι der Pastoralbriefe' (*Zeitschrift für die Neutestamentliche Wissenschaft*, xx, 1921).

G. Kittel and G. Friedrich, *Theologisches Wörterbuch zum Neuen Testament* (esp. articles on γενεαλογία, γνῶσις, διάκονος, ἐπίσκοπος, μῦθος, πίστις, πρεσβύτερος, σπένδομαι).

W. Lütgert, *Die Irrlehrer der Pastoralbriefe* (Gütersloh, 1909).

C. Maurer, 'Eine Textvariante klärt die Entstehung der Pastoralbriefe auf' (*Theologische Zeitschrift*, iii, 1947).

B. M. Metzger, 'A Reconsideration of Certain Arguments against the Pauline Authorship of the Pastoral Epistles' (*Expository Times*, lxx, 1958).

W. Michaelis, 'Pastoralbriefe und Wortstatistik' (*Zeitschrift für die Neutestamentliche Wissenschaft*, xxviii, 1929); *Pastoralbriefe und Gefangenschaftsbriefe* (Gütersloh, 1930); *Einleitung in das Neue Testament* (2nd ed., Bern, 1954).

O. Michel, 'Grundfragen der Pastoralbriefe' (*Auf dem Grund der Apostel und Propheten*: Festschrift für D. T. Wurm, Stuttgart, 1948).

R. Morgenthaler, *Statistik des Neutestamentlichen Wortschatzes* (Frankfurt a.M., 1958).

C. F D. Moule, *The Problem of the Pastoral Epistles: A Reappraisal* (*Bulletin of the John Rylands Library*, 1965).

O. Roller, *Das Formular der paulinischen Briefe* (Stuttgart, 1933).

C. Spicq, 'Pastorales (Épîtres)' (*Supplément au Dictionnaire de la Bible*, Fasc. 36. Paris, 1961).

H. Windisch, 'Zur Christologie der Pastoralbriefe' (*Zeitschrift für die Neutestamentliche Wissenschaft*, xxxiv, 1935).

38

THE FIRST EPISTLE
TO TIMOTHY

1. ADDRESS AND GREETING. i. 1-2

(1) Paul, an apostle of Christ Jesus commissioned by God our Saviour and Christ Jesus our hope, (2) to Timothy, my true child in faith: grace, mercy, and peace from God the Father and Christ Jesus our Lord.

Ancient Greek letters had a standardized opening formula comprising the sender's name, the addressee's name, and a brief salutation—usually just 'Greeting'. While conforming to this pattern, Paul introduces significant modifications of his own. He writes, for example, in the first person, tends to dwell on the status of himself and his correspondents as Christians, and gives the normally colourless good wishes a specifically Christian content. His revised formula developed over the years; as it appears in the Pastorals, it is still undergoing development, but at the same time faithfully reflects the stages it had reached in his earlier correspondence.

Following his regular practice since Galatians (except in Philippians and Philemon, where he was not concerned to appeal to his authority), Paul starts off with the reminder that he is **an apostle of Christ Jesus.** By this he means that he is no mere representative of a local church (for 'apostle' used in this sense, cf. 2 Cor. viii. 23; Phil. ii. 25), but the Lord's personally chosen ambassador, charged to bear witness to his resurrection and proclaim his gospel. This insistence is important in his eyes as adding weight to his message. It has been questioned whether a loyal colleague like Timothy needed such reassurances, but they have point if the letter was written with an eye to being read out to the Ephesian congregation, in which he had many ill-wishers.

Paul's right to the title had often been contested, but here as elsewhere (e.g. Rom. i. 1 and 5; Gal. i. 1) he claims that it had been divinely bestowed; he had been **commissioned by God**

our Saviour and Christ Jesus our hope. Usually he refers his apostolic status to 'the will' of God (1 Cor. i. 1; 2 Cor. i. 1; Eph. i. 1; Col. i. 1; 2 Tim. i. 1), but his present language is stronger. 'Commission' (Gk. *epitagē*) connotes an order, and is often used of royal commands which must be obeyed. It vividly conveys Paul's consciousness that, so far from being only a privilege, apostleship involves responsibility; the apostle is a man under orders from God.

The commission had come to him, presumably at his conversion, from God and Christ, whose action he does not distinguish. The description of God as **Saviour** is characteristic of the Pastorals (1 Tim. ii. 3; iv. 10; Tit. i. 3; ii. 10; iii. 4), and outside them is found in the N.T. only in Lk. i. 47 and Jud. 25. On the rare occasions when Paul employs the term elsewhere (Phil. iii. 20; Eph. v. 23; 2 Tim. i. 10; Tit. iii. 6), he applies it to Christ (see note on 2 Tim. i. 10). The O.T. provided abundant precedent for calling God 'our Saviour' or 'my Saviour' (e.g. Ps. xxv. 5; xxvii. 1; 9; Hab. iii. 18; Is. xii. 2; Ecclus. li. 1), and Paul's usage here is clearly based on Jewish devotional practice. There is thus no need to regard it as a Christian correction of the growing custom of saluting the emperor as saviour.

The whole expresssion, as **Christ Jesus our hope** confirms, has an eschatological slant. God is **our Saviour** because in the coming of Jesus he has inaugurated a redemptive process which he will consummate for his chosen on the last day. Christ is **our hope** (*a*) in a general way, since we have set our hopes on him (cf. Col. i. 27: 'Christ in you, the hope of glory'), and (*b*) more precisely, because we eagerly look forward to his 'manifestation' (1 Tim. vi. 14), when the salvation of which we enjoy a foretaste will be bestowed in full measure.

2   In addressing Timothy as **my true child** (the Greek noun is the intimate *teknon*) **in faith** Paul is underlining their relationship of trust and affection, and also, probably, recalling that he had converted and ordained (2 Tim. i. 6) his young colleague. For their meeting and collaboration, see Introduction, p. 1. The implication of **true** (lit. 'legitimate', 'born in lawful wedlock') is that there is nothing spurious in the latter's Christianity. By **in faith** Paul does not mean 'in the faith', which gives too concrete a sense. The force of the expression may be instru-

mental, 'through faith', emphasizing that it is as a result of his faith that Timothy is Paul's spiritual child: cf. 1 Cor. iv. 15. Or it may denote the sphere of their relationship, in which case *ib.* iv. 17 ('my dear, faithful child in the Lord') provides a parallel.

Outside the Pastorals Paul's regular salutation is, 'Grace to you and peace . . .' Here and in 2 Tim. i. 2 he inserts **mercy** and, probably for the sake of the rhythm, cuts out 'to you'. 'Grace' (Gk. *charis*) is a Christianized version of the pagan 'Greeting' (Gk. *chairein*). 'Peace', on the other hand, was the usual Jewish salutation, and there is evidence (Tob. vii. 12 in S text; 2 Bar. lxxviii. 2) of a Jewish blessing 'mercy and peace', which Paul himself adapts in Gal. vi. 16. His use, here and in 2 Tim. i. 2 (nowhere else) of a Jewish greeting, revised in a Christian sense, is probably deliberate, pointing to the common background of thought and idiom which, as Jews, he and Timothy shared.

Paul substitutes **from God the Father and Christ Jesus our Lord** for his customary 'from God our Father and the Lord Jesus Christ'. It is a mistake to regard this and the other changes mentioned above as betraying that the paragraph does not come from him. The contrary inference is more plausible, for an imitator would have taken care to model his greetings exactly on the formula in the letters he had before him.

2. A WARNING AGAINST FALSE TEACHERS.
i. 3-11

(3) As I requested you when I was going to Macedonia, you should stay on at Ephesus so as to charge certain persons not to teach novelties, (4) or give their minds to interminable fables and genealogies, which promote speculations rather than God's saving plan, which works through faith. (5) The object of my charge is love issuing from a pure heart, a good conscience, and sincere faith. (6) Through missing these some have swerved aside after futile verbiage, (7) wanting to be teachers of the law, but having no clear idea either of what they are

saying or of the things about which they dogmatize. (8) We are well aware that the law is excellent, provided one treats it as law, (9) realizing that law is not made for the righteous man, but for the lawless and insubordinate, the impious and the sinful, the irreligious and the profane, for parricides and matricides, murderers, (10) fornicators, homosexuals, kidnappers, liars, perjurers, and whatever else is antagonistic to the wholesome teaching. (11) Such is the gospel with which I have been entrusted, which tells of the glory of the blessed God.

This passage immediately raises the question of Paul's recent movements. According to the usual interpretation, he has himself been working along with Timothy at Ephesus, and having left the city is now repeating, formally and officially, the gist of the instructions which he had previously given him by word of mouth. To many it has seemed incredible that he should have thought it necessary to do this, especially as his verbal communication must have been more detailed and impressive. They have therefore pointed out that the Apostle's language does not strictly require Ephesus to have been his starting-point, but is consistent with his travelling to Macedonia from, e.g., the west, his original instructions having taken the form of summary notes on which he is now enlarging. Such a journey, they argue, agrees better with iii. 14 and iv. 13, where the Apostle speaks of going (not returning) to Ephesus.

While by no means impossible, this reconstruction of events is on the whole less likely than the generally accepted one. There is no mention of written instructions in 3, the more natural interpretation of which is that Paul had given them to Timothy personally. We also gain the impression that he has a first-hand acquaintance with the situation and personalities in Ephesus. Its supporters in any case exaggerate the difficulties in the ordinary view, overlooking both the official character of the letter and Paul's motive in writing it. He expects it to be read out publicly at Ephesus, and probably elsewhere in the surrounding district also, and then to be preserved in the church's archives. He therefore selects for repetition points in his original charge which he considers useful for general consumption. At the same time, since he is anxious to buttress Timothy's authority, he adapts the whole tone of the letter to this end.

In the original the sentence beginning **As I requested** 3 **you** . . . is an awkward anacoluthon; as not infrequently with Paul (e.g. Rom. ii. 17 ff.; v. 12 ff.; ix. 22 ff.), his thought runs on so precipitately that he passes into a second sentence before properly finishing the first.

We know nothing about the journey referred to in **when I was going to Macedonia** (i.e. the Roman province so named covering the northern part of Greece and including Philippi, Thessalonica, and Beroea among its leading towns), except that it cannot be fitted into the Apostle's career as known from Acts and the earlier letters. Like the other events immediately envisaged in the Pastorals, it must belong to the obscure period subsequent to his release from his first Roman imprisonment. See Introduction, pp. 6-10. Ephesus was the principal city of Asia Minor, the seat of the provincial governor and a religious centre of great importance. It could boast of the famous temple of Artemis or Diana (Acts xix. 23 ff.), and the new worship of the emperor was strongly established there. The foundation of its Christian community may be attributed to Aquila and Priscilla, whom Paul left in Ephesus when hurriedly passing through *en route* for Caesarea (*ib*. xviii. 19), but he himself laboured there for well over two years (*ib*. xx. 31). Not least because of the system of communications radiating from it, the city was a key-point in the Church's strategy, and we can readily understand Paul's eagerness to have a man whom he can trust stationed in it as leader. There is a hint in the verb **stay on** (Gk. *prosmeinai*) that Timothy may have wanted to make a move; hence the Apostle's insistence that his continued presence is indispensable.

Timothy's commission is immediately defined; it is **to charge certain persons not to teach novelties.** . . . In other words, he must make a stand against the dissemination of erroneous teaching. The verb translated **charge** (Gk. *paraggellein*) is a military term meaning 'give strict orders'. Timothy's position, we note, is an authoritative one; he is nothing less than an apostolic delegate, and as such can afford to take a strong line.

As the letter is a semi-public one, the identity of the leading errorists is not revealed. As in i. 6; 19; vi. 10; 21 (cf. 1 Cor. iv. 18; 2 Cor. x. 2; Gal. i. 7; Phil. i. 15), they are referred to, vaguely but ominously, as **certain persons,** but we may be sure that there was little doubt in the minds either of Timothy or of the congregation generally who they were.

The false teaching is first described in general terms as **novelties:** the verb (Gk. *heterodidaskalein*), a coinage of the Apostle's (or of his secretary's), literally means 'to teach a different doctrine', i.e. different from Paul's own, and suggests that there is an accepted norm of apostolic teaching. It is then 4 defined more specifically as **interminable fables and genea-logies.** These words come tantalizingly near disclosing the content of the heresy, but their interpretation is far from clear. Many moderns, following Irenaeus and Tertullian (who supposed that the Apostle was refuting Valentinus in advance), explain them as referring to Gnosticism of the fully developed type which flourished in the middle of the second century. By **fables** they understand the elaborate myths by which Gnostic thinkers sought to solve the problem of evil, and by **genea-logies** the families of descending emanations, or aeons, by which they bridged the gulf between the unknowable supreme God and the material order. Against this we should note: (*a*) the Gnostic systems of aeons were never, so far as we know, called genealogies; (*b*) had he had them in mind, we should have expected the writer to go more fully into their content instead of being satisfied with a passing, imprecise allusion; (*c*) we should also have expected a much sharper, more far-reaching criticism than that they encouraged idle speculation and contentiousness; and (*d*) the fables are expressly labelled 'Jewish' in Tit. i. 14, while in *ib*. iii. 9 'genealogies' are lumped with 'controversies about the law'.

The clear implication of the last point is that the background of the false teaching was Jewish. It has therefore been suggested that the **fables and genealogies** must have had to do with allegorical or legendary interpretations of the O.T. centring on the pedigrees of the patriarchs. Much of the rabbinical Haggadah consisted of just such a fanciful rewriting of Scripture; the Book of Jubilees and Pseudo-Philo's *Liber antiquitatum biblicarum,* with its mania for family-trees, are apt examples. It has also been shown that in post-exilic Judaism there was a keen interest in family-trees, and that these played a part in controversies between Jews and Jewish Christians. Viewed in this light the errorists are Judaizers who concentrate on far-fetched minutiae of rabbinical exegesis to the detriment of the gospel.

No interpretation, however, can be entirely satisfactory which fails to recognize that the heresy was not exclusively either Jewish or Gnostic, but a mixture of both. The very formula **fables and genealogies,** which had been a Greek cliché from Plato's time, confirms its syncretistic character. In the present context it probably denotes Gnostic speculations based on the O.T., and Jeremias may be right in connecting this, so far as **fables** is concerned, with the creation story. On the other hand, it seems probable that the two words are to be taken closely together, the latter defining the former, and that by **genealogies** Paul means family-trees in the strict sense. In his account of the Gnostic sect known as the Ophites (*Haer.* i. 30, 9), Irenaeus gives an interesting example of how the family-trees of Genesis could be worked up into myths, and it is possible that Paul had something of the sort in mind. It seems fruitless, however, in view of the complete lack of evidence, to try to pin down his reference precisely. All we can infer from his general tone is that these Jewish Gnostic efforts at exegesis did not have the cosmological range or Christological implications of, for example, the Colossian heresy; the ideas behind them were probably simpler and more elementary.

Even so Paul is unhappy about the errorists' treatment of the O.T., which in his view leads only to idle **speculations.** The word has a pejorative ring, but in using it he is not denying, as critics sometimes suppose, the Christian's right, and duty, to reflect about his faith. Rather he is condemning the mass of pseudo-problems which the heretics' exegesis engenders. The real end of Bible study should be an apprehension of **God's saving plan.** The Greek noun so translated (*oikonomian*: better attested than *oikodomēn*, i.e. 'edification') originally connotes the management of a house or household, but with Paul it refers either to God's redemptive purpose accomplished in history (Eph. i. 10; iii. 9), or to the responsibility, or stewardship, which

God entrusts to his chosen delegates to secure its realization (1 Cor. ix. 17; Col. i. 25; Eph. iii. 2). If the latter is the sense here, as the majority of critics think, Paul's meaning is that the errorists' exegesis fails to promote the faithful discharge of God's stewardship. The former, however, seems preferable, since it makes a more effective contrast with the purely imaginary fancies with which the false teachers' heads are full. If this is correct, the divine plan **works through faith** in the sense that it is apprehended, and so becomes effective, through faith on the part of those who accept Christ.

5   The ultimate **object** of Paul's **charge,** as of all Christian moral preaching, is not merely negative. If its initial purpose is to check error, it has the further and more positive aim of establishing **love** in the Ephesian congregation in place of the spirit of contentiousness which the errorists have sown there. This mutual charity can only spring **from a pure heart, a good conscience, and sincere faith.**

Paul's mention of **a pure heart** recalls the sixth Beatitude, as well as numerous O.T. passages (e.g. Gen. xx. 5 f.; Job xi. 13; Ps. xxiv. 4; li. 10) in which purity of heart is applauded. In Scripture the heart is the centre and source of a man's entire mental and moral activity; if purity is lacking there, he obviously cannot radiate Christian love. Nor can he unless his **conscience** is **good,** i.e. not only free from self-reproach but orientated by the Holy Spirit. He also needs a **faith** in Christ which involves no pretence but expresses itself in positive acceptance of his way of life (cf. Gal. v. 6: 'faith working through love'). It has been objected that Paul could never have qualified faith as **sincere,** since there can be no question of insincerity in the soul's direct relation to God. But this is making too fine a point; he can speak (Rom. xii. 9; 2 Cor. vi. 6) of 'sincere love', despite the fact that love which is insincere is no more love than insincere faith is the genuine article. The point is that, while faith itself cannot be insincere, it is possible to deceive onself or others that one possesses it.

'Conscience' (Gk. *suneidēsis*) occurs twice, or thrice, in the LXX; in the N.T., apart from Jn. viii. 9 (so most MSS), Hebrews, and 1 Peter, it is found only in the Pauline letters and in speeches attributed to Paul (Acts xxiii. 1; xxiv. 16). The term, and the idea behind it, were popular with the Stoics, and also with Philo; Paul seems to have borrowed it from his Gentile environment. Its basic meaning is a man's inner awareness of the moral quality of his own actions (e.g. Rom. ii. 15; ix. 1; 2 Cor. i. 12), but conscience can also pronounce on the actions of others (1 Cor. x. 28 f.; 2 Cor. iv. 2; v. 11). Passages like Rom. xiii. 5 and 1 Cor. viii. 10 suggest that Paul thought of it as a guide to life, and it is clear from *ib.* viii. 7-12 that he recognized that it could be imperfectly informed.

In the Pastorals he takes the notion deeper. While speaking of the conscience of rebellious heretics as 'branded' or 'seared' (1 Tim. iv. 2) or 'polluted' (Tit. i. 15), he describes that of faithful Christians as 'good' (1 Tim. i. 5; 19) or 'pure' (*ib.* iii. 9; 2 Tim. i. 3). In the Acts passages he is represented as referring to his own conscience as 'good' or 'free from offence': cf. also Heb. ix. 14; x. 22; xiii. 18; 1 Pet. iii. 16; 21. There is little evidence for this usage in Greek literature of the first century, although Philo (*De spec. leg.* i. 203) has the expression 'from a pure conscience'. The occurrence of the Latin equivalent (*bona,* al. *mala, conscientia*) was much more frequent in writers like Cicero and Seneca, and some have detected here the growing influence of western ideas and idioms on the Apostle in his later years. Primarily, a good or pure conscience is one that is free from feelings of guilt. In Christian writers, however, it contains more far-reaching implications as well. Conscience is closely linked with faith, since through baptism the Christian has his sins forgiven and by the influx of the Holy Spirit undergoes that 'renewal of mind' which enables him to 'prove what is the will of God' (Rom. xii. 2) as well as to perform it. Thus in Rom. ix. 1 Paul protests that his conscience bears him witness 'in the Holy Spirit', i.e. the Spirit is the principle which informs and inspires it. His use of 'a good conscience' in the Pastorals, with the suggestion that it is part of the endowment of the man of faith and cannot be possessed by one who lacks true faith, is only the logical extension of this underlying conception.

It is **Through missing these** indispensable qualities that 6 the false teachers, in Paul's opinion, **have swerved aside** from the right track, and have landed themselves in what amounts to nothing more than a mass of **futile verbiage.** The former verb

(Gk. *astochein*: cf. vi. 21; 2 Tim. ii. 18) may have the more positive sense of 'fail to aim at', as is suggested by the description of the errorists' character in vi. 3-5: cf. Ecclus. viii. 9. It is characteristic of Paul in the Pastorals (vi. 20; 2 Tim. ii. 16; Tit. i. 10) to dismiss their teaching as so much idle chatter (Gk. *mataiologia* here). Both these words occur only in the Pastorals (though for the latter cf. Rom. i. 21), while 'swerve aside' (Gk. *ektrepesthai*) occurs only in them (v. 15; vi. 20; 2 Tim. iv. 4) and in Heb. xii. 13. All three belong to the higher *koinē* and illustrate its influence on these letters.

The Jewish character of the false teaching, and also probably its preoccupation with Scriptural exegesis, come out in the state-7 ment that its exponents desire **to be teachers of the law.** This is an honourable title in the N.T., and in Acts v. 34 is applied to Gamaliel. Paul throws it back at them ironically, for as he sees it the use to which they put their misguided exegetical methods proves that they **have no clear idea either of what they are saying or of the things about which they dogmatize.** It is not that they are Judaizers of the kind, for example, attacked in Galatians who desire to impose the full ceremonial law upon Christians. Rather they read out of the law, i.e. the legal portion of the O.T., fantastic myths and ascetical prescriptions (cf. iv. 3) which serve to show that they have missed the point both of the O.T. itself and of the gospel.

This leads the Apostle to a characteristic digression about the place and function of the law. The slighting tone of his reference to **teachers of the law** might appear to contain a reflection on the law itself. So he hastens to reassure Timothy, and those to whom the letter is to be read out, that of course **We,** i.e. well-8 informed Christians, **are well aware that the law is excellent** (for the concessive formula 'we are aware . . .', cf. Rom. ii. 2; iii. 19; viii. 28; 1 Cor. viii. 1; 4; 2 Cor. v. 1), **provided one treats it as law.** His point is that Christians who have accepted the gospel and live by the Spirit fully appreciate the place of the law and its precepts in the working out of God's purpose; as he remarks in Rom. vii. 12 and 14, it is 'holy' and 'spiritual' (cf. also 2 Tim. iii. 15-17). At the same time its limitations must also be recognized; even though it is the law given by God to Moses, it is not the gospel but remains a species of law. And we must acknowledge **that law,** i.e. law of whatever kind, **is not** 9 **made for the righteous man, but for** people who are still under the domination of sin.

Although the approach is different, the attitude to the law set out here is fully in line with that expounded in Rom. vii. 7-25 and Gal. v. 13-26. In the latter passage, for example, it is clearly implied that the law applies only to those who are under the influence of the flesh and who in their lives follow its promptings. Many think that Paul, with his reverence for the law, could never have been responsible for the statement that it is not intended for the righteous. Its bluntness, however, is greatly reduced if we observe (*a*) that it is law in general (including of course the Mosaic law) that he is referring to, and (*b*) that **righteous** does not simply mean 'honest, respectable character', but connotes the Christian who lives by faith (Rom. i. 17; v. 19; Gal. iii. 11; Heb. xii. 23). Such transitions from one sense of law to another are common enough in Paul (e.g. Rom. ii. 14; vii. 23; Gal. v. 14; 23). The sharpness of his language here is to some extent conditioned by the position of the errorists, who are apparently singling out and twisting O.T. precepts in accordance with their arbitrary ideas.

Paul proceeds to elaborate his point by enumerating types of people for whom, as opposed to Christians, law in general, and the law of Moses in particular, have a very direct relevance. If he strikes us as choosing unnecessarily shocking examples, we should remember that it is characteristic of him to use lurid colours when he is portraying human conduct apart from the gospel (e.g. Rom. i. 24-32; Gal. v. 19-21). His list takes the form of a catalogue of vices of a kind which occurs frequently (sometimes with a parallel catalogue of virtues) in the N.T.: e.g. Rom. i. 28 ff.; 1 Cor. v. 10 f.; 2 Cor. xii. 20 f.; Gal. v. 19-23. Similar catalogues were used by the Qumran sect and also by contemporary Hellenistic and Hellenistic-Jewish circles. The Christian lists were probably modelled on the latter, and this explains the general terms in which they are usually cast. They exhibit a good deal of overlapping, and it is evident that the early Church soon amassed a substantial body of hortatory material which could be brought into play on the appropriate occasion.

What is particularly interesting in the present list is that it is

largely based on the Decalogue. Thus it opens with six rather general epithets, arranged in pairs—**the lawless and insubordinate, the impious and the sinful, the irreligious and the profane**—which cover offences against God and can perhaps be taken as representing the first table of the Decalogue. It then castigates separately violators of the first five commandments of the second table. **Parricides and matricides** represent flagrant examples of the breaking of the Fifth Commandment, **mur-**
10 **derers** of the Sixth. **Fornicators and homosexuals** are transgressors of the Seventh, which was interpreted as embracing sexual vice in all its forms, and **kidnappers** of the Eighth, since in rabbinical exegesis stealing was held to include traffic in human beings (cf. Ex. xxi. 16; Dt. xxiv. 7). **Liars** and **perjurors** clearly offend against the Ninth.

Paul rounds off his catalogue, rather in the manner of Rom. xiii. 9 and Gal. v. 21, with the all-inclusive **and whatever else is antagonistic to the wholesome teaching.** Coming at the end of an inventory of the grossest offences, some have found this a grotesque climax, but in fact it vividly reflects the contrast Paul habitually draws between the works of the flesh and the fruits of the Spirit. This is the first appearance of the expression **wholesome teaching** (Gk. *hugiainousa didaskalia*) which is characteristic of the Pastorals (2 Tim. iv. 3; Tit. i. 9; ii. 1: for the same idea, cf. 1 Tim. vi. 3; 2 Tim. i. 13; Tit. i. 13; ii. 2; 8), but is found nowhere else in the N.T. According to many it is a convincing token of the 'bourgeois' Christianity of the letters, and betrays a rational approach to ethics which is alien to Paul's spirit. On the other hand, an imitator is not likely to have so repeatedly attributed to him an idiom which is found in none of his acknowledged letters, while nothing is more common than for a man, at a certain stage of his life, suddenly to adopt a turn of phrase which strikes him as apt and then work it to the death. The Apostle borrows the present metaphor from current philosophical jargon, in which 'wholesome' connoted 'sound' or 'reasonable', and uses it here to designate the authentic Christian message as applied to conduct. It expresses his conviction that a morally disordered life is, as it were, diseased and stands in need of treatment, viz. by the law, whereas a life based on the teaching of the gospel is clean and healthy. This is the kind

of conviction which is liable to have loomed larger in his mind
in his later years.

The clause which follows, **Such is the gospel . . .** (lit. 11
'according to the gospel . . .'), applies to all three preceding
verses, claiming that the teaching they contain about the limited
role of the law is not simply Paul's personal opinion, but a real
element in the revelation he has received. The typically Pauline
with which I have been entrusted (cf. 1 Cor. ix. 17; Gal. ii.
7) at once traces this back to his call on the Damascus road and
is a reminder of the divine authority of his message. The gospel
tells of the glory of the blessed God (this translation is preferable to 'the glorious gospel' of AV and RSV) because, in
contrast to the law, which only serves to bring to light the sin-
fulness of men, it reveals in the person of Christ the divine
power, majesty, and compassion. The same idea, that through
Christ, who is God's image, the brightness of his glory is made
manifest to believers, comes in 2 Cor. iv. 4. The adjective
blessed (Gk. *makarios*), common enough in Hellenistic Judaism
(e.g. Philo) as a description of God, is applied to him only here
and in vi. 15 in the Bible. The idea it conveys is, not that God is
the object of blessing, but that he contains all blessedness in
himself and bestows it on men. Its occurrence here, instead of
the more usual, and characteristically Semitic, epithet *eulogētos*
(Rom. i. 25; ix. 5; etc.), illustrates the more cultivated Hellenistic
idiom which marks the Pastorals in distinction from the other
letters.

3. PAUL AND THE GOSPEL. i. 12-17

**(12) I am grateful to him who gave me strength, Christ
Jesus our Lord, because he considered me trustworthy
and appointed me to his service, (13) in spite of my
previously having been a blasphemer, persecutor, and
bully. I was shown mercy, however, because I had acted
ignorantly in unbelief. (14) Indeed, our Lord's grace,
with the faith and love which we have in Christ Jesus,
was superabundantly bestowed on me. (15) It is a trustworthy saying, deserving whole-hearted acceptance, that**

Christ Jesus came into the world to save sinners—of whom I am the first. (16) But it was for this reason that I was shown mercy, so that in me first Jesus Christ might demonstrate the full extent of his patience, thus giving an illustration of the kind of people who were going to believe in him and so come to eternal life. (17) To the King of the ages, the incorruptible, invisible and only God, be honour and glory for ever and ever. Amen.

This powerful passage links up naturally with what precedes. Paul's reference in 11 to **the gospel with which I have been entrusted** prompts him to recall, with amazement and gratitude, his experience of God's superabundant grace, as a result of which he has been transformed from an embittered foe to an apostle of Christ, the prototype and example of others whom he will similarly call and equip for his service. While reminding Timothy and the Ephesian church generally of his apostolic standing, it also conveys a hint, for the former's benefit, of the limitless power of the gospel to change sinners and strengthen them for God's work.

12   The original of **I am grateful** is *charin echō*, which is the normal Greek for 'I thank', but which Paul employs only here and in 2 Tim. i. 3. His regular expression is *eucharistō*. If there is any significance in the change beyond assimilation to the conventional idiom, it may possibly reflect the influence of residence in the west, since the Latin equivalent is *gratiam habeo*. The Greek participles translated **gave me strength** (the variant reading 'gives me strength' is probably an assimilation to Phil. iv. 13) and **appointed,** like the verb **considered,** are all in the aorist; Paul is looking back to the memorable occasion when **Christ Jesus our Lord** confronted him on the road to Damascus. What evokes his special gratitude is that, in spite of his behaviour, Christ judged him **trustworthy;** we recall his statement in 1 Cor. iv. 2 that the quality *par excellence* demanded of one of God's stewards is 'that he be found trustworthy'. The word chosen (Gk. *pistos*) consciously echoes **entrusted** (Gk. *episteuthēn*) in 11 above.

As in 1 Cor. xv. 9 ff. and Gal. i. 13 ff., Paul uses the strongest language about his conduct before his conversion; he wants to

throw into relief the wonder of God's choice of him. He had
previously been **a blasphemer,** not only in denying Christ 13
himself but in forcing others to follow his example (Acts xxvi.
11). He had been a **persecutor and bully,** harrying the Church
and its members. Nevertheless he can say gratefully, **I was
shown mercy** (the passive verb *eleēthēn* is typical: cf. Rom. xi.
30 f.; 1 Cor. vii. 25; 2 Cor. iv. 1) in spite of everything. It is
absurd to see in **I had acted ignorantly** (Gk. *agnoōn*) 'an
example of the intellectualistic interpretation of Christianity
which characterizes the Pastorals . . . derived from the Stoic
conception of natural religion' (F. D. Gealy following Dibelius).
Paul is simply availing himself of the distinction, conventional
in Judaism (Lev. xxii. 14; Num. xv. 22-31) and also in the
Qumran sect, between 'unwitting' and 'presumptuous' sins,
linking **unbelief** with his ignorance. He does not claim that as
a result he was without guilt, but mentions the fact as explaining
how his career prior to his conversion became the object of
God's compassion rather than his wrath. In his case the prayer,
'Father, forgive them, for they know not what they do' (Lk.
xxiii. 34), has found fulfilment.

Not only did God call him, persecutor though he was, but
our Lord's grace . . . was superabundantly bestowed on 14
him. By **grace** he means, as always, God's undeserved favour
towards sinful men (cf. Rom. v. 20). The compound verb which
he uses (Gk. *huperpleonazein*) is a N.T. hapax which is paralleled
by similar compounds with *huper*, mostly hapaxes, which are
found in the other letters (Rom. v. 20; viii. 26; 37; 2 Cor. x. 14;
Phil. ii. 9; 1 Thess. iv. 6; 2 Thess. i. 3). The divine **grace**
brought with it **faith** to replace his previous **unbelief,** and **love**
instead of the brutal aggressiveness he had displayed to those
who should have been his brothers. This **faith** and **love** are
characterized as **in Christ Jesus** (cf. 2 Tim. i. 13), a phrase
which, as the translation attempts to bring out, is much more
than a periphrasis for 'Christian'. Those who so limit its meaning argue that where 'in Christ' has the full mystical sense usual
in Paul it is used of persons, not qualities. But faith and love are
not qualities hanging in the air but always belong to persons;
even if he remains unmentioned, their personal possessor is
always implied. It is here suggested that they are the visible

expression of the Christian's living relationship with his Saviour.

Faith and love are similarly coupled together in 1 Thess. i. 3; Eph. i. 15; iii. 17; vi. 23; Phm. 5. It has been objected that they are here treated in an un-Pauline fashion as moral qualities 'separate from grace and given in addition to it' (E. F. Scott), or even that they 'are results of justification, not its condition' (F. D. Gealy), but this is to misunderstand the passage. Paul's language connects them in the closest possible way with **our Lord's grace.** As D. Guthrie aptly comments, 'Paul would readily agree that apart from the operation of divine grace, love and faith would be impossible, yet without the latter there would be no evidence of the former'.

15   Paul now interjects a striking formula, **It is a trustworthy saying,** which is found, with or without the elaboration **deserving whole-hearted acceptance,** in four other contexts in the Pastorals (iii. 1; iv. 9; 2 Tim. ii. 11; Tit. iii. 8), but nowhere else. It has a solemn ring, and in each case is used to introduce, or follow, a citation, probably drawn from early catechetical or liturgical material, to which he wishes to draw attention. The formula itself, or at any rate the first part (**It is a trustworthy saying**), has Jewish precedent, e.g. the prayer following the Shema; but close parallels to the wording of both parts can be found in Greek literature and contemporary inscriptions. Their use provides further evidence of the cultivated style of the Pastorals.

The quotation which the formula here introduces, **Christ Jesus came into the world to save sinners,** seems to Paul aptly to epitomize what he has been saying. The Apostle himself does not normally speak of Christ coming into the world; the stress on the incarnation is more Johannine (e.g. Jn. i. 9; iii. 17; xii. 46 f.; xvi. 28) than Pauline. The words, however, echo Christ's own statement to Zacchaeus (Lk. xix. 10), 'The Son of Man came to seek and save what was lost'. The sentence is probably an excerpt, familiar enough to Timothy, from some primitive creed or liturgy. But the mention of **sinners** awakens in the Apostle a sudden outburst of self-abasement—**of whom I am the first** (he means foremost as well as first in order). This exclamation is in the spirit of his confession in 1 Cor. xv. 9 that he, who had once persecuted the Church, is 'the least of

the apostles', and in Eph. iii. 8 that he is 'the very least of all
the saints'. These parallels show that, so far from there being
anything morbid or unreal in the words, they are thoroughly in
accord with Paul's psychology, and it is difficult to imagine
anyone attributing them to him.

The present, **I am,** deserves notice. Although his sins have
been forgiven, Paul still regards himself as a sinner, or rather as
having the status of sinner-redeemed, dedicated to ever deeper
penitence and service.

It is precisely here, in the fact that he is the first and foremost
of sinners, that Paul discerns the reason for God's gracious
dealing with him. **I was shown mercy,** he claims, taking up 16
and repeating the verb of 13 and **first** from 15, **so that in me
first Jesus Christ might demonstrate the full extent of his
patience.** The divine **patience** (cf. esp. Ex. xxxiv. 6; Num.
xiv. 18) is, of course, God's readiness to put up with ill-treatment, insult, and provocation; and this has been signally displayed in Christ's attitude to Paul, whom so far from punishing
as he deserved he has actually made his chosen vessel. Moreover,
what has happened to Paul is, as it were, a rough outline sketch
(such is the sense of Gk. *hupotupōsis*, here translated **illustration**) of what will be the blessed experience of countless others
who will similarly be given grace **to believe in him,** i.e. accept
him in faith and place their trust in him. For the verb 'believe'
with *epi* and the dative, cf. Rom. ix. 33; x. 11 (citing Is. xxviii.
16, which may be in Paul's mind here too). As a result of this
faith they will be made sure of **eternal life,** i.e. the blessed life
of the world to come of which believers have a foretaste here.
Paul is thus the clinching proof that no one need despair of the
divine compassion reaching him.

This passage, which began as a quiet thanksgiving but rose to
heights of emotion as Paul recalled God's amazing mercy to
himself, reaches its natural climax in a solemn doxology. For
his use of doxologies elsewhere cf. Rom. xi. 36; xvi. 27; Gal. i. 5;
Phil. iv. 20; Eph. iii. 21. The formula he employs here, like
the parallel one in vi. 15 f., is almost certainly a liturgical one
borrowed from the pre-Christian Hellenistic synagogue. The
first title, **king of the ages** (Gk. *basilei tōn aiōnōn*) is probably 17
suggested by **eternal life** (Gk. *zōēn aiōnion*) in 16. It is a Jewish

cult-formula which is found in Tob. xiii. 7 and 11 and is echoed
in many Jewish prayers today. It stresses that God is the supreme king who governs all the ages from the creation of the
world, including the age of the Messiah himself, until the end of
time. The description of God as **incorruptible,** i.e. immune
from decay, immortal, reflects Greek philosophical conceptions,
but Paul had used it in Rom. i. 23. The epithets **invisible** and
only are commonplaces of Jewish thought about the Godhead;
the former has parallels in Rom. i. 20; Col. i. 15, and the latter
in Rom. xvi. 27; 1 Cor. viii. 4-6.

The doxology concludes with the Hebrew verbal adjective
Amen, which was pronounced in the synagogues in assent to
doxologies or benedictions of the high-priest. From this it
passed to the Christian liturgy: cf. 1 Cor. xiv. 16; Gal. i. 5;
Heb. xiii. 21. It has been suggested (J. Jeremias) that the reader
of the letter was supposed to pause at the end of the doxology
proper so that the listening congregation could say, 'Amen'.

4. PAUL'S CHARGE TO TIMOTHY. i. 18-20

**(18) This charge I entrust to you, my son Timothy, rely-
ing on the prophecies once made about you, so that
braced by them you may fight the good fight, (19) armed
with faith and a good conscience—through rejecting the
latter some have made shipwreck of their faith. (20)
Among these are Hymenaeus and Alexander, whom I
delivered over to Satan so that as a result of chastisement
they might cease being blasphemous.**

Paul now reverts to the theme of his letter, from which his
attack on the errorists in 6 ff. and the personal outburst which
followed it diverted him. But before defining his charge in
detail, he solemnly reminds Timothy of the supernatural tokens
attending his call, which give the Apostle himself confidence in
his choice, and which should also inspire his young disciple to
enter wholeheartedly into his foreordained role.

18   By **This charge I entrust to you** Paul means Timothy's

responsibility for extirpating heresy and establishing sound teaching; the word rendered **charge** (Gk. *paraggelia*) consciously repeats the noun and its cognate verb used in 5 and 3. What he desires to emphasize now is that its assignment to Timothy is not something arbitrary, but accords with God's will as expressed through his prophets. If Paul has selected him for this arduous task, he has done so **relying on** (lit. 'according to') **the prophecies once made about you.** An alternative translation is 'the prophecies which pointed me to you'; the verb can bear either sense, and a decision between them is difficult. Paul is thinking about some occasion, or perhaps occasions, still vivid in Timothy's memory, on which prophets expatiated on the young man's fitness for God's service. This may have taken place at his ordination, which we are told was accompanied by prophetic activity (iv. 14), or his appointment at Ephesus, or in the course of some other episode in his career. The story of the commissioning of Barnabas and Saul in Acts xiii. 1-3, with its mention of prophets and of the clear declaration of the Holy Spirit, supplies an instructive illustration.

Paul reminds Timothy of these prophecies **so that braced by them** (lit. 'in them') he **may fight the good fight,** i.e. the battle, by its very nature noble, against perversions of the gospel message. Paul is fond of military metaphors, and in particular likes to depict the apostolic leader as a Christian warrior (1 Cor. ix. 7; 2 Cor. x. 3; Phil. ii. 25; 2 Tim. ii. 3 f.). A previous description of the Christian's necessary equipment had included faith and love as his breastplate, and the hope of salvation as his helmet (1 Thess. v. 8: cf. Eph. vi. 11-16 for a variant account). Here he merely bids Timothy be **armed with faith and a 19 good conscience,** these being specially relevant to his forthcoming campaign. The two are conjoined three times in all in this letter (cf. i. 5; iii. 9), which suggests the close connexion in his mind between religion and morality.

Paul is particularly concerned to stress the importance of having a rightly ordered conscience which is free from reproach (see note on 5 above): **through rejecting the latter some have made shipwreck of their faith.** The participle is a strong one, suggesting a positive spurning of conscience rather than mere carelessness. The Greek rendered **their faith** could be translated 'the faith', i.e. the Christian faith objectively understood, and this gains support from vi. 21 and 2 Tim. ii. 18. But the subjective sense agrees better with the previous verse as well as with the stress on faith in the whole chapter. The point Paul is making is the sound one that 'more often than we know, religious error has its roots in moral rather than intellectual causes' (E. F. Scott).

He then, as a warning, cites two tragic examples of men 20 whose moral laxity has led to their faith being ruined: **Among these are Hymenaeus and Alexander,** two fellow-workers, apparently, at Ephesus. We learn from 2 Tim. ii. 17 that the former was guilty of the erroneous belief that the resurrection was already past. The latter has been identified with the Alexander who tried to speak at the riot stirred up by Demetrius at Ephesus many years previously (Acts xix. 33), but beyond the coincidence of their name, a very common one in any case, there is nothing to support this. It is much more likely that he is the copper-smith mentioned in 2 Tim. iv. 14 as having greatly injured the Apostle.

So deplorable is their case that Paul has solemnly **delivered** them **over to Satan,** an expression which recalls the sentence he had passed on the incestuous Corinthian (1 Cor. v. 5). The formula was a technical one, probably derived from Job ii. 6, and connoted excommunication, i.e. the expulsion of the sinner from the church, the realm of God's care and protection, and the formal handing of him over to the power of Satan. In the mind of the primitive Church this did not simply mean that he left the Christian congregation and resumed a peaceful life in pagan society; such a man was thought to be really exposed to the malice of the Evil One, and physical disaster was fully anticipated. It is practically certain, for example, that in 1 Cor. v. 5 Paul expected his sentence to be followed by the guilty man's death. Cf. also the fate of Ananias and Sapphira (Acts v. 1-11) and the blinding of Elymas (*ib.* xiii. 11). In the present case Paul is not envisaging the actual death of Hymenaeus and Alexander; the object of his ban was **so that as a result of chastisement they might cease being blasphemous,** which suggests that he looked for their restoration to a better frame of mind in this world. But the verb used (Gk. *paideuthōsin*) is a strong one; it conveys the idea of stern punishment rather than instruction, and we must infer that illness, paralysis, or some other physical disability was in the Apostle's mind.

5. THE ORDERING OF PUBLIC WORSHIP. ii. 1-15

(1) First of all, then, I urge that supplications, prayers, intercessions, and thanksgivings be offered for all men, (2) for sovereigns and all who occupy high office, so that we may lead a quiet and peaceable life in entire godliness and gravity. (3) This is excellent, and acceptable to God our Saviour, (4) who desires all men to be saved and attain knowledge of the truth. (5) For there is one God, and also one mediator between God and men, Christ Jesus, himself man, (6) who gave himself as a ransom for all—thus bearing testimony at God's good time. (7) For this I was appointed a herald and apostle (I am speaking the truth and not telling lies) to teach the nations in faith and truth. (8) So it is my wish that in every place the men should pray raising holy hands, without anger or quarrelsomeness. (9) Women similarly, in becoming costume, should adorn themselves modestly and chastely, not with elaborate hair-styles, or with gold or pearls or expensive clothing, (10) but, as befits women who claim to be religious, with good deeds. (11) A woman ought to learn quietly, with complete submissiveness. (12) I do not allow a woman to teach or wield authority over a man; she ought to keep quiet. (13) For Adam was created first, and then Eve; (14) and Adam was not deceived, but it was the woman who was deceived and fell into transgression. (15) She will be saved, however, through child-bearing, provided they continue in faith and love and sanctification, combined with chastity.

This section, dealing with the importance of public worship and the conduct appropriate at it, and the following chapter with its directions for the ministry, form the earliest manual of church order we possess. The necessity of clear regulations for congregational gatherings was speedily realized in the primitive Church, and as early as 1 Cor. xiv we find Paul concerned about the misunderstandings and disorder caused by the un-supervised exercise of 'prophecy' and 'talking with tongues', as well as by the eagerness of women to assert themselves at meetings. His golden rule was that whatever was done in church should be done 'decently and in order' and should contribute to edification, i.e. building up the faithful (1 Cor. xiv. 40; 26).

1   Paul's first requirement is **that supplications, prayers, in-tercessions, and thanksgivings be offered for all men.** The precise distinction between these terms need not be pressed; his object is to insist on the centrality of prayer rather than to provide a systematic analysis of its types. The mention of **thanksgivings** (Gk. *eucharistias*), however, deserves notice. As in 1 Cor. xiv. 16 f., we should probably see here a reference to the eucharist, which from earliest times was regarded as in essence a prayer of blessing and thanksgiving to God for all his goodness, from the creation of the world to the sending of his Son to suffer, die, and rise again for man's salvation.

Paul's chief concern is that Christian intercession should be **for all men;** this is confirmed by his emphatic reminder in 4 and 6 that God wants *all* men to know the truth and that Christ gave his life for *all* mankind. We must infer that there was an exclusivist spirit in sections of the Ephesian community, prob-ably connected with the Jewish-Gnostic strain in the errorists' thinking. Paul makes it plain that narrowness of this kind offends against the gospel of Christ.

2   In particular Christians should pray **for sovereigns and all who occupy high office.** The former term (lit. 'kings') designated the emperor in the east, and since it is used here in the plural, the inference has been drawn that the letter must date from after 136, when the emperors had colleagues associ-ated with them. The injunction is general, however, and the plural covers not only the Roman emperor (in the present case Nero), but local rulers as well. Those **who occupy high office,** too, is a general description for prominent officials of

almost any kind. Christianity was to have good grounds for hostility to the state, and Revelation shows that such an attitude became common in some circles. But the N.T. testifies to considerable loyalty to the imperial and civic authorities: e.g. Rom. xiii. 1 ff.; 1 Pet. ii. 14; 17; Tit. iii. 1; Acts *passim*. In Judaism sacrifice was regularly offered in the Temple and intercession made in the synagogues for the pagan civil power: cf. LXX Jer. xxxvi. 7; Bar. i. 10-13; Ezr. vi. 10; 1 Macc. vii. 33. The custom soon took root in Christianity, and such prayers were established in the liturgy by the end of the first century (1 *Clem.* lxi). In general Christianity down the ages has inculcated respect for the civil power, whether Christian or not, at any rate until it begins to exercise an intolerable tyranny. The theological basis has been the conviction that earthly power and authority have their appointed place in the providential ordering of the world (cf. Rom. xiii. 1 ff.).

Two reasons are advanced for such prayers. The first (the second is given in 3-6) is that, as a beneficent result of it, Christians may expect to **lead a quiet and peaceable life in entire godliness and gravity.** In other words, not being exposed to the suspicion of disloyalty, they will be allowed to practise their religion without fear of disturbance and to lead the morally serious lives appropriate to it. The two terms translated **godliness** (Gk. *eusebeia*) and **gravity** (Gk. *semnotēs*) both belong to the higher *koinē*; they are only used by Paul in the Pastorals, and provide a further illustration of their distinctive style. The former (cf. iii. 16; iv. 7 f.; vi. 3; 5; 6; 11; 2 Tim. iii. 5; Tit. i. 1) designates the religious attitude in the deepest sense, the true reverence for God which comes from knowledge; the latter (cf. iii. 4; Tit. ii. 7) connotes moral earnestness, affecting outward demeanour as well as interior intention. Together they represent the Hellenistic counterpart of the Hebraic 'holiness' (Gk. *hosiotēs*) and 'righteousness' (Gk. *dikaiosunē*) combined in Lk. i. 75. They sum up, as has often been pointed out, the religious ideal of the letters, with its accent on settled piety expressing itself in a well-ordered life, which many (see Introduction, pp. 17f.) find it hard to associate with Paul. On the other hand, (*a*) the words themselves may be due to his secretary; and (*b*) we cannot exclude the possibility that Paul's attitude underwent a considerable change as a result of passing years and altered circumstances.

Paul now comes to his second, more profound and theological 3 reason. **This,** he states, **is excellent, and acceptable to God our Saviour.** General intercession, he means, and intercession for rulers in particular, is a good thing in itself, but in addition it pleases God, whose nature it is to save (for **our Saviour,** see on i. 1). While he is the actual Saviour of us Christians (that is 4 the force of **our**), he also **desires all men to be saved,** i.e. to escape the divine wrath on the last day, and, as an indispensable preliminary to this, to **attain knowledge of the truth.** This latter phrase is used by Paul only in the Pastorals (2 Tim. ii. 25; iii. 7; Tit. i. 1: cf. Heb. x. 26), although the word for **knowledge** (Gk. *epignōsis*) is a favourite of his and he elsewhere speaks of 'the truth of the gospel' (Gal. ii. 5; 14) or 'the truth' (*ib*. v. 7; Rom. ii. 8; 2 Cor. vi. 7). It is yet another example of the Hellenistic diction of the letters. 'Knowledge' includes not only rational apprehension on the believer's part, but also acceptance by faith, while 'truth' is the whole revelation of God in Christ; in the Pastorals it almost connotes Christian orthodoxy. The whole expression, to **attain knowledge of the truth,** has a distinctly Johannine ring, and is equivalent to 'be converted to Christianity'.

All down Christian history this sentence has provoked intense heart-searching and controversy. How is God's will to save all to be reconciled with (*a*) the almost universal belief that not all are in fact saved, and (*b*) the teaching about predestination expounded by the Apostle himself elsewhere (e.g. Rom. ix.)? What is above all clear is that all the subtle qualifications which have been proposed (e.g. Tertullian's suggestion that **all** means 'all whom he adopted', and Augustine's that it denotes 'all the predestined, because every type of mankind is among them') are artificial and out of place. The same applies equally to the much more sensible distinction, made by fathers like John Chrysostom, Theodore of Mopsuestia, and John Damascene, between God's antecedent, general will that all whom he created should share in his beatitude, and his subsequent will that all who refuse to accept his free grace should be punished. The truth is that all the profound questions which later theology

was to raise were remote from the Apostle's mind. In affirming
the universal scope of God's will to save he was probably conscious of taking issue with (a) the Jewish belief that God willed
the destruction of sinners and the salvation of the righteous
alone, and (b) the Gnostic theory that salvation belonged to the
spiritual élite alone.

To clinch his argument Paul inserts in 5 and 6 what is almost
certainly (cf. the four compact, balanced, rhythmical clauses)
an extract from a catechetical or liturgical formula which was
probably already familiar to his readers. It is a bi-membered
one of a kind which he cites elsewhere: cf. esp. 1 Cor. viii. 6.
The first clause affirms the basic tenet of Judaism, repeated at
every synagogue service and by pious Jews daily (Deut. vi. 4-9),
there is one God. The linking conjunction **For** shows that the 5
statement is advanced in support of what precedes, and it is
noteworthy that Paul elsewhere (e.g. Rom. iii. 29) makes the
oneness of God the foundation of the universality of the gospel.
The second member continues: **and also one mediator between God and men, Christ Jesus, himself man.** It thus
excludes on the one hand Jewish ideas of Moses (Gal. iii. 19) or
angels (Heb. ii. 6 ff.; Test. xii Patr., Dan. vi) acting as intermediaries, and on the other all the intermediary deities, Gnostic
aeons, etc., accepted in pagan circles. Christ can fulfil this
unique role precisely because he is **himself man.** We have
here, in summary form, the conception of the second Adam,
the inaugurator of a new, redeemed humanity, which Paul expounds in Rom. v. 12 ff.; 1 Cor. xv. 21 f.; 45 ff. It has been
objected that he nowhere else calls Christ mediator, reserving
the description for Moses (Gal. iii. 19), but against this we
should note (a) that we are almost certainly dealing here with a
citation, and (b) that in any case Paul's teaching about the re-
demption is essentially mediatorial since, according to it, human
beings are restored to fellowship with God through Christ and
his work on their behalf.

The confession proceeds to define this work: **who gave 6
himself as a ransom for all.** This is a free version of Christ's
own statement (Mk. x. 45) that the Son of Man came 'to give
his life as a ransom for many'. Since Paul is not setting out a
theory of the Atonement of his own but citing what has become

a theological cliché, it is fruitless to speculate about the complex of ideas lying behind it. The important words for him were **for all;** it is the fact that Christ died for all men, without any kind of favouritism, that makes it obligatory for Christians to pray for them all without distinction.

The clause which follows—**thus bearing testimony at God's good time** (lit. 'the testimony at his own times')—is enigmatic; the MS variants show what difficulty early exegetes had with it. Many take it as part of Paul's citation, but the formula is neater without the appended tag; indeed it is hard to see its relevance. Much more probably we should understand it as a comment of the Apostle's standing in loose apposition (cf. Rom. xii. 1; 2 Thess. i. 5 for the construction) to the preceding statement. What Paul is saying is that, by dying for all mankind in accordance with the divine plan, Christ has borne over-whelmingly convincing witness to God's desire for the salvation of all men. He bore it **at God's good time,** i.e. at the decisive moment in history which God in his providence had fixed for the accomplishment of his purpose (cf. Rom. v. 6; Gal. iv. 4). This interpretation is confirmed by Tit. i. 3, but since the expression (Gk. *kairois idiois*) can also have a future reference (vi. 15: cf. 2 Thess. ii. 6), some prefer this meaning here. They thus explain the text as meaning that Christ's act of sacrifice was 'the testimony to appointed times to come', the 'time' particularly envisaged being the final redemptive event. It is doubtful, however, whether the Greek will yield this, and in view of the mention of Christ's saving death a reference to the past seems in any case more appropriate.

As a final argument Paul appeals to his own special role in
7 the propagation of the gospel. **For this,** he exclaims, i.e. in order to spread abroad precisely this testimony, declared in Jesus Christ, of God's universal will to save, **I was appointed a herald and apostle ... to teach the nations in faith and truth.** The **I** is emphatic, and **appointed** echoes the claim of i. 12 that Paul's ministerial status is due entirely to the divine initiative. The accent, however, falls on the final clause, and to bring this out he interjects vehemently, **I am speaking the truth and not telling lies** (cf. the protesting language of Rom. ix. 1; 2 Cor. xi. 31; Gal. i. 20). The fact that God himself has

chosen him (cf. Acts ix. 15; xiii. 47; xxii. 21) to preach the gospel to **the nations,** i.e. the Gentile world and not just the Jews, is clinching proof of God's will to save all men, and therefore of the obligation to pray for them all.

This interpretation has the advantage of giving full value to the final clause, and of making the whole verse the logical development of 5 and 6. The vehement parenthesis is best explained as highlighting Paul's claim to have been assigned the mission to the Gentiles as against the errorists' exclusivist ideas; with their Judaizing tendencies they may well have been critical of evangelizing non-Jews. Thus the parenthesis looks forward, as in Rom. ix. 1. A widely supported alternative explanation is that Paul is, in his customary manner, defending his apostolic status; the parenthesis thus looks backwards to **a herald and apostle.** This is quite possible, for Paul was always sensitive about his authority, and while Timothy needed no reassurance about it, there are hints (see on i. 1) that it may have been questioned in some circles in Ephesus. This view, however, does not account for the surprising violence of Paul's protest, and by introducing the irrelevant issue of his apostleship fails to integrate the verse satisfactorily with what precedes. On either interpretation **in faith and truth** go closely with **to teach** . . . and denote (*a*) the subject, or content, of Paul's instruction, or (*b*) the fidelity and veracity with which he imparts it.

From the universal scope of prayer Paul passes to the dispositions and demeanour appropriate to it. He begins courteously but firmly with, **So it is my wish** . . . using a verb (Gk. 8 *boulomai*) which in Hellenistic Judaism conveys a note of authoritative command. His first ruling is **that in every place the men should pray.** . . . In the Jewish synagogue only men were permitted to recite the prayers; the stress on sex suggests that this convention may have been breaking down at Ephesus (for Corinth much earlier, cf. 1 Cor. xi. 5 ff.; xiv. 33 ff.), and this is confirmed by 11 ff. below. Prayer is to be offered **in every place,** i.e. wherever the gospel is preached; the expression recalls Mal. i. 11, but is almost technical in Paul (1 Cor. i. 2; 2 Cor. ii. 14; 1 Thess. i. 8). He then comes to his main point: at prayer the men of the congregation must raise **holy hands,**

without anger or quarrelsomeness. The outward gesture is futile, and indeed blasphemous, unless the heart within is free from ill-will. We recall the express teaching of Jesus (Mk. xi. 25; Mt. v. 23 f.; vi. 12) that genuine prayer is impossible for those who are unforgiving or who nourish grudges. The most general attitude for prayer in antiquity, for pagans, Jews and Christians alike, was to stand with hands outstretched and uplifted, the palms turned upwards. The frescoes of *orantes* in, e.g., the Roman catacombs provide vivid illustrations from the life of the early Church.

Paul then turns to the female members of the congregation: 9 they **similarly, in becoming costume, should adorn themselves modestly and chastely.** Since women are not allowed to lead the prayers, it has been suggested that he has moved away from the subject of public worship and is thinking of female dress and behaviour in general. This is unlikely in itself, however, and both the loosely attached adverb **similarly** and 11 ff. make it clear that he is laying down rules for dress and deportment at prayer-meetings. While his remarks conform broadly to the conventional diatribe against female extravagance, what is probably foremost in his mind is the impropriety of women exploiting their physical charms on such occasions, and also the emotional disturbance they are liable to cause their male fellow-worshippers. This is brought out by **modestly** and **chastely,** which in the original are represented by the nouns *aidōs* and *sōphrosunē*. The former, used only here in the N.T., connotes feminine reserve in matters of sex (the French *pudeur*). The latter (only here, ii. 15 and Acts xxvi. 25 in N.T.) basically stands for perfect self-mastery in the physical appetites, and was one of Plato's four cardinal virtues (cf. Rep. iv. 430 e). As applied to women it too had a definitely sexual nuance.

It is not Paul's idea that women attending church meetings should lack adornment. Certainly they should not trick themselves out **with elaborate hair-styles, or with gold or pearls or expensive clothing.** Whether or not these items are borrowed from the armoury of contemporary moral lecturers, their mention seems to point to the presence of comfortably off converts in the Ephesian church. The noun translated **elaborate hair-styles** (Gk. *plegma*) refers to the practice of plaiting or braiding the hair, which was a regular feature of the coiffure of fashionable women, Jewish and pagan, in the first-century Graeco-Roman world. The Apostle wants the feminine section of the congregation to make themselves attractive, **but, as** 10 **befits women who claim to be religious, with good deeds.** The alternative rendering 'as befits women who give proof of their religious profession by good works' is syntactically possible, but the contrast between adorning oneself with fine trappings and with a life of Christian service gives much the most natural sense. The noun translated **to be religious** (Gk. *theosebeia*) occurs only here in the N.T., and the whole expression reflects the influence of the higher *koinē*.

The emphasis on **good deeds** (a phrase which might be less misleadingly rendered 'deeds of charity') in the Pastorals is remarkable. They are required from the church as a whole (Tit. ii. 14; iii. 8; 14), but especially from its officers (*ib*. ii. 7) and better-off members (1 Tim. vi. 18), and also from its women-folk and widows (here and *ib*. v. 10). The explanation lies, of course, in Paul's practical objective in writing the letters, although the possibility cannot be excluded that the errorists were so absorbed in their futile speculations that they had lost all appreciation of the ethical side of religion. Three points should be noted. (*a*) An insistence on the practical exercise of charity, though much less prominent in the acknowledged Paulines, is by no means absent from them (e.g. Rom. ii. 7; 2 Cor. xi. 8; Eph. ii. 10; Col. i. 10). (*b*) The gospels abound in evidence that our Lord's teaching, as it was passed down and understood in the primitive Church, placed immense store by deeds of charity (cf. esp. Mt. xxv. 31-46). (*c*) There is no suggestion in the Pastorals, any more than in the gospels, that the good deeds of Christians are done with the motive of acquiring merit. On the contrary, such hints as they give seem to indicate that the good men do is the work of God in them (2 Tim. ii. 21), and they strongly repudiate any idea that salvation depends on good works (*ib*. i. 9; Tit. iii. 5).

After dress and outward adornment Paul touches on the part women should play at church meetings. **A woman,** he lays it 11 down, **ought to learn quietly, with complete submissiveness.** The issue was a burning one, for whereas in the Jewish

synagogue silence was expected of women, we have evidence
that a new spirit of emancipation was spreading in the young
Christian congregations. In 1 Cor. xi. 4-15 Paul requires women
who pray or prophesy aloud at meetings to wear a veil; the
impression left is that he grudgingly recognizes the position,
presumably because the women concerned were under the influence of the Spirit. In *ib.* xiv. 33-36 he absolutely forbids
women to address the congregation and imposes silence on
12 them. In the same way he adds here, **I do not allow a woman
to teach . . . she ought to keep quiet.** For a woman to teach
in church, he suggests, is tantamount to her wielding **authority
over a man,** i.e. domineering, or laying down the law to, him;
and this, he implies, is contrary to the natural order. His repeated insistence on the point may be due to a suspicion on his
part that the Ephesian errorists were exploiting the readiness of
religiously minded women to claim what he considered an unbecoming prominence for themselves.

Paul advances two arguments in support of his ban. The first
13 is that **Adam was created first, and then Eve.** In other
words, what is chronologically prior is taken to be in some
sense superior. He had made the same point in 1 Cor. xi. 8,
pointing out that 'man did not come originally from woman,
but woman from man', and deducing from it her dependence
on the male. His second argument is based on the Biblical
14 account of the Fall: **Adam was not deceived, but it was the
woman who was deceived and fell into transgression.**
Paul is of course not questioning Adam's guilt, which he freely
acknowledges elsewhere (e.g. Rom. v. 12 ff.), and which in the
final assessment must have been all the greater since he sinned
with his eyes open. His point is that since Eve was so gullible a
victim of the serpent's wiles, she clearly cannot be trusted to
teach. If we are to follow Paul's reasoning, we must recall that
like other exegetes, Jewish and Christian, he regards Adam and
Eve as historical persons, but also as archetypes of the human
race. Their characters and propensities were transmitted to
their descendants, and in their relationship can be seen fore-
shadowed the permanent relationship between man and woman.
The prophecy of Gen. iii. 16 that Eve's desire would be to her
husband and that 'he shall rule over you' was clearly in his

mind, and equally clearly he regards it as applying to the entire female sex.

The preceding discussion might leave the impression that woman lies under God's permanent displeasure, and Paul hastens to correct this. **She will be saved, however,** he adds, 15 referring of course (as the future indicates), not to Eve, but to woman in general. But she will achieve this, not through performing masculine tasks like teaching in church, but **through child-bearing.** Her path to salvation, in other words, consists in accepting the role which was plainly laid down for her in Gen. iii. 16 ('in pain you shall bring forth children'). Even this, however, demands further qualification, since motherhood is the common lot of all women, and in any case salvation is not procured by mere works. So the Apostle adds, as a second and vital condition, **provided they continue in faith and love and sanctification, combined with chastity.** The transition to the plural **they** is awkward, and has led interpreters to postulate either 'the husband and wife' or 'their children' as the missing subject of **continue.** But it is as difficult to accept such an abrupt change of subject as to believe that Paul is arguing that a mother's salvation depends on the Christian behaviour of her children. The awkwardness disappears when it is recalled that in the whole paragraph he has been either speaking of women in the plural (9 f.) or speaking and thinking of woman generically.

This seems to be the only natural interpretation of the passage, unpalatable though the attitude to women implied may be by contemporary Christian standards. Commentators have proposed a variety of alternative exegeses, ranging from 'she shall be saved through the child-bearing', i.e. through the birth *par excellence* in which the Blessed Virgin brought the Saviour into the world, to Moffatt's 'However, women will get safely through childbirth, if . . .'. As regards the former, it is true, of course, that the child-bearing of Mary has undone the mischief of Eve, but it seems incredible that Paul should have expected his vague 'through the child-bearing' to be understood, without further explanation, of Christ's nativity. The latter, as well as yielding an intolerably banal sense, can only be extracted from the Greek with difficulty. The key to the passage, however, is

clearly Gen. iii. 16, with its prediction that motherhood is
woman's appointed role. If she sticks to this instead of usurping
masculine functions, and fulfils it in the right spirit, she will
obtain salvation. It is also likely that, in laying such stress on
the importance of child-bearing for women, Paul is aiming a
shaft at the false teachers, who had disparaging views about sex
(1 Tim. iv. 3), and whose later Gnostic successors, according to
Irenaeus (*Haer*. i. 24. 2) declared that 'marriage and the beget-
ting of children are of Satan'.

In the last resort a woman's salvation will depend on her
spiritual state, i.e. on her **faith** in Christ, the sincerity of her
love for her fellow-Christians, and her **sanctification,** or the
degree in which her married life is consecrated and not merely
carnal (for the word, see esp. 1 Thess. iv. 3; 4; 7). And these
gifts must be **combined with chastity;** the word is the same
(Gk. *sōphrosunē*) as is used in 9 above, where its nuance was
noticed.

6. DIRECTIONS FOR MINISTERS. iii. 1-13

**(1) It is a trustworthy saying, 'Anyone who aspires to
oversight sets his heart on a worthwhile job'. (2) The
overseer should therefore be above reproach, the husband of one wife, clear-headed, self-controlled, dignified,
hospitable, a skilled teacher, (3) not a slave of drink or
given to violence, but magnanimous, free from quarrelsomeness and attachment to money, (4) a man who
manages his own household well, keeping his children
in submission with unruffled dignity—(5) if a man cannot manage his own household, how will he look after
God's church? (6) He should not be a recent convert, so
that he may not get swollen-headed and incur the judgment of the devil; (7) and he ought also to have a good
reputation with outsiders, so that he may not incur
slander and get caught in the devil's trap. (8) Deacons
similarly should be serious, consistent in what they say,
not given to heavy drinking nor greedy for dishonest
gain, (9) holding fast the mystery of the faith with a clear**

conscience. (10) These, too, should have a preliminary
testing, and should then serve as deacons if no fault has
been found in them. (11) Women deacons similarly
should be serious-minded, not given to gossip, temperate,
reliable in everything. (12) Let deacons be husbands of
one wife, managing their children and their own households properly. (13) For those who have served well as
deacons secure a good standing for themselves as well
as great assurance in their faith in Christ Jesus.

Paul passes naturally from public worship to the qualities to
be looked for in the church's office-bearers. Although these are
frequently mentioned in the N.T., they nowhere receive such
detailed treatment as in the Pastorals (for the bearing of this on the
question of date and authorship, see Introduction, pp. 14-16; 28).
In this section the male officials are designated 'overseers' (Gk.
episkopoi) and 'deacons' (Gk. *diakonoi*), exactly as in Phil. i. 1.
Later (v. 17 f.: also Tit. i. 5) 'elders' (Gk. *presbuteroi*) are also
mentioned, and the relation between overseers and elders is a
major problem: see note on v. 17. Though the technical designation is there lacking, these ministers are almost certainly to be
identified with the 'leaders' (Gk. *proïstamenoi*; the same verb is
used twice in 4 f. below) to whom Paul refers in Rom. xii. 8
and 1 Thess. v. 12, and the 'pastors' whom he mentions in
Eph. iv. 11, as well as with the 'helpers' and 'administrators'
of 1 Cor. xii. 28.

There has been much discussion about how these functionaries emerged in the primitive Church. At the earliest stage
Spirit-inspired apostles, prophets, teachers, and miracle-
workers enjoyed great prestige in the Pauline congregations, and
the Apostle himself admits (1 Cor. xii. 28) that God had assigned
them their special precedence. Nothing indicates, however, that
these exercised pastoral and administrative oversight, and it is
doubtful whether their special pneumatic gifts would have
equipped them for it. From every point of view it seems probable that, side by side with them though lacking their popular
éclat, there always existed officials of a more practical kind
charged with what can broadly be described as pastoral responsibility. At first they must have been volunteers, like the members

of Stephanas's household (1 Cor. xvi. 15), but as time went on they must have gradually acquired official recognition. That such was in fact the situation is the clear implication of the passages cited above, which also seem to indicate that Paul was increasingly concerned to see that ministers were paid proper respect and recognized as possessing spiritual gifts. It will be argued later that they were normally selected, as was natural, from the board of elders which had a general superintendence over the affairs of each community.

Paul opens his discussion by quoting a tag which Timothy
1 was presumably expected to recognize: **Anyone who aspires to oversight sets his heart on a worthwhile job.** Since **oversight** (Gk. *episkopē*) does not necessarily refer to ecclesiastical office but can connote any kind of administration, this may possibly be a current proverb commending ambition for office in general. If so, it may reflect the growing reluctance among responsible people in the first and second centuries to undertake civic duties. An ecclesiastical reference, however, seems on the whole preferable, and if this is correct, the maxim suggests a situation in which deliberate efforts were being made to increase the esteem attaching to overseers and thus encourage good candidates to offer themselves for the position. It is interesting to note that the *Didache*, which may well have been written only a few years later, insists (xv. 1 f.) in precisely the same spirit on the desirability of choosing 'overseers and deacons who are worthy of the Lord . . . for they too fulfil among you the ministry of prophets and teachers'. On either interpretation Paul's object in quoting the tag is (*a*) to vindicate the importance of the practical ministry, and (*b*) to add force to his plea that church officers should possess the highest qualities.

According to the text printed above, Paul prefaces his maxim with the words, **It is a trustworthy saying.** This is the familiar formula of the Pastorals (see on i. 15), and raises two problems. (*a*) Exegetes have questioned, in ancient as well as modern times, whether it does not rather refer back to ii. 15. While it usually precedes its citation, the formula on occasion (iv. 9; Tit. iii. 8) follows it, and it is conceivable that Paul inserts it here to round off, as it were, the teaching he has just given about the salvation of women. On the other hand, neither

ii. 15 nor any of the verses immediately preceding strikes one as a maxim which might have been current in the apostolic Church, whereas iii. 1b has all the style and ring of a proverbial saying. (*b*) Instead of **trustworthy** (Gk. *pistos*) a few authorities read *anthrōpinos* (lit. 'human'). Several critics argue that *pistos* is the easier and more obvious reading, and therefore reject it in favour of *anthrōpinos*, which they translate 'popular'. The MS evidence for it, however, is very weak, and it can be accounted for as a disparaging marginal comment by some scribe who, failing to grasp Paul's point, considered the saying lacking in spiritual weight and therefore all too 'human'.

Having stressed the worthwhileness of the office, Paul can logically insist that **The overseer should therefore be above 2 reproach,** etc. The traditional rendering 'bishop' for Gk. *episkopos* has been deliberately rejected as misleading. The later episcopate, based on the conception of one bishop presiding in each area and having complete authority over it in all departments, developed out of the first-century 'overseers', but there are such important differences between the two offices that it seems desirable to use distinct terms for them. In the N.T. outside the Pastorals *episkopos* is found only in Phil. i. 1, Acts xx. 28, and 1 Pet. ii. 25 (with reference to our Lord). In the contemporary Greek world the term was used to denote a wide variety of functionaries, e.g. inspectors, civic and religious administrators, finance officers. It was formerly thought by many that the apostolic Church must have borrowed the title from this last usage, since the Christian *episkopos* had the finance of the congregation (poor relief, etc.) under his care. On the other hand, if we can trust the Pastorals and are right in identifying the 'leaders' and 'pastors' of the other Paulines as *episkopoi*, it is clear that their responsibilities covered a much wider field than finance alone. They had charge, for example, of the church's external relations and as its representatives entertained visiting Christians. In the congregation itself they exercised a teaching and pastoral ministry, and had authority to discipline members. In general they presided over its affairs as a father does over his family and household. It is therefore interesting to note that they find their closest parallel in the 'overseers' (in Hebrew *mebaqqer*) of the Qumran community.

According to the *Manual of Discipline* (esp. vi. 10 ff. and 19 ff.)
and the *Damascus Document* (esp. xiii. 7-16; xiv. 8-12), these
had the duty of commanding, examining, instructing, receiving
alms or accusations, dealing with the people's sins, and generally
shepherding them. It thus seems more than likely that the term,
and the administrative system it represented, passed into the
Church from heterodox Judaism.

In spite of its use in the singular both here and in Tit. i. 7, it
is extremely likely that **The overseer** is to be understood
generically, and that a plurality of such officials is presupposed.
This is borne out not only by the parallels in Phil. i. 1 and Acts
xx. 28, but by the interchangeability, or at any rate overlapping,
of overseers with elders (cf. v. 17; Tit. i. 5-7). There is in any
case no suggestion of the later 'monarchical' episcopate in these
letters. The singular may have been prompted by the singular
Anyone (in Gk. 'if anyone') in 1 above. For Paul's partiality for
the generic singular, cf. his discussion of widows in v. 4-10,
where he speaks of 'the widow', etc., in spite of having the
plural in v. 3.

The list of qualities which follows has sometimes surprised
readers by its generality; it has even been said, rather unfairly,
that it contains nothing specifically Christian, much less adapted
to a Christian minister. Two comments may be made. First,
analogous paradigms of virtues and vices, designed for different
callings (e.g. rulers, generals, doctors) were popular in the contemporary Hellenistic and Hellenistic Jewish world, and these
too were cast in remarkably general terms. The influence of
such paradigms is discernible elsewhere in the N.T., including
Paul's letters (e.g. Col. iii. 18-iv. 1; Eph. v. 22-vi. 9). The fact
that he is modelling his advice on them, here and elsewhere in
the Pastorals, accounts, in so far as is necessary, for its apparent
flatness and colourlessness. But, secondly, this aspect has been
greatly exaggerated. Every one of the qualities demanded was
appropriate in an overseer, and some of them had a direct
relevance to his functions. If the modern reader is sometimes
tempted to think that Paul pitched his requirements surprisingly
low, he should remember that standards of conduct were not
high in Asia Minor in the first century, that the people for whom
the letters were written had recently come out of, and probably

74

still had close contacts with, a pagan environment, and that the Apostle was a realist.

The catalogue opens with an all-embracing requirement; the overseer must **be above reproach.** That is, he should present 2 no obvious defect of character or conduct, in his past or present life, which the malicious, whether within or without the church, can exploit to his discredit. In particular, his sexual life must be exemplary, and the highest standards can be expected of him: he must be married only once. Re-marriage, whether after divorce in the case of a converted pagan or after the decease of his first wife, is frowned upon as unbecoming in a minister of Christ. It is equally forbidden to deacons (iii. 12) and elders (Tit. i. 6), and counts as a disqualification in aspirants to the order of widows (v. 9).

This is the plain meaning of **the husband of one wife.** Alternative interpretations proposed are (a) that the words are directed against either keeping concubines or polygamy, i.e. having more than one wife at the same time—suggestions which are improbable in the extreme, since neither of the practices can have been a live option for an ordinary Christian, much less a minister; (b) that they merely stipulate that the overseer should be a married man—this is in harmony with the high value the letter places on marriage (iv. 3), but is most unlikely in itself, and in any case makes the emphatic **one** in the Greek meaningless; (c) that their object is merely to prescribe fidelity within marriage, a suitable paraphrase being 'not lusting after other women than his wife'—but this is to squeeze more out of the Greek than it will bear. On this matter, as on many others, the attitude of antiquity differed markedly from that prevalent in most circles today, and there is abundant evidence, from both literature and funerary inscriptions, pagan and Jewish, that to remain unmarried after the death of one's spouse or after divorce was considered meritorious, while to marry again was taken as a sign of self-indulgence.

Paul certainly shared this view, and while permitting a widow to marry again esteemed her more blessed if she abstained from a second marriage (1 Cor. vii. 40). In general, while opposed to the ultra-asceticism which discountenanced marriage and applauded unnatural feats of self-denial (cf., e.g., his criticism of 'spiritual unions' in 1 Cor. vii. 36-38), he had a great respect for complete sexual abstinence, where it was possible, regarding it as a gift from God, and also held that periodical restraint within marriage was spiritually valuable (*ib.* vii. 1-7). In the context of such presuppositions it was natural to expect the Church's ministers to be examples to other people and content themselves with a single marriage. In the early Christian centuries, we should note, second marriages were not absolutely forbidden, but were regarded with distinct disapproval.

The overseer should in addition be **clear-headed,** a word (Gk. *nēphalios*: in the N.T. only here and in iii. 11; Tit. ii. 2) which originally connotes abstinence from alcohol, but which here, since drunkenness is expressly stigmatized in the next verse, probably has the wider, metaphorical sense. This is in line with Paul's use of the related verb *nēphō* in 1 Thess. v. 6 and 8: cf. 1 Pet. iv. 7.

The next two adjectives, **self-controlled** (Gk. *sōphrōn*: it may have the same nuance as the related noun *sōphrosunē* in ii. 9, where see note) and **dignified,** bring out essential traits in the overseer's character and external deportment respectively, while the third, **hospitable,** underlines that in his official capacity he has the duty of keeping open house both for delegates travelling from church to church and for ordinary needy members of the congregation. Cf. Paul's instructions to his correspondents (Rom. xii. 13) to 'minister to the needs of the saints and practise hospitality with enthusiasm'. This mutual service, at once charitable and diplomatic, played a great part in the daily life of the primitive Church, is abundantly attested (v. 10; Heb. xiii. 2; 1 Pet. iv. 9; 3 Jn. 5 ff.; 1 *Clem.* i. 2; Hermes, *Mand.* viii. 10), and fell primarily on the overseer (Tit. i. 8).

A further important aspect in the overseer's functions is indicated in the request that he should be **a skilled teacher.** The overseers are probably to be identified with that group within the body of elders who are 'occupied with preaching and teaching' (v. 17, where see note). These duties are more fully specified in Tit. i. 9 as comprising (*a*) loyalty to the apostolic tradition, (*b*) readiness to instruct the congregation in it, and (*c*) vigilance in confuting those who pervert it.

3   The overseer must further be on his guard against being

a slave of drink. The epithet (Gk. *paroinos*: only here and Tit. i. 7 in the N.T.) is a strong one; what is condemned is not drinking wine, but drunkenness. The same warning is given to deacons in iii. 8, and to elder-overseers in Tit. i. 7. Modern people are sometimes surprised that Paul should have thought it necessary to make such a ruling, but the danger must have been a real one in the uninhibited society in which the Ephesian and Cretan congregations were placed. We recall that at Corinth some Christians had been in the habit of getting drunk at the Lord's Supper (1 Cor. xi. 21). In such an atmosphere, so far removed from the bourgeois respectability of much modern Christianity, it was particularly desirable for the clergy to keep clear of intemperance and its unseemly consequences. Some of these may be hinted at in **or given to violence.** Literally translated, the Greek means 'not a giver of blows', and the reference may be to the brutality in which intoxication often results. More probably, however, Paul is hinting at the rough treatment the impatient overseer might be tempted to administer to irresponsible or recalcitrant members of his flock. Three centuries later the *Apostolic Constitutions* (VIII. xlvii. 27) found it necessary to depose bishops or other clerics guilty of such conduct.

From these prohibitions the Apostle passes to other qualities which, in spite of a superficially negative form, are really positive in content. By **magnanimous** (Gk. *epieikēs*) he means the gracious condescension, or forbearingness, with which the Christian pastor should deal with his charges, however exasperating they may on occasion be. Cf. Tit. iii. 2: the related noun *epieikeia* is used in 2 Cor. x. 2 of Jesus himself, the model of such understanding patience. So far from exhibiting **quarrelsomeness,** he should, it is implied, radiate a spirit of peace and mutual charity in the congregation. Finally, he should be **free from . . . attachment to money** (Gk. *aphilarguros*: only here and in Heb. xiii. 5 in the N.T.). This requirement, which is again made of the elder-overseer in Tit. i. 7, has both a general bearing, undue concern for money being unbecoming in a Christian, but in addition contains an allusion to the function of the *episkopos* as keeper of the community purse and as responsible for the charitable relief administered in its name.

A further, and crucial, test is added: the overseer must be

4 **a man who manages his own household well, keeping his children in submission with unruffled dignity.** It is taken for granted that he will normally be a married man, and as such he should see that his family life is exemplary. The idea is echoed in the ordinal in the *Book of Common Prayer*, where candidates for the priesthood are asked, 'Will you be diligent to frame and fashion your own selves, and your families, according to the doctrine of Christ, and to make both yourselves and them, as much as in you lieth, wholesome examples and patterns to the flock of Christ?' Some have taken the last three words as applying to the children (cf. Moffatt's '. . . keep his children submissive and perfectly respectful'), but the noun **dignity** (Gk. *semnotēs*) seems more appropriate to the father's attitude. The point is that he must maintain strict discipline, but without fuss or resort to violence.

The underlying reason for this stipulation is brought out, in a rhetorical question characteristic of Paul's style (e.g. 1 Cor.
5 xiv. 7; 9; 16): —**if a man cannot manage his own households, how will he look after God's church?** The word **church** has no article, and might be translated 'a church of God's', i.e. any local congregation. The Apostle sees its life and problems reflected in microcosm in those of the human family, and implies that essentially the same qualities are needed for leadership in both: for the analogy, cf. Eph. ii. 19 ('members of God's household'); v. 28-vi. 9. Without going into a detailed analysis, the comparison, and in particular the use of the verbs **manage** and **look after,** throw a revealing light on the role of the first-century overseer in the congregation.

6   The demand that the overseer **should not be a recent convert** has been hailed as 'an unguarded admission that the Pastorals are considerably later than the time of Paul' (E. F. Scott). It certainly rules out an early date in the Apostle's ministry, but is quite consistent with a date after his first Roman imprisonment, by which time the Ephesian church had been in existence at least a dozen years. It is significantly absent from the parallel instructions about overseers for the Cretan church, which had only recently been founded (Tit. i. 6). The term for **recent convert** (Gk. *neophutos*) literally means 'newly planted'; this is its only occurrence in the N.T., but Paul uses the same

metaphor for converting people to the faith in 1 Cor. iii. 6.

The temptation to promote recent converts, especially ones of social rank and influence, must have been great in a youthful church like that at Ephesus, but the dangers are obvious. In particular Paul singles out that of becoming **swollen-headed.** The Greek verb *tuphousthai* (only here and in vi. 4; 2 Tim. iii. 4 in the Bible) literally means 'to be filled, or enveloped, with smoke'. It is always used metaphorically, and connotes the beclouding of the mind and judgment, here as the result of conceit engendered by over-rapid advancement.

The real danger in which the conceited upstart stands is that he **may . . . incur the judgment of the devil.** This expression has caused needless difficulty to commentators. Because the Greek word *diabolos* when used in the plural in the Pastorals (iii. 11; 2 Tim. iii. 3; Tit. ii. 3) has the meaning 'gossips', 'slanderers', some have thought that it must bear that sense here. So the translation 'may . . . incur the criticism of malicious gossips' has been proposed. This provides, however, an intolerably weak climax, for we have been expecting a much direr fate for the conceited neophyte. In any case *diabolos* in the singular can in a Christian context only mean the devil, and this is the only sense it can bear in 2 Tim. ii. 26, and much the most likely in the next verse. If this is agreed, two interpretations are possible, depending on whether the genitive is taken as objective or subjective. If the former, the meaning will be 'incur the sentence passed on the devil'; if the latter, 'incur the sentence which the devil will carry out on him'. Either is possible, but the former does nothing to prepare the way for 7, and introduces ideas about the devil's fate which are irrelevant to the context. The latter, on the contrary, is fully in harmony with the idea contained in 7, and also with the matter and spirit of i. 20.

As leader and representative of his flock, the overseer **ought 7 also to have a good reputation with outsiders,** i.e. among non-Christians, Jewish and pagan, in the locality. It is always important for Christians, as Paul frequently impressed upon his correspondents (1 Cor. x. 32; Phil. ii. 15; Col. iv. 5; 1 Thess. iv. 12: also vi. 1; Tit. ii. 5) to aim at this, and this applies particularly to the clergy, by whose character and conduct the world tends to judge the church. The pastor who fails in this respect is liable to **incur slander,** since unsympathetic outsiders will put the most unfavourable interpretation on his slightest word or deed. In that event he may well **get caught in the devil's trap.** This last phrase could be rendered 'trap set by the slanderer' (see note on 6 for the double sense of Gk. *diabolos*), and this translation has sometimes been accepted. It must be objected, however, that this not only gives *diabolos* (in the singular) a very unlikely sense, but also adds little or nothing to the preceding **incur slander.** On the other hand, the picture of the devil setting snares to discredit the overseer, and through him the church, is in harmony with 2 Tim. ii. 26, and also with the general conception of his activities set out in the Pastorals.

8   Paul brackets **Deacons** closely with the overseer; precisely the same juxtaposition meets us in Phil. i. 1, as well as in second-century documents like Ignatius's letters. The implication must be that, although they were subordinate in rank, the functions of deacons covered much the same ground as those of *episkopoi*. The primary meaning in the N.T. of *diakonein*, from which 'deacon' is derived, is to serve in a menial capacity, such as waiting at table (e.g. Lk. xvii. 8; xxii. 26 f.; Jn. xii. 2), and Jesus taught that the role of his disciples, like his own, could be fittingly compared with that of someone who serves at meals. It was the term 'deacon', or servant, which he employed to express his own revolutionary ideal of human relationships as mutual service involving complete self-sacrifice (Mk. x. 43-5; Mt. xx. 26-8). By a natural transition, therefore, every kind of service in the propagation of the gospel is in the N.T. described as a *diakonia*, or ministry. The work accomplished by Paul and Barnabas on the first missionary journey is one (Acts xii. 25); in particular, the task of collecting alms for the Jerusalem congregation, to which Paul gave high priority, counted in his eyes as one too (Rom. xv. 31; 2 Cor. viii. 4; etc.). An apostle is a 'deacon of Christ' (*ib.* xi. 23: cf. iv. 1; Rom. xi. 13). Paul describes himself as 'a deacon' of the Church (Col. i. 25), and in this letter speaks of Timothy as 'a deacon of Christ Jesus' (iv. 6: cf. 2 Tim. iv. 5).

The origin of a specific order of deacons in the primitive Church has been much discussed, but remains wrapped in ob-

scurity. The traditional explanation, viz. that it is to be sought
in the appointment of the Seven (they are nowhere actually
termed 'deacons') in Acts vi, is almost certainly wrong.
Stephen and his companions were not strictly ministers in any
sense analogous to the deacons of the later apostolic and post-
apostolic ages. They were *ad hoc* representatives of the interests
of the Hellenists with the Twelve, and are depicted as evangelists disputing, teaching, and baptizing alongside them. The rise
of deacons as a regular order of ministers must have been
closely connected with that of the *episkopoi* (see above, pp. 71-74),
whose associates they were. If the *episkopoi* were the 'administrators' (lit. 'governments') mentioned by Paul in 1 Cor. xii. 28,
the deacons must have been the 'assistants' (lit. 'helps') to
whom he refers in the same breath. Their subordinate, auxiliary
role is brought out (*a*) by the absence of any suggestion that
they were responsible for teaching or hospitality, and (*b*) by the
hints that their preliminary scrutiny was, if anything, more
rigorous than that of the overseers.

Though often dismissed as colourless and general, the list of
qualities required of deacons in fact bears a close relation to
their duties. It is fitting, in the first place, that they should be
serious (Gk. *semnos*), an adjective which covers at once inward
temper and outward bearing. The cognate noun has already
been used to designate an essential quality in Christians in
general (ii. 2) and overseers in particular (iii. 4). The expression
rendered **consistent in what they say** (Gk. *mē dilogous*) has
been taken to mean 'no tale-bearers', the reference being to the
opportunities for malicious tittle-tattle which deacons had in
their house-to-house pastoral work. A literal translation, however, would be 'not double-talkers', and so it is likely that the
true sense is either 'not saying one thing while thinking another'
or (more probably) 'not saying one thing to one man and a
different thing to the next'.

The warning against being **given to heavy drinking** echoes
in more precise terms the counsel of sobriety given in 3 to the
overseer. So too **nor greedy for dishonest gain** is parallel to
free from . . . attachment to money in the same verse,
although the adjective (Gk. *aischrokerdēs*: only here and in Tit.
i. 7 in the N.T.) is a much stronger one. It may, as some have

thought, carry an allusion to doubtful occupations which deacons should be careful to avoid, but Paul is probably thinking rather of the temptations to which their responsibilities in regard to the alms, poor relief, and finance generally of the congregation might expose them.

9 Most important of all, however, deacons must be men of Christian conviction, **holding fast the mystery of the faith with a clear conscience.** The accent here is on the concluding words, and Paul is insisting on the intimate relation between sound belief and a conscience free from stain and self-reproach; without the latter, the former must be sterile. For **conscience,** see note on i. 5. As so often in the Pastorals, **the faith** stands for the Christian faith regarded as an objective body of teaching: cf. iv. 1; 6; v. 8; vi. 10; 2 Tim. iii. 8. The basic meaning of **mystery,** in Judaism as in Christianity of the apostolic age, is a divine secret which has now been divulged. So when Paul uses it in Col. i. 26 f. (and in Rom. xvi. 25 if authentic), what he has in mind is God's redemptive plan which has been kept hidden from the beginning, but has at last been made manifest, to those with eyes to see, in the coming of Christ. Since Christ himself is the focal point of the divine plan, the Apostle can speak succinctly of 'the mystery of Christ', i.e. which consists in Christ (Col. iv. 3), and if it were fully expounded, it would comprise the key-articles of the Christian kerygma or creed. Thus **the mystery of the faith** is equivalent to the totality of hidden truths, inaccessible to reason and made known only by divine revelation (cf. iii. 16; Eph. iii. 4).

Many students, especially those who question the authenticity of the letters, are doubtful of this interpretation. According to them, **mystery** has in this passage lost the characteristically Pauline sense (cf. 1 Cor. ii. 7; iv. 1; xiii. 2; xiv. 2; xv. 51), and either denotes what transcends ordinary comprehension or has become a mere piece of heavy theological jargon. The references given above, however, indicate that the gulf between the exegesis proposed and Paul's normal usage is by no means so wide as these critics suggest. It may also be questioned (*a*) whether the Pastorals anywhere imply that 'men cannot understand the gospel' (E. F. Scott), and (*b*) whether, even in the post-apostolic age, 'mystery' was used to connote simply truths which pass understanding and have to be accepted with blind faith. Even Ignatius, for example, when he speaks of 'three mysteries to be cried aloud' (*Eph.* xix. 1), gives the word a sense strictly in line with the Pauline.

These, too, i.e. the deacons no less than the overseers, 10 **should have a preliminary testing.** Only **if,** after careful screening as regards their character, past conduct, and general suitability, **no fault has been found in them,** are they to be permitted to **serve as deacons.** Some have thought that a probationary period or a formal examination is envisaged, and either or both are possible. On the whole, however, in view of the parallelism with 7, some less formal consideration of their record seems implied; the requirement of the Twelve that the Seven should be 'men of good reputation' (Acts vi. 3) provides a parallel. Even so, Paul's language seems to suggest that the scrutiny was stricter for deacons than for overseers; e.g. the term **testing** is not used of the choosing of the latter.

The following verse contains a puzzle which will probably never be solved to everyone's satisfaction. Despite the translation **Women deacons similarly,** the original Greek has only 11 'Women similarly' (no article before the noun). It is agreed on all hands that Paul cannot, in a passage concerned with special groups, be interjecting a reference to the women of the congregation in general. The words could, however, mean, 'Let their wives [i.e. of the deacons] similarly . . .', and many commentators prefer this rendering. But if this is the sense, (*a*) we should have expected the definite article before 'Women', or at least the genitive pronoun after it, or some other turn bringing out that they were 'their wives'; (*b*) it is very strange that only deacons' wives are singled out for mention, since the overseers' wives occupied an even more influential position; (*c*) the adverb **similarly,** repeated from 8, leads us to expect a fresh category of officials, as does also the list of parallel, if not identical, qualities. For these reasons the translation **Women deacons** is likely to be the correct one. The absence of the article is, if anything, a point in its favour, **Women** being used almost adjectivally—'deacons who are women'. It has been asked why, if Paul meant deaconesses, he did not use a separate technical term, but a sufficient answer is that the N.T. does not know one. Phoebe, for example is simply called 'deacon (Gk. *diakonos*) of the church at Cenchreae' in Rom. xvi. 1. Their lack of a technical word for deaconesses is a small but significant pointer to the primitiveness of the Pastorals.

The emergence of the order of deaconesses in the primitive Church is very obscure, as is the relation between it and the order of widows (see C. H. Turner, 'Ministries of Women in the Primitive Church' in *Catholic and Apostolic*, ed. H. N. Bate, 1933). The office developed greatly in the third and fourth centuries, and is described in *Didascalia* (third cent.) and *Apostolic Constitutions* (second half of fourth cent.). In 112, however, Pliny in his well-known letter to Trajan (*Ep.* x. 96) mentions a couple of deaconesses, using the technical term *ministrae*, and there is every reason to suppose that female officiants were required for duties in connexion with women (e.g. pastoral work with the sick and poor, assistance at baptism, carrying official messages, etc.) from the beginning. The hints contained in Rom. xvi. 1 and this passage are evidence that this was the case, and the brief list of qualities demanded supplies further confirmation. Like their male counterparts, they must be **serious-minded** and **temperate** in the use of alcohol, and in addition must resist the temptations of **gossip** to which their pastoral functions would lay them open.

Paul then returns to the male deacons, insisting that, like the 12 overseers, they should be **husbands of one wife,** i.e. marry only once in their lifetime (see note on 2 above), and should give proof of their fitness for pastoral office by **managing their children and their own households properly.** He then touches on the rewards in store for them if they carry out their duties successfully and in the right spirit. In the first place, 13 **those who have served well as deacons secure a good standing for themselves,** i.e. they ensure that their office, for all its modest title and appearance of subordination, is one of influence and respect in the community at large.

The word translated **standing** (Gk. *bathmos*: a N.T. hapax) literally means either 'base', 'foundation' (e.g. of a pedestal), or 'stair', 'step'. Figuratively it can be used to denote a degree of advancement or rank (e.g. in the army), or in religion a stage in the soul's growth in knowledge (so in Clement of Alexandria) or in its heavenly progress (so in the *Corpus Hermeticum*). One widely accepted exegesis therefore refers it here to a step in the ministry; Paul is promising deacons that, if they serve loyally, they can hope for promotion to the rank of overseer. Though this is the meaning of the word in later writers and liturgies, it seems out of context here, and it is in any case unlikely that anything like a precisely ordered ladder of ecclesiastical promotion was in force in the first, or even early second, century. Others have taken it in a Godward sense; faithful deacons will make spiritual progress, or will even establish a closer relationship between themselves and God. This again brings in alien ideas, and overlooks the connexion between this verse and the preceding one; the transition from the possession of humdrum virtues like those mentioned above to heavenly rewards seems much too abrupt. For these reasons it seems most likely that the Apostle is thinking of the repute and influence the deacons will have with the congregation; his encouragement to them is parallel to his description of the overseer's office as 'a worthwhile job'.

This, however, is not their only reward; they will also find themselves endowed with **great assurance in their faith in Christ Jesus.** 'Assurance' (Gk. *parrhēsia*) is, with its cognates, a favourite with Paul. Its basic meaning in all contexts is the peculiar courage and confidence which the true apostle brings to his preaching of the word. Usually it is confidence before men (2 Cor. vii. 4; Phil. i. 20; 1 Thess. ii. 2), but sometimes confidence in drawing close to God (Eph. iii. 12). Here the **assurance** promised to the faithful deacons probably includes both; they will be conscious of an increasing boldness in proclaiming the gospel, and also of an ever-deepening confidence in their approach to God. And this **assurance** has its roots and motive force **in their faith in Christ Jesus.** For the expression, which means much more than 'Christian faith' (B. S. Easton), see on i. 14. The Apostle's meaning is illustrated by Eph. iii. 12, where he describes his assurance as based on 'the confidence born of trust in him' (NEB).

7. GOD'S HOUSEHOLD AND THE CHRISTIAN MYSTERY. iii. 14-16

(14) I am writing you these instructions in the hope of coming to you shortly, (15) but in case I should be held up, so that you may know the behaviour suitable in God's household, that is, a church of the living God, a pillar and buttress of the truth. (16) Yes, beyond all question great is the mystery of our religion—'Who was manifested in flesh, vindicated in spirit, gazed on by angels, proclaimed among the nations, believed in throughout the world, taken up in glory.'

This section has been well described (M. Dibelius) as 'the caesura' of the letter, i.e. the dividing point which gives it significance. Not only does it form the bridge between the first part, with its instructions about prayer and the ministry, and the practical directions of the second part, but by highlighting the true functions of a church it provides the theological basis for the rules and regulations, as well as for the onslaught on false teaching, which make up the body of the letter. The gist of Paul's message is that order, in the widest sense of the term, is necessary in the Christian congregation precisely because it is God's household, his chosen instrument for proclaiming to men the saving truth of the revelation of the God-man, Jesus Christ.

The syntax of the first two verses is clumsy; Paul would have expressed his meaning more logically had he written, 'Although I hope to come to you shortly, I am sending you these written instructions so that, in the event of my being held up, you may know. . .'. For the situation envisaged, and the argument that

14 it bears traces of artificiality, see note on i. 3. The **instructions** cover the entire charge contained in the letter. Since there is a real possibility of delay, Paul naturally wants to set it down in writing, especially as his advice about church order and the necessity of maintaining sound teaching is clearly intended for a wider audience than Timothy alone. This applies particularly to the present passage, with its implied suggestions about the responsibilities of church membership.

The translation **the behaviour suitable in God's house-** 15
hold assumes that the Greek means 'how *one* ought to behave',
not 'how *you* ought to behave'. In favour of the latter, which
was preferred by several of the fathers (also AV), are (*a*) the
singular verb **so that you may know,** and (*b*) the fact that it
rested with Timothy more than anyone else to see that Paul's
ideals were realized at Ephesus. On the other hand, the verb
'to behave' (Gk. *anastrephesthai*) is a comprehensive one and
aptly covers the conduct expected from, and the mutual relations of, all the groups discussed. To understand it as applying
to the Ephesian church generally also consorts better both with
the semi-public character of the letter and with the idea of the
congregation as God's family.

The original of **God's household** has been translated by
many 'God's house', the Gk. *oikos* being given the sense of
'building'. This is perfectly possible and is supported by (*a*) the
architectural metaphors in the second half of the verse, and (*b*)
Paul's language elsewhere (e.g. 1 Cor. iii. 9; 16 f.; Eph. iv. 12).
In this passage, however, Paul is clearly picking up the thought
of iii. 4; 5; 12, where *oikos* means 'household' (cf. 2 Tim. i. 16;
Tit. i. 11) and the analogy between a church and a human
family is explicitly or implicitly present. He speaks of Christians
forming a family with one another in the faith in Gal. vi. 10 and
with God in Eph. ii. 19.

It is such a family or household, made into a unity by its
divine Head, that each congregation, or **church of the living
God,** forms. As in iii. 5, there is no definite article before
church, and this suggests that Paul is thinking primarily of
the particular local community. His comment may carry implications for the Church universal, but no doctrine of it is
explicitly set forth here. Paul frequently describes God as
living (iv. 10; 2 Cor. iii. 3; vi. 16; 1 Thess. i. 9). He borrows
the epithet from the O.T., where it serves to bring out the
contrast between Yahweh and dead idols.

The local congregation, Paul adds, is **a pillar and buttress
of the truth.** As in the Pastorals generally (see on ii. 4), **the
truth** stands for the full revelation of God in Christ, but carries
the nuance of 'the orthodox faith'. The choice of word here is
motivated by conscious opposition to the errorists about to

be denounced in iv. 1 ff. What Paul is saying is that it is the function and responsibility of each congregation to support, bolster up, and thus safeguard the true teaching by its continuous witness. We should note (a) that **buttress** is probably a more accurate rendering of the Greek *hedraiōma* (nowhere else found) than 'foundation' or 'ground' (AV), and (b) that the local church is described as **a pillar,** etc., not 'the pillar, etc.', because there are many local churches throughout the world performing this role.

Two other interpretations of the passage should be mentioned. It has been proposed that **pillar and buttress of the truth** should (a) be taken as in apposition to Timothy, the understood subject of **you may know** above, or (b) be attached to what follows and made to qualify **the mystery of our religion.** The latter can be dismissed at once. It involves a tautology, since **the mystery of our religion** is not the support of the truth but the truth itself; and the anticlimax of **beyond all question great** coming after **pillar and buttress** is intolerable. The former is slightly more plausible. But, in the first place, there is far too much matter intervening between the words and **you may know** to allow of their being connected with that verb; in the second place, the subject of discussion is not Timothy but the function of the church. Exegetes have had recourse to these expedients because they have imagined that, as ordinarily interpreted, the passage must imply that the church is somehow the foundation or ground of the gospel, whereas the exact opposite is the case (1 Cor. iii. 11). But if the translation and explanation given above are correct, the alleged difficulty is non-existent. Paul's sole concern is to emphasize that the members of each local community should be a strong bulwark of the gospel against the assaults of false teachers.

The mention of **the truth** stimulates the almost ecstatic out-
16 burst, **Yes, beyond all question great is the mystery of our religion.** The adverb rendered **beyond all question** (Gk. *homologoumenōs*) means 'by common consent', and expresses the unanimous conviction of Christians. In some MSS it is broken up into two words, *homologoumen hōs*, i.e. 'we confess that . . .', but this is quite unnecessary and destroys the note of solemn emphasis. As in 9 above, **the mystery** stands for God's

88

redemptive plan which has been kept secret from all ages but has now been revealed. The original of **our religion** is the Gk. *eusebeia*, so characteristic of the Pastorals: see note on ii. 2. The whole phrase, which for all intents and purposes is equivalent to 'the mystery of faith' in 9 and 'the truth' in 15, might be paraphrased, 'The saving revelation which lies behind, and finds expression in, Christian faith and life'.

The formula **great is the mystery . . .**, it has been pointed out, is strangely like the cry, 'Great is Artemis of the Ephesians' (Acts xix. 28; 34). There is inscriptional and other evidence that the latter was a regular cult acclamation at Ephesus in the first century. The resemblance is probably mere coincidence, but it is just conceivable that Paul is deliberately framing his own Christian claim in terms which repudiate the pagan claim so often heard at Ephesus.

In justification of his high estimate of **the mystery of our religion,** Paul epitomizes its content in an excerpt from a primitive hymn about Christ. That it is a hymn, not a credal fragment or piece of catechetical material, is borne out by the careful parallelism of the strophes, the rhythmic diction, and the deliberate assonance (very marked in the Greek) of the six third person singular aorist verbs. For the similar use of a hymn, cf. 2 Tim. ii. 11-13. The quotation is only a fragment, a complex relative clause opening with the pronoun **Who** (Gk. *hos*) without any principal clause. This evidently caused difficulty to early exegetes and scribes, some of whom tried to amend the text so as to produce a smooth-flowing sentence. Thus the majority of Western witnesses substitute the neuter *ho* (='which') for *hos*, so linking the clause with **the mystery of our religion.** A number of later MSS read *theos* (='God') for *hos*, which gives the translation 'God was manifested . . .' (so AV). Both these variants are clearly secondary, being attempts to eliminate the superficial disjointedness of the true text. Unquestionably *hos* has the best MS support and represents the true text, and there can in any case be no doubt that Christ, not God, must be the subject of the following verbs. The absence of an antecedent is explained by the fragmentary character of the passage cited.

The essence of the Christian mystery, Paul affirms (cf. Col. i.

27), is Christ himself, incarnate and glorified. The missing antecedent clause must have mentioned him by name; now in six compact strophes the relative clause sets out key-moments in his glorification. Since the excerpt is a mere fragment and the language of hymnody tends to be cryptic, it is not possible to identify all of these exactly, but the first at any rate is absolutely clear. It stresses the incarnation, stating that Christ **was manifested in flesh,** i.e. appeared on earth as a real man. As in the related Christological passages Rom. i. 3 (probably an extract from catechetical material) and 1 Pet. iii. 18, **flesh** stands for the God-man's humanity and not, as so often in Paul, for the flesh as the seat of sin. For the verb 'manifest' (Gk. *phanerousthai*) cf. Heb. ix. 26; 1 Pet. i. 20; Paul himself does not use it of the incarnation, although speaking (2 Tim. i. 10) of Christ's 'appearing' (Gk. *epiphaneia*). His pre-existence is probably, though not necessarily, implied.

The second strophe, **vindicated in spirit,** is more difficult. Since **vindicated** (Gk. *edikaiōthē*) literally means 'justified' or 'declared righteous', M. Dibelius argues that what is affirmed is Christ's exaltation to the divine sphere, the sphere of righteousness. Admittedly this entails giving 'justified' a sense it has nowhere else in the N.T., but this is not a serious problem, especially as the passage is a citation. The real problem is how to extract this meaning from the Greek, for **spirit** does not naturally suggest 'the sphere of spirit'. If this interpretation is rejected, we are left with two alternatives. (*a*) If **spirit** is taken as strictly parallel to **flesh,** the two expressions must stand for the divine and human elements in Christ's being respectively, as in Rom. i. 3 and 1 Pet. iii. 18. The clause will then affirm that, while the Saviour appeared on earth as true man, he was **vindicated,** i.e. declared righteous and shown to be in fact Son of God, in respect of his spiritual nature, a reference to the resurrection being implied. (*b*) Others, giving **in** an instrumental sense and reading **spirit** as denoting the Holy Spirit, prefer the rendering, 'He was declared righteous through, or by means of, the Holy Spirit'. The meaning will then be that, although Christ was crucified as a malefactor, God vindicated him and declared him to be righteous when, through the Holy Spirit (cf. Rom. viii. 11), he raised him from the dead. It is difficult to decide between these two exegeses, especially as in primitive thought no clear distinction was drawn between Holy Spirit and the Lord's spiritual nature. If a choice must be made, it should probably be in favour of (a) in view of the manifest parallelism between **flesh** and **spirit** and the consequent difficulty of giving **in** before the latter an instrumental sense.

The third strophe, **gazed on by angels,** has been much discussed, but its broad meaning is really beyond dispute. Attempts have been made to explain it as referring either to the messengers (the Greek word translated **angels** can equally well signify 'messengers') who reported Christ's resurrection, or to the angels who attended his earthly life (Mk. i. 13; Lk. ii. 13; xxiv. 23; Jn. i. 51), or to 'the fuller knowledge of Christ's person which was opened out to the heavenly host by the incarnation' (J. H. Bernard, quoting 1 Pet. i. 12 and Eph. iii. 10 in support). All these exegeses, however, make the mistake of assuming that Christ's incarnate experiences are in view and thus miss the point the hymn is making. What it is in fact stressing is the worship accorded by angelic powers to the ascending, glorified Christ. Illuminating parallels are furnished by Phil. ii. 9 f.; Col. ii. 15; Heb. i. 6, where his exaltation is represented as a triumph over the world of spirits which elicits their adoration. The theme was elaborated in popular early Christian teaching: cf. *Ascension of Isaiah*, xi. 23.

The remaining three strophes present relatively fewer problems. The fourth, **proclaimed among the nations,** affirms the world-wide preaching of the gospel of Christ. 'Nations' (Gk. *ethnē*) is ambiguous, and can denote either the nations of the earth, i.e. mankind, or the Gentiles in particular. Our decision between these alternatives must be determined by the view we take of the structure of the hymn as a whole (see next paragraph). The fifth, **believed in throughout the world,** which emphasizes the universal acceptance of the gospel preached, is again ambiguous, since **world** (Gk. *kosmos*) can mean either the entire created universe or simply the whole of mankind. Finally, **taken up in glory,** which might seem a mere repetition of previous allusions to Christ's exaltation, contains in fact much more than that. 'Glory' is a technical term for the dazzling brightness with which God's presence is encompassed. Thus the whole phrase implies, not just that Christ ascended, but that he has been taken up into the realm of the divine glory, there to reign with the Father.

Further light on the bearing of the hymn can be obtained by a study of its structure and plan. According to some there are two verses, each containing three lines. On this view the first three strophes have as their theme the successive phases in Christ's exaltation—his incarnation, his resurrection, his ascension through the higher sphere of the angelic powers; while the last three strophes dwell on the universality of his reign—among the Gentiles (or perhaps mankind as a whole), in the whole world (or perhaps the entire universe), in heaven itself. The chief objections to this arrangement are: (a) the two sets of significant moments which are intended to be highlighted do not in fact stand out at all clearly; and (b) it completely overlooks the manifest parallelism between **flesh** and **spirit, angels** and **nations,** and **world** and **glory.** This parallelism makes it practically certain that the hymn is really arranged in three couplets, each containing a carefully designed antithesis. First, Christ incarnate and thus in the form of a servant is seen vindicated at his resurrection. Secondly, Christ receives the worship of angels and is preached to the nations of mankind, i.e he is brought to the knowledge of all rational beings, celestial and terrestrial. Thirdly, he is accepted both throughout the entire created universe (cf. Col. i. 23) and in the heavenly realm itself.

Working on this basis, J. Jeremias has suggested that the pattern influencing, no doubt unconsciously, the unknown author's mind must have been that of the ancient enthronement ritual of Egypt and the Near East generally. This involved three successive acts—the king's exaltation and acceptance of divine attributes, the presentation of the now deified king to the circle of the gods, and his enthronement. He sees parallels to the first of these in Christ's elevation to the realm of divine being in the first couplet, to the second in the proclamation of his lordship to angels in heaven and mankind on earth, and to the third in the acceptance of his reign implied in the last two strophes. This proposal is ingenious and attractive, and Jeremias discerns

a parallel in Heb. i. 5 ff.; but (a) there are difficulties in working
out his scheme (e.g. if it is accepted, the deliberate parallelisms
seem to lose their point), and (b) it is doubtful whether the
superficial similarity of patterns is more than a coincidence.

8. A WARNING AGAINST FALSE ASCETICISM.
iv. 1-5

**(1) The Spirit expressly states that in the last times some
will abandon the faith, paying attention to deceptive
spirits and the teachings of devils, (2) as a result of the
hypocrisy of liars whose consciences have been branded,
(3) who forbid marriage, and bid one abstain from foods
which God created to be partaken of with thanksgiving
by people who believe and have come to know the truth.
(4) For everything created by God is good, and nothing
is to be rejected provided it is received with thanksgiving; (5) for then it is sanctified by the word of God
and prayer.**

After his brief digression extolling the Christian mystery,
Paul addresses himself once again to the errorists, whom he
has scarcely touched on since ch. i. That an attack was to be
launched was hinted in iii. 15, with its mention of correct
behaviour in the Christian congregation. This time he fastens
on the heretics' practical advice, with its bias in favour of a
basically un-Christian asceticism, and he contrasts with it the
authentically Christian kind of self-discipline.

Such false teaching might be a problem for the Church, were
it not that it has already been forewarned: **The Spirit expressly 1
states that in the last times some will abandon the faith.**
It is of course impossible to identify the prophecy. Critics who
deny Pauline authorship sometimes claim that the writer is
thinking of Paul's own warning prediction to the Ephesian
elders (Acts xx. 29 f.), but even on their assumption this is
unnecessary. The belief that false teaching resulting in apostasy
would have to be reckoned with in the period before the

Parousia was deeply embedded in primitive Christian thought. We have examples in the Lord's logion recorded in Mk. xiii. 22 and in 2 Thess. ii. 3; 11 f.: cf. also 2 Tim. iii. 1 ff. The Qumran sect, apparently, shared the view that 'at the end of the days' blasphemers would arise (see *Habakkuk Commentary* ii. 5 f.). Passages like Acts xi. 27 f.; xiii. 1 f.; 1 Cor. xiv give illustrations of the way in which the Spirit conveyed his warnings to the community.

For **the faith** in the objective sense, see on iii. 9. The falling-away, or apostasy, has been prophesied for **the last times.** This is a better translation than the more common, and literal, 'in later times'. The expression is equivalent to 'in the last [Gk. *eschatais*: here *husterois*] days' in 2 Tim. iii. 1. The fact that this critical epoch is equated with the present indicates that the hope of the imminent Parousia is still alive. The apostates' lapse, Paul explains, is due to their **paying attention to deceptive spirits and the teachings of devils;** in other words, he detects in it the malefic stratagems of Satan and his allies, much as he had discerned their influence at work in the Corinthian opposition (2 Cor. ii. 11) and, more generally, in men's resistance to the truth (*ib.* iv. 4; Eph. ii. 2).

These demons, however, employ human agents; thus the 2 apostasy comes about **as the result of the hypocrisy of liars whose consciences have been branded.** These are of course the false teachers themselves, who are therefore described as **liars** (lit. 'false-speakers'). In accusing them of **hypocrisy** Paul is insinuating that their air of devotion and ethical rigour is only a specious mask. In addition they are people who are in the service of Satan and in consequence have their **consciences** stamped with the brand-mark which indicates his ownership. The verb used (Gk. *kaustēriazein*: nowhere else in the Bible) means 'to brand with a hot iron'. A possible alternative inter-pretation (preferred by RSV) is that their consciences have been 'cauterized', i.e. made insensible to the distinction between right and wrong. This would agree with Paul's description (Eph. iv. 19) of pagans who have no knowledge of Christ as 'dead to all feeling'. It is difficult to be sure which is right, but brand-marks indicating the owner's title were stamped on the fore-heads of slaves, and this idea perhaps harmonizes better with the suggestion that the errorists are the instruments of demonic powers.

Paul now proceeds to define a particular aspect of their doctrine: the errorists **forbid marriage, and bid one abstain 3 from foods** . . . (there is no **and bid one** in the original: the infinitive 'to abstain' is attached to **forbid** by zeugma). As regards the former point, the discouragement of marriage, as of sex generally, was a definitely Gnostic trait, and came to the fore in the great second-century Gnostic systems. It was based on the dualism which was integral to Gnosticism, the principle being that matter, including the human body and its functions, was evil and that the religious man should do his best to live emancipated from it. Such ideas were alien to Judaism generally, although Josephus reports (*Bell. Iud.* ii. 8. 2) that the Essenes disparaged marriage. This has tempted many to identify the heretics as Gnostics proper, but this is to ignore the Jewish background of their teaching and the fact that all the main features of developed Gnosticism are absent from it (see Introduction, pp. 11 f.). There is evidence of a negative attitude to sex, not perhaps so radical as this, in the Corinthian church (1 Cor. vii. 1 ff.: esp. 36 ff.), and Paul had earlier dealt with this in his sensible way. What we have to do with here is not so much thorough-going Gnosticism as an incipient tendency in that direction manifested by converted Jews in a syncretistic environment. It is noticeable that, while implicitly condemning it, Paul does not refute it by argument. The explanation probably is that he has already made his views on the naturalness and propriety of marriage abundantly clear in his treatment of the qualities required in office-bearers.

He produces a reasoned case, however, against the heretics' food regulations. The precise nature of the abstinence demanded is not clear, although we can perhaps deduce from v. 23 that it involved teetotalism, while Tit. i. 10 ff. suggests that it had some connexion with Jewish ritual food prohibitions. The strict vegetarianism discussed in Rom. xiv. 1 ff. provides an instructive parallel. As in that passage, we are probably justified here in inferring a fusion of Gnostic and Jewish elements, although Paul seems to imply that the Ephesian prohibitions were based on a more explicit dualism which stigmatized matter as evil,

This may account for the vehemence of his attack here as contrasted, for example, with his relative mildness in Rom. xiv. 1 ff.
He realizes that asceticism which draws its motive force from
dualism presupposes salvation by man's own efforts as well as
violating the doctrine of creation set out in Gen. i ('God saw
that it was good') and taken up in Ecclus. xxxix. 16; 25-27.

In the light of this he argues that **God created** these foods
which they ban with the specific object of their being **partaken
of with thanksgiving by people who believe and have
come to know the truth.** The insistence on **thanksgiving**
echoes Paul's teaching in Rom. xiv. 6; 1 Cor. x. 30; Phil. iv. 6:
see below on the following verse. The words are emphatic and
are to be linked closely with what follows: the Christian who
believes and has entered into the fulness of God's revelation
(for **the truth** as equivalent, in the Pastorals, to the full
Christian gospel, see on ii. 4) has a special reason for acknow-
ledging with gratitude that all material things come from him.

The great principle abolishing all food laws and taboos is
4 then set out: **For everything created by God is good.** It
had been enunciated, in the context of a discussion of Jewish
ritual regulations, by Christ himself (Mk. vii. 19), and had been
confirmed in Peter's remarkable experience described in Acts
x. 9-16. Its inescapable corollary is that **nothing is to be
rejected,** the sole condition being **that it is received with
thanksgiving.** Paul is referring, not to gratitude in general,
but to gratitude as expressed in grace at meals: cf., e.g., 1 Cor.
x. 30. In Judaism the saying of grace was conceived of as no
mere formality, and the gospels relate how Jesus always blessed
God before a meal and offered thanks after (e.g. Mk. vi. 41;
viii. 6; xiv. 22 f.; Lk. xxiv. 30). The passages listed in the
previous paragraph illustrate the importance of grace-saying in
Paul's eyes.

5   The next words, **for then it is sanctified by the word of
God and prayer,** are intended to counter the scruples of possible doubters. However common or unclean a particular form
of food may conventionally be held to be, the fact that we have
blessed God for it from the bottom of our heart and thereby
acknowledged that it is his gift to us, should make it all right in
the eyes of the most scrupulous. The sentence does not claim

that an additional sanctification, over and above its intrinsic
goodness as God's creature, is imparted to food by saying grace.
What it states is that the grace sets the food in its true perspective and in that way enables us to regard it as sacred. By
the word of God we are not to understand, as some propose,
God's creative word, as if the sanctification had a twofold
source, the divine word by which the food was brought into
existence and the human prayer. The whole sentence, as **for**
indicates, is intended to explain **provided it is received with
thanksgiving.** Correctly interpreted, therefore, **the word of
God** and **prayer** should be taken closely together as expressing
a single idea; the latter is the actual prayer of blessing and
thanksgiving, and the former the excerpts from Scripture
which, according to Jewish custom, formed its content.

9. THE POSITIVE ATTITUDE EXPECTED OF TIMOTHY. iv. 6-16

**(6) If you put these suggestions before the brothers, you
will be an admirable minister of Christ Jesus, sustained
by the words of the faith and of the admirable doctrine
which you have followed. (7) But have nothing to do with
those profane old wives' fables. Train yourself rather for
sound religion. (8) For 'while bodily training is beneficial
up to a point, sound religion is beneficial all the way',
since it holds the promise of life here and now and of life
to come. (9) This is a trustworthy saying, deserving
wholehearted acceptance. (10) For it is to this end that
we toil and struggle, because we have set our hope on
the living God, who is Saviour of all men, especially of
those who have faith. (11) Command and teach these
things. (12) Let no one underrate you because you
are young, but be an example to believers in speech,
in behaviour, in love, in faith, in purity. (13) Until I
come, devote yourself to Scripture reading, exhortation,
and teaching. (14) Do not leave unused the special gift
which is in you, which was bestowed upon you to the**

**accompaniment of prophecy along with the laying on
of hands for ordination as an elder. (15) Give your mind
to these things, busy yourself with these things, so that
your progress may be obvious to all. (16) Look to yourself and your teaching; stick to the directions given. For
in acting thus you will save both yourself and those who
listen to you.**

Paul now addresses Timothy personally, explaining how he
is to fulfil the tasks outlined and in particular deal with the
false teaching. The advice is almost wholly constructive. No
attempt is made to denounce or refute; all the emphasis is on
Timothy's duty to make himself a model to his flock. By setting
them an example of Christian faith, devotion, and conduct, he
will distract their attention from heresy, and at the same time
will be able to give full and fruitful play to the spiritual endowment he possesses in virtue of his ordination.

6   Timothy is to **put these suggestions before the brothers.**
The verb used (Gk. *hupotithesthai*) contains no note of authority
or peremptory command. As John Chrysostom observes, 'He
did not write "ordering", he did not write "instructing", but
"suggesting", that is, as if giving advice'. The **suggestions**
are the principles summarized in 1-5 and reaffirmed in more
general terms in 7-10 below. The members of the Ephesian
church are called **brothers,** a word in which the feeling of
belonging to a family is still fresh (cf. v. 1; vi. 2; 2 Tim. iv. 21).

By acting so Timothy will prove himself **an admirable
minister of Christ Jesus.** The Greek for **minister** (*diakonos*)
is the same as that for 'deacon'; although it is in process of
becoming specialized (see note on iii. 8), the word still retains
its more general meaning (e.g. 1 Cor. iii. 5; 2 Cor. xi. 23), and
can be applied to any apostle or apostolic man carrying out
Christ's work. The effective accomplishment of this ministry,
however, presupposes that he is **sustained by the words of
the faith and of the admirable doctrine which** he has
followed, i.e. diligently studied and perseveringly practised.
The participle is in the present tense (lit. 'nourishing yourself
on'), and suggests that feeding upon the truths of the gospel
must be Timothy's daily task. For the metaphor of food or

drink applied to Christian teaching, cf. 1 Cor. iii. 2. Again (see
on iii. 9) **the faith** stands for the Christian faith objectively
regarded; **doctrine** (Gk. *didaskalia*), too, as in i. 10; vi. 1; 3;
possibly 2 Tim. iii. 10; iv. 3; Tit. i. 9; ii. 1; 10, has the sense of
the objective body of Christian teaching. Critics who consider
the letters pseudonymous interpret the passage as counselling
loyal adherence to the Pauline tradition, now canonized and
regarded as the authentic version of the gospel. There is no
difficulty, however, about taking it in its natural sense as hinting
that the best refutation of error lies in a positive presentation of
the Christian faith.

In direct antithesis to **the words of the faith,** etc., stand
those profane old wives' fables which the heretics hawk 7
around in support of their misguided asceticism as well as their
other errors. For **fables** see note on i. 4. Timothy must **have
nothing to do with** these. They are **profane** (Gk. *bebēlos*), a
word which connotes what is radically separate from and opposed to the holy, and which Paul uses in the Pastorals (cf. i. 9;
vi. 20; 2 Tim. ii. 16) to suggest that the heretics' teaching has
no real religious basis or content. In fact, they are only fit for
superstitious old women (Gk. *graōdeis*: a sarcastic epithet which
was frequent in philosophical polemic and conveys the idea of
limitless credulity). Instead of attending to such follies, Timothy
should **Train** himself **for sound religion** (Gk. *eusebeia*: see
note on ii. 2), i.e. so that he may grow in true Christianity. The
comparison between the Christian life and athletic exercise or
sport is, of course, a favourite with Paul: cf. esp. 1 Cor. ix. 24-27.
His choice of it here is prompted by the thought that, just as the
sectaries subjected themselves to ill-judged forms of physical
self-discipline, so there is a genuinely Christian self-discipline
which Timothy ought to practise. It consists, however, not in
unnatural forms of abstinence, but, we may presume, in general
self-control, continuous devotion to the gospel tradition, and
perhaps most of all (as iv. 10 suggests), accepting cheerfully the
cross of suffering which all Christians must expect.

Timothy's objective, Paul has just laid it down, must be, not
the merely negative subjugation of his physical nature, but advancement in **sound religion.** In support of this he quotes
what, by its jingle, sounds like a proverbial tag, **'while bodily** 8

training is beneficial up to a point, sound religion is beneficial all the way'. As originally formulated, this apothegm must have been directed against the excessive training of athletes, which we know was the subject of sharp criticism in Stoic and Cynic circles. In the present passage, of course, athletic training as such is not under discussion, and a reference to it is strictly irrelevant. Paul introduces the quotation (*a*) because the juxtaposition of **Train** (a metaphor from athletics) and **sound religion** in the previous sentence suggests it; (*b*) because the allusion to **sound religion** with which it closes admirably clinches the advice he has just given Timothy; and (*c*) because the phrase **bodily training,** with its complete lack of spiritual overtones, strikes him as a suitable caricature description of the exclusively physical self-discipline practised by the sectaries.

On the whole this seems the most satisfactory way of understanding this difficult passage. Some have proposed that both **Train** (Gk. *gumnaze*) in 7 and **bodily training** (Gk. *sōmatikē gumnasia*) in the present verse should be taken metaphorically as referring to ascetic self-mortification. On this interpretation the two verses could be paraphrased, 'Engage by all means in the mortification of the body, but in doing so make advancement in true religion your aim, and not merely the subjugation of your natural impulses. Such exclusively bodily asceticism has its limited place in the Christian life, but it is sound religion itself which alone leads to salvation'. This has the advantage of getting rid of the awkward and, at first sight, pointless allusion to athletics. It also draws support from other N.T. passages where self-denial and asceticism for strictly Christian motives are encouraged (Mk. ix. 29; 1 Cor. vii. 5; viii. 13; ix. 27). It is doubtful, however, whether the Greek words *gumnaze* and *gumnasia* can without qualification bear the meaning required; and it also seems incredible that, after denouncing the sectaries' asceticism as devilish, Paul should end up by conceding that physical mortification has a limited value.

The concluding words, **since it holds the promise of life here and now and of life to come,** define the blessings which the man who gives himself to **sound religion** can look for. They seem to echo words of our Lord recorded in the gospel

tradition which offer precisely this reward to those who renounce
all for his sake (Mt. xix. 29; Mk. x. 30; Lk. xviii. 30). For the
same promise, cf. Tit. i. 2. We can sum up Paul's point by
saying that true Christian piety (i.e. *eusebeia*) does not involve
physical asceticism as a necessary element; where this is practised, there should be a higher purpose in view, as in the
passages listed in the previous paragraph. True Christianity
consists rather in ever renewed submission to the control of the
Spirit, with the cheerful acceptance of toil and suffering (see 10
below) and the practice of those virtues which are the fruit of
the Spirit. Eternal life, both in this world and in the world to
come, is the crown which those who embark on such a course
can expect.

If the first half of the sentence is, as proposed above, a current
tag criticizing excessive athleticism which Paul has taken over
for his purposes, these concluding words about the promise of
life cannot of course have formed part of it. They must have
been added in passing by the Apostle himself, or may perhaps
have been present in the Christian adaptation of the apophthegm
which he quotes. They, too, have a proverbial quality and, as
we have seen, crystallize ideas about the faithful Christian's
eternal reward which come down from the teaching of our Lord
himself. Paul is almost certainly referring to them when he
interjects, **This is a trustworthy saying, deserving whole-** 9
hearted acceptance. For the formula, see note on i. 15. It can
refer either forward, as in i. 15, or back, as in Tit. iii. 8. Some
have argued that here it refers forward to 10, but (*a*) this only
takes up the thought of 8 and gives it a practical application,
and (*b*) its vocabulary (cf. 'toil', 'struggle', 'hope', 'God our
Saviour') is distinctive of the Pastorals. On the other hand, the
second half of 8 has the epigrammatic quality and also the weight
of Christian significance which we look for in one of the 'faithful
sayings'; it is easy to understand how the mention of the promise
of life prompted Paul to make this comment.

After his brief outburst he resumes the thread, and the next
words, **For it is to this end,** look back to the promise of eternal 10
life touched on in 8. It is with the object of securing that blessed
life, the Apostle states, that **we toil and struggle** (cf. Col. i. 29:
'to this end I toil and struggle'). A number of MSS substitute

'suffer reproaches' (Gk. *oneidizometha*) for **struggle**, and this
may be the correct reading (so AV), having been replaced by
copyists with **struggle** under the influence of Col. i. 29; but
the received text has the weightier support and fits the context
better. Paul is continuing his athletic metaphor (cf. esp. 1 Cor.
ix. 25, where he speaks of struggling for a wreath that will not
wither away), but his interest has switched from Timothy's
spiritual wrestling to achieve **sound religion** to the labour and
buffeting which he and his associates have to put up with (and
put up with cheerfully) in their efforts to spread the gospel.

If they can endure all this confidently and without fainting,
it is **because we have set our hope on the living God.** For
this description of God, see note on iii. 15. Paul singles it out
here because, as himself **living** and the source of life, God can
bestow life on others and can therefore be relied on to fulfil the
promise of 8. The perfect **we have set our hope** (cf. 1 Cor. xv.
19; 2 Cor. i. 10) should be noted; it implies a continuous state
of hope, not just a single act. And a further ground of our confidence is the knowledge that God **is Saviour of all men,
especially of those who have faith.** For the idea of God as
Saviour, see on i. 1. The statement, which means much more
than that God is Preserver (D. Guthrie), repeats the thought of
ii. 4 (see note), where it is affirmed that God wills the salvation
of all men. The distinction between **all men** and **those who
have faith** does not necessarily (as some who are sceptical of
Pauline authorship hold) reflect the outlook of the post-apostolic
age, when it was realized that actual believers were only a
fraction of mankind. The emphatic **all**, as in ii. 4 and 6, is
aimed at the exclusivist ideas of the errorists: see note on ii. 4.
In adding **especially of those who have faith** Paul is no
doubt giving expression to his conviction that the certainty of
salvation belongs in an especial degree to those who have accepted Christ: cf. Rom. viii. 29, where he states that it is for
those who love God and are called according to his purpose that
all things work together for good. Even so, as the adverb
especially reminds us, he is not denying that others may
obtain salvation. His main object in this passage, however, is
not to discuss the deep issues of predestination and grace, but
merely to make it clear beyond all doubting that those who

make a genuine effort to practise *eusebeia* and lead a fully Christian life, placing their hope in the living God, will not be disappointed.

Paul's advice, starting with the peremptory **Command and 11 teach these things,** now assumes an extremely personal tone as he encourages his deputy to assert himself with vigour. The verb **Command** is a strong one, with military overtones, and implies that Timothy must speak authoritatively: see on i. 3. We must infer that the Apostle was worried about Timothy's diffidence, and that the latter was not too happy about standing on his own feet. As such the passage is extremely lifelike, and confirms the impression left by 1 Cor. xvi. 10 f. that he was a timorous person of whom people were prone to take advantage. Those who regard the letter as pseudonymous must assume that the author deliberately brought in these personal touches so as to create an air of verisimilitude. On their view his instructions, although apparently addressed to Timothy, are in fact intended for all young men who might be called to similarly responsible office in the Church. This account illustrates one of the difficulties of the theory of pseudonymity. It is not easy to see why a later writer should have singled out young men for advice of this kind, still less why he should have imagined that young men were likely to occupy positions of such unusual responsibility in the local congregation. On the other hand, the stress on the recipient's youth and diffidence is entirely natural if we assume that it is Paul who is writing to Timothy.

In **these things** Paul has no particular instructions in view; he is thinking of all the various pieces of advice given in the letter so far. His next remark, **Let no one underrate you 12 because you are young** (lit. 'despise your youth'), though of course primarily meant as an encouragement to Timothy himself, was also intended to produce a salutary effect on the Ephesian congregation generally. Some have detected here a proof that the letter cannot have been written in the early or middle sixties since Timothy could not properly be described as a young man then. This emphasis on youth, they argue, is best taken as 'an indication that the addressees are the clergy subordinate to the writer' (F. D. Gealy). This latter suggestion is highly artificial and implausible; it presupposes a congregation in which the office-bearers were (what must have been very unusual) predominantly youthful. Actually at the date of writing Timothy, who need not have been born before 30, may well have not been much beyond his middle thirties. According to the ancient usage the description 'young man' (Gk. *neos*, etc.) could be applied to a full-grown man of military age. Polybius (xviii. 12. 5) speaks of Flaminius as 'young' because he was only thirty, and Irenaeus (*Haer*. ii. 22. 5) explicitly states that one could aptly be called 'young' up to forty. We recall that Luke designates Paul a young man at the time of Stephen's death, when he must have been about thirty (Acts vii. 58). As a much older man, probably in his sixties, Paul was therefore perfectly in order in addressing Timothy in this way. Moreover, if the situation is historical, quite a number of members of the Ephesian community, including no doubt some of the elders, must have been considerably older than Timothy, and may well have chafed at being lectured to, and at having their conduct dictated by, so relatively young an official, all the more so if he was not of a forceful, assertive character.

To offset the handicap of youth, Timothy is invited to **be an example to believers.** This is a truly Pauline touch; the Apostle expected the Christian leader to be a model to others (Phil. iii. 17; 2 Thess. iii. 9). Five spheres in which it is important that he should do this are mentioned. First, **in speech** refers to his day-to-day conversation (his preaching will be touched on later), and **in behaviour** to the general conduct of his life; both should presumably be marked by great propriety and Christian grace. The remaining three terms denote interior qualities which nevertheless colour a man's outward deportment—**love,** i.e. fraternal charity in the full Christian sense; **faith,** by which is probably meant 'faithfulness' or 'fidelity' (cf. Rom. iii. 3; Gal. v. 22); and **purity** (Gk. *hagneia*: also v. 2), which covers not only chastity in matters of sex, but also the innocence and integrity of heart which are denoted by the related noun *hagnotēs* in 2 Cor. vi. 6.

We have already learned from iii. 14 that Paul plans a visit to 13 Ephesus; in the meantime, **Until I come,** Timothy is bidden to **devote** himself energetically to his public ministerial functions. The list is interesting and important, and its brevity is

possibly indicative of its very early date. Had it been compiled
in the second century as a mirror for church leaders, it would
almost certainly have been fuller and more precise, and a reference to the sacraments would have been natural.

In the Greek the words translated **Scripture reading, exhortation,** and **teaching** are each preceded by the definite
article; this shows that they are recognized items in the congregational meeting for worship. **Scripture reading** (lit. 'the
reading') denotes, primarily, the public reading of the O.T.,
which at this time was the Church's Bible. This was a feature
of the synagogue service (Lk. iv. 16; Acts xv. 21; 2 Cor. iii. 14),
and was immediately adopted by the Christian congregations.
This is in fact the earliest reference to the use of Scripture in
the Church's liturgy. Specifically Christian documents, however, like the letters of Paul and other leaders or the revelations
of prophets, were also read out (Col. iv. 16; 1 Thess. v. 27;
Rev. i. 3), and this practice is probably also envisaged here.
Public reading in the ancient world called for some technical
accomplishment, for the words in the codex were not divided.
From the middle of the second century at any rate the function
was delegated to an official called *lector* or *anagnōstēs* (e.g.
Hippolytus, *Trad. ap.* xii; Tertullian, *De praescr.* xli).

By **exhortation** is meant the exposition and application of
Scripture which followed its public reading, in other words the
sermon. So we read in Acts xiii. 15, 'after the reading of the law
and the prophets, the synagogue officials sent this message to
them: "Brothers, if you have anything to say to the people by
way of exhortation, let them hear it"'. On the other hand,
teaching signifies catechetical instruction in Christian doctrine;
this too had its place in meetings for worship from the earliest
times, and it is evident that a great deal of catechetical material
is embodied in the N.T. writings, including the Pauline letters.
Paul mentions both these functions together in Rom. xii. 7,
implying that their exercise called for a special *charisma*, or
endowment, of the Spirit.

The question facing Timothy, diffident and unsure of himself
as he is, must be whether he has the knowledge, ability, and
soundness of judgment to carry out these tasks successfully.
The Apostle meets his unspoken doubts with a forthright and

14 bracing answer: he possesses a **special gift,** and provided he
does not **leave** this **unused,** he should be amply equipped to
face any demands. The reference is of course to the grace of the
Holy Spirit which Timothy had received on the occasion of his
ordination or consecration to his office, and which will be without fruit if it is neglected: cf. 2 Tim. i. 6. In Paul's letters (e.g.
Rom. xii. 6 ff.; 1 Cor. xii. 4 ff.) *charisma*, or 'gift', denotes a
special endowment of the Spirit enabling the recipient to carry
out some function in the community. When he wrote 1 Corinthians, his correspondents were inclined to attach an exaggerated importance to the more specifically 'pneumatic'
endowments, like speaking with tongues and prophecy. One
of his objects in 1 Cor. xii was to correct this and to persuade
them that, properly understood, the more routine functions of
running the day-to-day life of the community were also 'gifts'
in this sense (cf. 1 Cor. xii. 28).

   The rest of the verse is of signal importance for our understanding both of the letter and of the emergence of Christian
institutions, and its exegesis raises certain problems. There is
no difficulty about the phrase **to the accompaniment of
prophecy.** It is parallel to '. . . the prophecies once made about
you' in i. 18 (where see note). Paul is recalling the endorsement
of the choice of Timothy by the Spirit-inspired utterances of
prophetic men (cf. Acts xiii. 1-3). There is also no difficulty
about **along with the laying on of hands.** Ordination or
appointment to office in the apostolic Church was modelled on
the contemporary Jewish rite for the ordination of rabbis. This
in turn found its inspiration in Joshua's ordination as described
in Num. xxvii. 18-23 and Deut. xxxiv. 9, at which Moses 'laid
his hands' ('leaned' or 'pressed' would be a more accurate
version) on his prospective successor. It was assumed that as a
result of the action Moses's spirit had been conveyed to Joshua;
he had, as it were, poured something of his personality into the
younger man and thereby made him his effective substitute.
Accordingly we find the apostles, or more probably the people,
laying or pressing their hands on the Seven at their appointment
(Acts vi. 6), and the prophets and teachers laying or pressing
their hands on Barnabas and Saul so as to consecrate them as
missionaries (*ib.* xiii. 3). This action of laying, or rather pressing,

hands on someone (the Hebrew verb is *samakh*), it should be noted, is entirely different from the 'placing' (Hebrew verb *sim* or *shith*) of the hands employed for blessings and healings, although the two are commonly confused and are rendered by the same Greek verb in both the LXX and the N.T.

It is over the interpretation of the whole phrase translated **along with the laying on of hands for ordination as an elder** that our problem arises. Literally rendered, the Greek gives, 'along with the laying on of hands of the presbytery', and this is the version that has been almost universally adopted. The picture it puts forward is of the whole body of elders at Ephesus, no doubt with Paul as their leader or chairman, participating in Timothy's solemn consecration and joining in pressing their hands on his head. The collective noun 'presbytery' (Gk. *presbuterion*) is awkward (why not 'of the presbyters'?), but it is by no means impossible that this is the correct translation. In later times, as we know, the presbyters ('elders') present at an ordination took their part in the laying on of hands, and the practice may go back to apostolic times. On the other hand, if this is the true meaning of the passage, it stands in apparent contradiction with 2 Tim. i. 6, which explicitly states that the special gift which Timothy possesses was bestowed 'by the laying on of my hands', and also probably with 1 Tim. v. 22, where Timothy himself is counselled not to be over-precipitate in laying hands on anyone. The former seems to imply that Paul alone ordained Timothy; and the implication of the latter that Timothy was to be sole ordainer can only be avoided by assuming that in this context the laying on of hands refers, not to ordination, but to some other rite such as the bestowal of the Spirit on a convert after baptism.

Various harmonizing expedients have been proposed. It can be argued, for example, that Paul's role at Timothy's ordination must in any case have been the preponderant one; that of the elders must have been one of simple cooperation and assistance. According to others, the absence of reference to the elders in 2 Tim. i. 6 may be explained by the very personal character of the context. Others argue that the present passage may reflect the primitive corporate form of ordination, while 2 Tim. i. 6 reveals its later modification in conformity with the emergence of the monarchical episcopate. None of these solutions, however, is wholly satisfactory, and the true one, as it seems, has been supplied by D. Daube.[1] His contention is that the Greek of this verse (*epithesis tōn cheirōn tou presbuteriou*: lit. 'laying on of the hands of the presbytery') is a rendering of the Hebrew *semikhath zeqenim*, a technical term whose literal translation is 'the leaning-on of elders', and which in effect meant, 'the leaning, or pressing, of hands upon someone with the object of making him an elder or rabbi'. In a Christian context it would mean 'elder-ordination' or, more generally, 'formal ordination to office'.

The adoption of this brilliant suggestion at once eliminates any difficulty about the collective noun 'presbytery', and of course does away with the contradiction between the three passages in 1 and 2 Timothy. The resulting picture is an alto-gether more probable one, since if Timothy was Paul's personal delegate, it would be natural for the Apostle himself to com-mission him, and the collaboration of the elders does not seem called for. At the same time, if this is the correct interpretation of the phrase, it is an important pointer to the very early date of the letter's composition. It is not easy to imagine a second-century writer, or even one living in the last decades of the first, using such a rabbinical idiom. The use of such language also suggests a primitive period when ministerial offices had not become properly demarcated. The net result is to confirm the traditional view that Timothy is a special, *ad hoc* apostolic delegate, and to render even more difficult the theory that he is the typical church leader or monarchical bishop who is being held up as a pattern to second-century clergy.

15   The admonition **Give your mind to these things, busy yourself with these things,** brings together the several points covered in the three preceding verses. The former verb (Gk. *meletān*) can mean 'meditate on' (so AV), but its predominant note is 'prosecute diligently' or 'practise', as an athlete trains; thus the sporting metaphor of 7-10 is echoed. The motive is still to establish Timothy's authority. If he pays heed to these directions, he will make **progress,** and it will **be obvious to all.** The congregation will take note of it, and will cease regarding

[1] See *The New Testament and Rabbinic Judaism*, London, 1956, pp. 244-246.

him as an inexperienced young man whose authority can be discounted. The word translated **progress** (Gk. *prokopē*) was used by the Stoics to denote the advances made by a novice in philosophy or ethics; it was used by Paul in Phil. i. 12 of the progress made in spreading the gospel, and in *ib*. i. 25 of the spiritual development of his correspondents.

He concludes with the twofold charge, **Look to yourself** 16 **and your teaching.** There is a clear hint that exclusive concentration on one or the other will be dangerous. The next clause is difficult; a literal rendering would be, 'Stick to them (Gk. *autois*)'. It is intolerable to take the pronoun 'them' as referring to **yourself and your teaching,** and we are therefore obliged to understand it as referring to **these things** in 15. Thus we get what is in effect a rather loose paraphrase, **stick to the directions given.**

Finally comes the incentive which Timothy, and every other minister of Christ, should hold before himself: **in acting thus,** i.e. according to the instructions laid down, **you will save both yourself and those who listen to you.** The first half of the sentence reminds us of the fear Paul had expressed in 1 Cor. ix. 27 that after all his preaching to others he might in the end find himself rejected. Timothy will be secure against that if he follows the advice given. He will also, as the result of his conscientious and devoted efforts, have the supreme joy of helping the flock entrusted to him, which depends upon his teaching and leadership, to attain salvation.

10. A RULE ABOUT PERSONAL RELATIONS.
v. 1-2

(1) Do not rebuke an older man harshly, but appeal to him as a father. Treat young men as brothers, (2) older women as mothers, and young women as sisters, with complete propriety.

At this point the tone and content of the letter change abruptly. The whole of the present chapter, and the first verses of the next, consist of advice to Timothy on dealing with various

classes of people in the community. The present section, a
general rule for governing behaviour towards old and young of
both sexes, appears to be modelled, both in structure and content, on some Hellenistic paradigm traditional in popular ethics.
There is a striking parallel, for example, in Plato's *Republic* (v.
463 c), where it is said of the Guardian: 'He will regard everyone
he meets as either brother or sister, father or mother, son or
daughter, grandchild or grandparent'. Similarly many funerary
inscriptions of the first centuries before and after Christ extol
those who have treated older people as parents and people of
their own age as brothers. A special nuance, of course, attaches
to the ideal as it is inculcated by a Christian teacher, since both
he and his auditors are aware of the profoundly spiritual sense
in which their relationship to Christ has made them fathers and
mothers, sisters and brothers to each other (cf. Mk. iii. 31-5).

1   So Timothy is admonished **not** to **rebuke an older man
harshly,** but to **appeal to him as a father.** The former verb
(Gk. *epiplēssein* connected with *plēktēs*, i.e. 'given to violence',
'striker'—cf. iii. 3) is a severe one and connotes rough treatment. The second verb, **appeal to** (Gk. *parakalein*), is much
kindlier, and comprises the ideas of exhortation, admonition,
and comfort. The noun translated **older man** (Gk. *presbuteros*)
could denote the official known as 'elder' or 'presbyter', as in
17 ff., and some (including NEB) render it so here. The context,
however, and above all the ethical paradigms already referred
to, confirm that it here connotes age. The problem of how to
administer rebukes constructively is always a difficult one for
those in authority, and never more so than when, as seems to
have been the case with Timothy, there is a discrepancy of age.

In the Greek there is no imperative verb representing **Treat,**
2 and the accusatives **young men as brothers,** as well as **older
women as mothers,** etc., are all, strictly speaking, governed
by **appeal to.** But there is little doubt that Paul has passed
beyond the truly Christian manner of finding fault. He is now
considering what should be Timothy's general relations with
the different groups in his flock, and so loosely subordinates
these clauses derived from the ethical paradigm to the verb he
has already used. He shows realism and frankness in slipping
in the hint that, in dealing with **young women as sisters,** his

delegate should be careful to act **with perfect propriety** (Gk. *hagneia*: lit. 'chastity').

11. REGULATIONS ABOUT WIDOWS. v. 3-16

(3) Officially recognize widows who really are widows. (4) But if a widow has children or grandchildren, let them learn to practise their religion first of all towards their own family and make a proper return to their forbears; for this is commendable in God's sight. (5) A widow who really is one and is absolutely alone in the world has her hope set on God and attends the prayers and supplications night and day. (6) On the other hand, a sensual-living widow is dead while still alive. (7) So issue these instructions too, so that the widows may be free from reproach. (8) Anyone who neglects to look after his relatives, especially members of his own family, has denied the faith and is worse than an unbeliever. (9) No widow should be on the official list unless she is over sixty, has been the wife of only one husband, (10) and has acquired a reputation for good works by looking after children, practising hospitality, washing the feet of Christians, relieving people in distress, and devoting herself to every sort of good work. (11) Do not admit younger widows, for when desire makes them restive against Christ they want to marry, (12) thus falling under the condemnation of breaking their original pledge. (13) At the same time they qualify as idlers, gadding round from house to house—and not only idlers, but gossips and busybodies, saying things they ought not. (14) It is my wish, therefore, that younger widows should marry, have children, manage a house, and give the Adversary no loophole for slander. (15) As it is, some have already gone astray after Satan. (16) If any believing woman has widows, she ought to support them, and the congregation should not have the burden, so that it may be free to support genuine widows.

This surprisingly long section throws a precious light on
conditions in, and the problems facing, the apostolic Church.
In Judaism widows were regarded as the object of special
solicitude (e.g. Deut. x. 18; xxiv. 17; Ps. lxviii. 5; Is. i. 17;
Lk. ii. 37), the obligation of the good Jew towards them being
deduced from the Fifth Commandment, and Christianity
naturally inherited this attitude. Such glimpses as we obtain
from Acts (vi. 1; ix. 39 ff.) reveal that at the very earliest stage
the community treated the widows in its midst as an important
responsibility, and that they for their part were grouped together as a body occupied in deeds of kindness to the poor. The
situation had not materially changed by the time the Pastorals
were written, but experience was forcing Christians to work
out a code for dealing with them. Two important points emerge
from the present passage. The first is that, while the church
remains fully alive to its duty in regard to widows, the need for
distinguishing between those whose condition really calls for its
support and those who are better left to the care of relatives
has become urgent. The second is that at Ephesus there is now
an officially recognized order of widows, with definite conditions
of entry which Paul, it appears, wants stringently observed, and
definite duties for those on the roll to perform. This is the first
clear allusion in Christian literature to the existence of such
an order; for its development in the second century, cf.Ignatius,
Smyrn. xiii. 1; *Polyc.* iv. 1; Polycarp, *Phil.* iv. 3; Tertullian, *De
virg. vel.* v. 9. Some editors try to distinguish between 3-8,
which in their view deal with widows who are the object of the
church's charitable concern, and 9-15, which treat specifically
of the actual order of widows. Their argument has some plausibility, but in fact the two themes overlap and merge. It is those
widows who are enrolled as such who qualify for official assistance, although the number in receipt of this must always have
been larger than that of those appointed to perform good
works.

3   Paul first lays down a general rule for Timothy, and through
him for the Ephesian church: **Officially recognize widows
who really are widows.** The imperative verb (Gk. *timā*)
literally means 'Honour', and has been taken by some as an
echo of the Fifth Commandment, which was certainly inter-

preted in Judaism as the basis both of the duty of children to provide for widowed parents and of the community's general responsibility towards the aged. But the context, without in the least excluding such a reference to the Commandment, suggests that the word, in addition to its normal meaning, has a more precise and technical nuance here (see note on 17 below, where 'double honour' also probably has a technical meaning). By **widows who really are widows** Paul means, as he later makes plain, not any and every woman whose husband is dead, but widows who (*a*) have no relatives who can be expected to support them, and (*b*) fulfil the qualifications listed in 5 and 9 ff. His motive in restricting the class so drastically is to ensure that the church's limited resources are expended where they are really needed.

For example, **if a widow has children or grandchildren,** 4 Paul suggests that these should **learn to practise their religion first of all towards their own family,** i.e. towards their widowed mother or grandmother as the case may be, and thereby **make a proper return to their forbears.** In other words, the burden of maintaining her should fall on them, not on the congregation. In the original **learn** has no expressed subject, and the translation and interpretation given assume that the implied one is **children or grandchildren,** in spite of the fact that they are the object, not the subject, in the preceding clause. The alternative is to make the implied subject 'widows with children or grandchildren', which would represent the Apostle as counselling widows with families to devote themselves to their care rather than to the charitable works expected of those enrolled in the official order. Since **widow,** however, is in the singular, and **learn** is in the plural, the strain on the syntax is wellnigh intolerable, and it is also difficult to see how by such conduct widows **make a proper return to their forbears.** The exegesis given above is much more natural, and is indeed demanded by the whole context.

Practical gratitude such as this, Paul suggests, is an expression of sound religion (*eusebeia*: the verb translated **practise their religion** is the Gk. *eusebein*—see note on ii. 2). It is also **commendable in God's sight;** this is a reference to the Fifth Commandment and, more generally, to the high valuation placed in the O.T. on the duty of children to provide for their parents.

5 In contrast the genuine widow, in Paul's definition, **is absolutely alone in the world.** Inevitably she **has her hope set on God** (the perfect tense of the verb indicates, as in iv. 10, that her attitude of mind is a settled and continuous one) for the simple reason that she has no one else to look to; the responsibility for her therefore legitimately falls on God's people. She demonstrates her reliance on God alone by the fact that she **attends the prayers and supplications night and day.** The strikingly similar picture drawn of the elderly prophetess Anna (Lk. ii. 37) illustrates the high esteem which in Judaism attached to such conduct on the part of widows. The presence of the article before **prayers** probably indicates that Paul is thinking of the congregation's meetings for worship. The order **night and day** is characteristically Jewish: cf. *ibid.*; 1 Thess. ii 9; iii. 10; 2 Thess. iii. 8; 2 Tim. i. 3.

6 **On the other hand,** there may be widows who, although without families and alone in the world, give no convincing evidence of fixing their hopes on God, but on the contrary are **sensual-living.** The verb used (Gk. *spatalō*) is a rare one, occurring only here and in Ezek. xvi. 49; Ecclus. xxi. 15; Jas. v. 5: it connotes abandonment to pleasure and comfort—it is quite unnecessary to infer that the women envisaged have actually descended to prostitution (B. S. Easton). A worldly-minded, self-indulgent widow like that **is dead while still alive** (for the idea, cf. Rev. iii. 1), and therefore can have no claim on the church's alms.

7 Paul urges Timothy to **issue these instructions too,** i.e. to add the criteria of genuine widowhood to the instructions given him in the first part of ch. iv. The **too** harks back to iv. 11, and the Greek *tauta paraggelle* ('give these orders') here corresponds to *paraggelle tauta* there. Paul is particularly insistent on this because he wants to ensure **that the widows may be free from reproach.** In other words, to include widows indiscriminately on the official list will do the reputation of the order no good.

8 The next verse, stigmatizing **Anyone who neglects to look after his relatives, especially members of his own family,**

repeats in more forthright language the principle laid down in 4, viz. that a widow who has close relations still alive should be looked after by them rather than by the congregation. The man who fails to observe this elementary duty has in effect, however eloquent his profession of Christianity, **denied the faith** (i.e. to all intents and purposes, not in the formal sense of apostasy: cf. Tit. i. 16) **and is worse than an unbeliever.** Presumably this is because even pagans, who do not know the Commandments or the law of Christ, recognize and set store by the obligations of children to parents. For similar appeals to pagan morality, cf. Rom. ii. 14; 1 Cor. v. 1; Phil. iv. 8. The verse comes in awkwardly, since the point has already been made, and some editors have therefore thought it displaced or a gloss. But the repetition, and the Apostle's sharper tone, may underline his exasperation at the selfishness of some families in the Ephesian church.

In 9 ff. Paul tackles, directly and postively, the qualifications for the order of widows, and hints at the duties involved. Throughout we get the impression of acute dissatisfaction with conditions in the Ephesian church. The first requirement is that **No widow should be on the official list unless she is** 9 **over sixty.** The imperative verb (Gk. *katalegestho*) literally means 'be enrolled'; it is the technical term for being placed on a recognized list or 'catalogue', and makes it absolutely clear that there was a definite order of widows. The age-limit of sixty is at first sight surprising, but in 11-13 Paul clearly indicates the kind of frivolous behaviour, particularly compromising in women with an official standing, to which widows less advanced in years might be tempted. Sixty was the recognized age in antiquity when one became an 'old' man or woman, and a woman's sexual passions might be deemed to have lost their dangers then. The fourth-century *Apostolic Constitutions* (III. i. 1 f.) accepted the same age-limit for widows, although it is interesting to observe that some texts of the late third century *Didascalia* (III. i) reduce it to fifty.

The stipulation that an officially enrolled widow should have **been the wife of only one husband** corresponds to the rule for overseers (iii. 2), deacons (iii. 12), and elders (Tit. i. 6), 'husband of one wife' there being the equivalent of 'wife of one husband' here. For the meaning, see note on iii. 2. Some interpret the formula as meaning a woman who has been faithful to her husband in marriage, but the reading given above is confirmed by the fact that in pagan, Jewish, and Christian inscriptions of the first centuries the noun *monandria* (lit. 'having one husband') is always applied, usually as a term of obvious eulogy, to widows who have been content with one marriage. Many commentators find this exegesis inconsistent with Paul's request in 14 that young widows should marry again, but they have missed the whole point of his argument. His advice to young widows is determined by a realistic appreciation of the emotional problem of a woman who has been left a widow while she is still in the prime of life. His general attitude is clear and logical: a single marriage followed by permanent widowhood after the husband's death is the ideal, and should be demanded of aspirants to the order of widows; but the strain which this would put upon women left in widowhood when still comparatively young would be excessive in most cases, and so it is better that they should remarry rather than risk exposing the church to scandal.

Members of the widows' order had practical duties to perform in the community; so the best testimonial a newcomer could produce was to point to zeal and efficiency in carrying out these tasks voluntarily. Hence she should have **acquired a reputation for good works.** For the emphasis on good works, or rather on the exercise of practical charity inspired by the gospel, in the Pastorals, see note on ii. 10. The specific examples listed give a fair, although not necessarily complete, picture of the tasks which members of the order undertook. The verb translated **looking after children** (Gk. *teknotrophein*) strictly means 'to rear children', i.e. one's own children, but it is absurd to suppose either that Paul is excluding childless candidates or that he is judging their suitability in the light of their record of bringing up children in the remote past; in any case widows with children still alive and available to report on the soundness of their upbringing should not, according to 4, be eligible. It is certain, therefore, that the word must be given the wider connotation suggested in the translation. One of the big problems facing the early Church was the care of orphans (cf. Hermas,

Mand. viii. 10; *Apost. Const.* III. iii. 2; etc.); it seems likely that the official widows were given charge of these.

The next words, **practising hospitality,** reveal that the widows had their part to play, alongside the overseers (cf. iii. 2), in the reception and entertainment of itinerant evangelists, preachers, messengers, and ordinary Christians travelling to and fro which formed a prominent feature in the daily life of the early Church. Cf. the example of Phoebe (Rom. xvi. 1 f.). One particular aspect of this is indicated in **washing the feet of Christians** (lit. 'saints'). This was a service to visitors which occupied a great place in Eastern hospitality; it was also an act betokening humility and love which Christ himself had recommended to his disciples (Jn. xiii. 14), and was therefore particularly important when the visitors were 'saints', i.e. members of the redeemed community. It was inevitable, also, that the numberless tasks included under **relieving people in distress** should, under the general supervision of the overseers, devolve upon the widows.

Paul now elaborates on, and gives frank reasons for, the age-limit he has prescribed, at the same time bringing out that membership of the widows' order entailed a formal engagement or vow. His first and principal reason is that sexual passion is still a potent factor in the make-up of young widows, so that **when desire makes them restive against Christ they want** 11 **to marry.** The language suggests that Christ is thought of as a spiritual bridegroom (cf. 2 Cor. xi. 2). Hence the desire to marry again, natural enough in young women who have lost their husbands, is in effect an act of unfaithfulness to him. Such a step, he adds, would involve them, if already admitted to the order, in **falling under the condemnation of breaking** 12 **their original pledge.** Evidently on joining it they would have bound themselves to chastity; the term translated **pledge** (Gk. *pistis*: lit. 'faith') points to a contract or engagement, more or less formal, of which the community probably had cognizance. It would therefore be dangerous for the women, and might lead to harm to the church, for them to be placed at a still susceptible age in the awful dilemma of having to choose between the strict continence appropriate to their office and the passionate promptings of their nature.

It is likely that Paul's advice, in this and also in what follows, was based upon experience. He now adds a second reason, viz. that young widows, being still active and full of energy, are liable if enrolled in the order to have too much free time on

13 their hands; hence **they qualify as idlers.** In the Greek the feminine adjective 'idle' (*argai*) and the verb 'they learn' (*manthanousin*) are simply juxtaposed, which has led commentators to infer that the infinitive 'to become' should be understood. Numerous parallels, however, prove that the verb *manthanein* ('to learn') with a substantive denoting a profession or occupation was an idiomatic construction signifying 'to qualify as such and such' (e.g. a doctor, wrestler, etc.). The translation adopted attempts to reproduce this idiom and at the same time to bring out the touch of sarcasm implied.

Thus if widows are enrolled too young, they are liable to exploit their new career by **gadding round from house to house,** no doubt under the pretext of carrying out charitable visits of the kind expected of members of the order. There is a danger, too, of their becoming **not only idlers, but gossips and busybodies, saying things they ought not.** If this gives the full meaning of the Greek, Paul is drawing a vivid picture of the mischief-making tittle-tattle to which he thinks that women still young enough to be in the social swim will be especially prone—although the Church's fuller experience has shown that neither older women nor male office-bearers are necessarily exempt from the same temptation. It is possible, however, that he is hinting at something more sinister. The word translated **busybodies** is *periergoi* (lit. 'over-careful', 'taking needless trouble'), the neuter plural of which (*perierga*) is used in Acts xix. 19 and certain magical papyri as a euphemism for 'spells' or 'magic arts'. He may therefore be expressing, in discreetly veiled language, the fear that irresponsible young widows, if encouraged to undertake house-to-house visiting, will resort to charms, incantations, and magical formulae in dealing, e.g., with sick people. On this interpretation **saying things they ought not** will contain an allusion to the spells and occult formulae used. Cf. Tit. i. 11 for a similarly veiled expression.

14 On these grounds Paul is positive in his own mind (**It is my**

wish, therefore) that **younger widows should marry, have children, manage a house.** It is not, according to his way of thinking, the theoretical ideal, but it is the only sensible course, having regard to the peculiar temptations to which lone women in the prime of life are exposed. Bearing children will satisfy the instinctive urges of their nature, and running a house will absorb their surplus energies. It is often argued that this advice proves that the writer cannot be the Apostle, since in 1 Cor. vii. 25 ff., while not opposed to marriage, he gave it as his opinion that in view of the imminence of the Parousia it was better for the unmarried to remain so. But (*a*) his Corinthian ruling was given many years previously, and it is agreed that as he grew older his sense of the nearness of the Parousia became dimmer; and (*b*) that ruling was in any case a general one, whereas here he is dealing with the very special case of widows. It is clearly his view that it is ideally better for anyone, man or woman, whose partner has died to avoid a second marriage, but his good sense and realism make him encourage second marriages where the strain involved in remaining single would be too great. This, as a matter of fact, is exactly the position he adopts in 1 Corinthians, where we find him (vii. 9; 36) specifically recommending marriage for (*a*) unmarried people and widows, and (*b*) partners in spiritual celibacy, provided they find it impossible to control their passions.

If these younger widows marry, there will be the further advantage that they will **give the Adversary no loophole for slander.** As always (cf. iii. 7; vi. 1; Tit. ii. 5; 8), Paul is anxious for the congregation to stand well with the outside world and to escape the scandal which slanderous talk will produce. The words translated **the Adversary** (Gk. *ho antikeimenos*) could refer either to the devil or to the church's human detractors (cf. 1 Cor. xvi. 9). The former is perhaps preferable in view of the use of the singular with the article; the thought also accords with iii. 6 f. It is unlikely, however, that Paul drew a sharp distinction in his own mind; the men and women who would tear the church's reputation to pieces were the instruments of the devil (cf. iv. 1).

Paul feels fortified in the advice he has given by the tragic fact that **As it is, some have already gone astray after** 15

Satan. He has in mind specific instances of widows who have
been admitted to the order under age and have either married
again or fallen into the other types of indiscretion or positive
misconduct he has been enumerating. For the verb 'go astray',
cf. i. 6. The statement betrays, some have argued, the fact that
the order of widows has been functioning for a considerable
time, but this is not necessarily implied. Length of time is a
relative matter, and the experience of two or three years would
be enough to give the Apostle a useful basis for his rulings.

The whole section on widows is awkwardly put together, and
in the next verse we are unexpectedly brought back to the
general question of the charitable support the congregation
16 owes them. **If any believing woman has widows,** Timothy
is told, **she ought to support them, and the congregation
should not have the burden** (Gk. *bareisthō*: cf. 2 Cor. i. 8; v. 4.
For its cognates used with a financial connotation, cf. *ib.* xi. 9;
xii. 16; 1 Thess. ii. 9; 2 Thess. iii. 8). The reason given for
this is **so that it may be free to support genuine widows,**
i.e. widows, in the sense defined in 5 above, who have no one
but God, and so his church, to look to.

The sudden shift in subject has puzzled commentators, and
some have concluded that this verse, which seems logically connected with either 4 or 8 above, has somehow got displaced.
But there is no MS evidence of this, and the abruptness of the
switch should not in itself disturb us, especially in an author
like Paul (cf., e.g., the structure of 1 Cor. vii and xiv). On the
assumption that the letter is a real one, he may well have remembered an important possibility he had overlooked and
hastened to include it before passing to the subject of elders.

The real problem concerns his meaning, and in particular
why believing (i.e. Christian) women, not believing men,
should be singled out. A number of MSS seek to solve it by
reading, 'If any believing man or believing woman'. If this is
correct and **widows** is glossed as 'relations who are widows',
the verse does little more than repeat the teaching of 4 and 8;
but the reading is poorly supported, and clearly represents an
attempt to produce a simple, straightforward text. Leaving this
on one side, we are left with two alternatives. First, **believing
woman** has been held to denote a widow (either one too young

to join the order or one qualified by age for it) who actually has
other widows, whether relatives or not, belonging to her household. Such a woman, Paul is suggesting, instead of marrying or
seeking to join the order, should expend her energies on looking
after these widows of her own, and so save the congregation the
trouble and expense. Against this, however, it is impossible to
narrow down the meaning of **believing woman** to 'widow';
and there is also the difficulty that, if she is a young widow,
ministering to other widows in her own house will provide no
relief for her emotional tensions, while if she is a woman of
more advanced years, there seems no reason why she should
limit her charitable efforts so drastically.

We are thus left with what is, after all, the only natural interpretation, viz. that Paul is envisaging the case of a comfortably off female member of the community, whether married
herself or single or a widow, whose household includes one or
more widows, not close relatives (that situation has already been
sufficiently dealt with), but servants or dependants or friends.
Such a woman is encouraged to make herself responsible for
their welfare instead of handing them over to the church's
charity, which has already too many calls upon it. The reason
why Paul does not impose the same obligation on a Christian
man of similar position should be obvious. If such a man were
unmarried or a widower, it would be most unsuitable for him
to take over responsibility for a group of widows; whereas if
he were married, the responsibility in all its practical aspects
would naturally devolve upon his wife.

12. DIRECTIONS ABOUT ELDERS. v. 17-25

**(17) Elders who exercise leadership well should be
deemed worthy of double remuneration, especially
those occupied with preaching and teaching. (18) For
Scripture says, 'You must not muzzle an ox treading
grain', and, 'A workman deserves his wages.' (19) Do
not entertain a charge against an elder except on the
evidence of two or three witnesses. (20) Those who do**

wrong you should publicly expose so that the rest may
be afraid. (21) I adjure you, in the sight of God and Christ
Jesus and the elect angels, to observe these rules without
prejudging the issue, doing nothing out of favouritism.
(22) Don't be in a hurry to lay hands on anyone, and
don't associate yourself with another man's sins; keep
yourself unstained. (23) Don't go on drinking only water,
but take a little wine for the sake of your digestion in
view of your frequent indispositions. (24) Some men's
sins are immediately obvious, running ahead of them to
judgment, but other men's trail behind them. (25) In the
same way good deeds too may be immediately obvious,
but even when they are not they cannot be concealed.

If we rule out iv. 14, this is the first mention in the Pastorals
of 'elder' (Gk. *presbuteros*) as a title of office; in addition to the
present passage it is also found in Tit. i. 5. J. Jeremias and
others have claimed that in both these contexts the word simply
means, as in v. 1 above, 'elderly man', and that there is therefore
no overt mention of an order of elders in these letters, any more
than in the acknowledged Paulines. Two difficulties they have
to face are (a) the reference to 'double pay' in 17 below, and
(b) Paul's statement in Tit. i. 5 that he left Titus in Crete
specifically in order that he might 'appoint *presbuteroi*'. The
former they attempt to dispose of by arguing that the meaning
of 'double pay' is that the stipend of elderly persons who undertake ministerial office (i.e. as overseers) is to be twice the
amount of the dole distributed to old men who depend on the
alms of the congregation. Since there is no hint of such a dole
paid to men elsewhere in the letters, this is very hard to accept.
As regards (b), they interpret 'appoint *presbuteroi*' as meaning
'appoint elderly persons as overseers', but this cannot be got
out of the Greek. If this were the sense, a second accusative
indicating the office would be required. A further objection to
the theory is its apparent, and highly improbable, corollary that
the church's administrative officials were drawn exclusively
from the ranks of the aged.

Apart from the Pastorals, we read of officials called elders or
presbyters in Acts xv (cf. also xi. 30; xvi. 4; xxi. 18), which

represents them as presiding with the apostles over the church at Jerusalem; xiv. 23, according to which Paul and Barnabas set up elders in every church on their journey through Asia Minor; xx. 17-38, which relates how the Apostle summoned the elders of Ephesus to Miletus; also in Jas. v. 14; 1 Pet. v. 1; 2 Jn. 1; 3 Jn. 1; Rev. iv; v; vii; etc. It seems certain that the primitive Christian communities, which even in pagan districts usually began from a Jewish nucleus and in any case were founded by ex-Jews like Paul, borrowed this patriarchal type of organization from Judaism. All over the world, in the Diaspora just as much as in Palestine itself, each Jewish community or synagogue had at its head a board of elders (the *gerousia*), who in earlier times at any rate were often called *presbuteroi*. Despite their name, they were not necessarily elderly persons, but represented the Jewish notables of the locality. They had a general responsibility for the financial and other affairs of the community, although the practical conduct of these was mostly delegated to an executive committee often known as 'the rulers' (Gk. *archontes*).

There is a widespread view that at the earliest stage of the Christian mission this patriarchal polity can only have been characteristic of the churches which sprang up in definitely Jewish areas, and confirmation of this is found in the absence of any mention of elders by name in Paul's acknowledged letters. As has been pointed out in the Introduction (p. 15), this is a very fragile premiss to support so far-reaching a conclusion, for the Apostle's silence need in no way be significant. It is in the highest degree likely, since this was the only method of organizing a community of which he had direct experience, that he would instinctively have established boards of elders wherever he founded a congregation, in Gentile just as much as in Jewish regions; and this, as we have seen, is precisely what Luke reports him as doing (Acts xiv. 23). There is no reason to suppose that his Gentile converts, who were perfectly familiar with the government of cities being in the hands of a senate, would have found this arrangement strange or unpalatable. It is conceivable, of course, that the title 'elder' caught on more rapidly where there was a predominantly Jewish element in the congregation, for it was reminiscent of the LXX; but the polity

itself must have normally been on patriarchal lines. This provides a much more natural and satisfactory explanation of the
universal prevalence of the order of presbyters by the end of
the first century than the hypothesis of the fusing together, at
some indeterminate date after Paul's death, of two alien types
of organization.

17   The importance of Paul's first requirement, that **Elders who
exercise leadership well should be deemed worthy of
double remuneration, especially those occupied with
preaching and teaching,** can scarcely be exaggerated; it
furnishes an invaluable clue not only to the local situation at
Ephesus, but to the embryonic beginnings of the ministry itself.
First, it defines the position of elders; their function is to
exercise leadership in each congregation. That is to say, they
exercise a general supervision over its affairs analogous to the
oversight exercised by the elders in a Jewish synagogue; for
the same verb applied to what are probably the same officials,
cf. Rom. xii. 8; 1 Thess. v. 12 (where Paul is insisting on respect
being paid to 'those who preside over you in the Lord').
Secondly, however, this text suggests that a distinction is beginning to emerge between the main body of elders who wield this
general oversight and the narrower group amongst them who
have more specific tasks to perform. This comes out clearly in
the reference to **those occupied,** etc., but is probably implied
in the expression **who exercise leadership well.** By this
must be meant, not simply those who have proved good elders
(the quality of their service cannot have been the basis of a
difference in remuneration), but those who have taken an active
and efficient, possibly full-time share in administration. The
most obvious examples of these must have been **those occupied
in preaching and teaching,** i.e. the overseers as distinct from
the deacons; we learn from iii. 2 and Tit. i. 9 that teaching was
their responsibility, and as the senior executive officials preaching must have fallen to them too. The word translated occupied
(Gk. *kopiōntas*) literally means 'labouring', but this sense should
not be pressed; the verb was technical in Paul's vocabulary for
ministerial activity (iv. 10; Rom. xvi. 12; 1 Cor. xv. 10; Gal. iv.
11; Phil. ii. 16; Col. i. 29; 1 Thess. v. 12).
  Thirdly, the passage reveals that, while all elders in virtue of

their office receive some kind of stipend or emolument, Paul is concerned to insist that the executive officials should receive twice as much as the rest, presumably because they devote more of their time and energies to their functions. The word rendered **remuneration** (Gk. *timē*) literally means 'honour', and many prefer to translate it so, some on the ground that the list of qualities expected of overseers and deacons in ch. iii can be taken as implying that they normally retained their secular jobs. Not much weight need be attached to the latter point, for the requirement that they should not be excessively keen on financial gains almost certainly refers to their administration of the community purse. Honour and respect in the congregation are of course included here, but the inference from 18 that financial, or at any rate material, rewards are primarily intended cannot be evaded. We have of course no idea of the character, scope or size of these, but the natural conclusion to be drawn from 18 is that the elders concerned are entitled to look to the church for their maintenance. This principle is in complete harmony with Paul's attitude as revealed elsewhere. While he preferred not to take advantage of it himself (1 Cor. ix. 3-18; 1 Thess. ii. 7-9), he always stood up vigorously for the right of the apostles and their coadjutors to be materially supported by the community.

Needless to say, this passage has an important bearing on the problem of date and authorship. In Asia Minor in the early second century, if we can trust Ignatius's letters, the line of demarcation between the executive officials (the bishop and his deacons) and the board of presbyters was firmly and clearly established, and there could be no question of the extraordinary prestige and dignity enjoyed by the bishop. The arrangements depicted here have an altogether more primitive air, for (*a*) the line of separation between the two types of ministers is still rather blurred, and (*b*) the right of the overseers to the enjoyment of special privileges was still, it would appear, not completely accepted, since the writer of the letter felt it necessary to press the point.

Paul backs his proposition that the church's ministers are entitled to material support with two citations. **For Scripture 18 says** is a thoroughly Pauline expression: cf. Rom. iv. 3; ix. 17; xi. 2; Gal. iv. 30; etc. The first of his citations is Deut. xxv. 4

(LXX version), a text which he applies in the same way in 1 Cor. ix. 9. The original intention of **'You must not muzzle'**, etc., was simply to secure that an ox was allowed an occasional bite as it moved round treading out corn, but in 1 Cor. ix. 9 Paul argues, in characteristically rabbinical fashion, that God cannot have had merely cattle in view when he caused these words to be written. So he finds in them unmistakable evidence that it is the divine will that the apostle, or Christian minister, should be supported by the congregation. He draws the same moral here. The second citation, **'A workman deserves his wages'**, does not come from the O.T., but is a logion attributed by Luke (x. 7) to Jesus. At first sight, therefore, it looks as if the Third Gospel is being quoted, and some have found in this convincing proof that the letter must date from the post-apostolic age. Others (e.g. C. Spicq) can see no reason why Paul should not be quoting an earlier draft of Luke's gospel, and claim that this is the first example of the N.T. being designated Scripture. There is certainly a problem here, but its solution does not necessarily entail either of these conclusions. The words **For Scripture says** may well refer strictly to only the former citation, the Lord's saying being loosely appended by way of explanation of confirmation. Alternatively the maxim may derive from some apocryphal writing which counted as Scripture in the Apostle's eyes. As has often been pointed out, Lk. x. 7 leaves the distinct impression that Jesus is appealing to a commonly accepted proverb.

The next two verses go closely together and deal with the situation, common enough in any community, of accusations being levelled against office-bearers. Paul requests Timothy 19 **not** to **entertain a charge against an elder except on the evidence** (AV's 'before', i.e. in the presence of, is incorrect) **of two or three witnesses.** This was a standing principle of Jewish legal procedure (Deut. xix. 15), and was evidently valued in the apostolic Church: cf. Mt. xviii. 16; Jn. viii. 17; 2 Cor. xiii. 1. It is not surprising that the Christians took it over; it was an enlightened rule which gave the Jew a protection almost unique in ancient codes of justice. Paul's point is that church leaders should not be at the mercy of frivolous or ill-natured complaints, but should enjoy at least the protection which any ordinary Jew could claim under the law.

On the other hand, when an elder's guilt is established in this way, Timothy **should publicly expose** him, **so that the rest** 20 **may be afraid.** Some lay stress on the present participle here translated **those who do wrong,** and explain it as meaning 'those who persist in wrong-doing', presumably after an initial, private remonstrance (Mt. xviii. 15); but this introduces an entirely fresh idea. Others understand the words as referring, not to elders, but to sinners in general, and interpret 20-22 as dealing with their censure and re-admission to the congregation; but this (*a*) involves too abrupt a change of subject-matter, and (*b*) presupposes a degree of development for the penitential system which we can hardly attribute to the first, or even early second, century. There is also much dispute as to whether **publicly** (lit. 'before all') implies before the assembled congregation or before the board of elders. We do not, however, hear elsewhere of such private sessions, and public exposure before the church suits the atmosphere of apostolic Christianity much better. On the other hand, **the rest** probably denotes the remaining elders.

A note of strong entreaty now comes into Paul's style as he urges Timothy **to observe these rules without prejudging** 21 **the issue, doing nothing out of favouritism.** It is difficult to escape the impression that he has in mind a concrete case, or perhaps cases, of scandal arising out of the preferential treatment which erring elders have received. He invokes **God and Christ Jesus and the elect angels** because the final judgment will be in their hands; Timothy must exercise his judicial functions as their representative, and also as one who will himself be judged by them. The angels are described as **elect** in contrast to the fallen angels: cf. *Od. Sal.* iv. 8. For the belief that they will take part in the last judgment, cf. 4 Esd. xvi. 67; Mt. xxv. 31; Mk. viii. 38; Lk. ix. 26; Rev. xiv. 10.

The command **Don't be in a hurry to lay hands on any-** 22 **one** almost certainly refers to ordination. This interpretation fits the context admirably; the realization of the liability of elders to fall into misconduct and of the awful judgment which awaits them if they do underlines the importance of using extreme care and deliberation when appointing such officials. It also accords with Paul's preoccupation in the Pastorals with the desirability of securing men of firm and proven character for the ministry. An alternative exegesis which has found much support explains the words as referring to the formal restoration of penitents. Paul's meaning will then be: 'after passing sentence on the guilty, don't be hasty in revoking it and readmitting the sinners to communion'. We know that in the third century and after penitents were readmitted by the laying on of hands (e.g. Cyprian, *Ep.* lxxiv. 12; Eusebius, *Hist. eccl.* vii. 2; *Apost. Const.* II. xviii. 7). Such considerations, however, as (*a*) the fact that elsewhere in the Pastorals the laying on of hands signifies ordination, (*b*) the absence of any other evidence for such a rite of readmission in the first century, and indeed in the second if the letter is assumed to be pseudonymous, and (*c*) the difficulty of supposing that by any of the dates suggested for the composition of the Pastorals the Church had evolved a formalized procedure of this kind for restoring sinners, seem to weigh decisively against it.

One sound reason why a chief pastor should exercise prudence in ordaining is to avoid associating himself **with another man's sins.** He could fairly be held in some degree responsible if the man whom he had ordained with improper haste became an occasion of scandal. So far from allowing that to happen, the Christian leader who is called upon to judge, and also to punish, others must (so Paul admonishes Timothy) **keep** himself **unstained** (lit. 'pure'), i.e. his own life must be absolutely above reproach.

23   The advice, **Don't go on drinking only water, but take a little wine for the sake of your digestion in view of your frequent indispositions,** seems at first sight to interrupt the connexion between 22 and 24 f., and critics have often assumed either that it has got misplaced or that it is a gloss which has crept into the text. There is no MS support for either of these surmises, and so far from being a likely intruder, the very banality of the verse strikes a note of authenticity. Believers in Pauline authorship have not been slow to point this out, adding that the Apostle's style is often disjointed. Actually it is by no means so irrelevant to the context as one might judge from a hasty glance. Paul has just urged Timothy to **keep** himself pure. This immediately reminds him that one of the measures

of self-discipline which his young disciple has adopted, and which in his opinion is unnecessary in itself as well as having a harmful effect on his health, is total abstinence. Hence he interjects this remark parenthetically in qualification of **unstained.** The advice will have even more point if we are justified in supposing (iv. 3 seems to support this) that the errorists erected total abstinence into a principle, thereby making nonsense of the theological truth that all God's gifts are good in themselves and remain so providing they are used in moderation and with an act of thanksgiving.

The beneficial effects of wine as a remedy against dyspeptic complaints, as a tonic, and as counteracting the effects of impure water, were widely recognized in antiquity, and modern travellers in Mediterranean countries have confirmed its value for the third at any rate of these purposes. The author of Proverbs (xxxi. 6) advises its use for maladies of both body and soul; Hippocrates (*De med. antiq.* xiii) recommends moderate draughts of wine for a patient for whose stomach water alone is dangerous; and Plutarch (*De sanit. praec.* xix) states that wine is the most useful of drinks and the pleasantest of medicines.

The Apostle now returns to his theme of the importance of taking pains to assess the character of prospective elders. There are people, he points out, whose **sins are immediately** 24 **obvious, running ahead of them to judgment**—a graphic way of saying that even the most inexperienced and undiscerning chief pastor has no excuse for not noticing them. The question has been asked whether the judgment is God's or Timothy's, but the former seems much preferable; even while they are still alive, such people cannot conceal the fact that they are incurring the divine wrath. There are others, however, whose sins **trail behind them,** i.e. will only be brought to light when they appear before the all-seeing Judge. The existence of such people underlines the necessity for extreme care in selecting ministers.

The same principle, Paul adds, operates with good men. In choosing candidates for the eldership Timothy will do well to remember that, while **good deeds too may be immediately** 25 **obvious,** and their doers in consequence have a sound claim to promotion, this is not always the case. It remains a fact, however, that even if a man's good deeds fail at present to attract the attention they deserve, **they cannot be concealed for ever.** That is to say, they will certainly come to light at the final judgment. The moral is that Timothy should not reject out of hand candidates who at first sight do not seem to possess the qualities demanded.

13. DUTIES OF SLAVES. vi. 1-2a

(1) All who are under the yoke as slaves should deem their masters worthy of complete respect, so that the name of God and the Christian teaching may not be exposed to scandal. (2) Slaves who have believing masters should not take liberties with them on the ground that they are brothers, but should be all the better slaves because the recipients of their good service are believers and beloved.

This section concludes the Apostle's advice for the several groups in the Ephesian church. Slaves formed an important element in the early Christian communities, and Paul in particular shows considerable concern for them: cf. 1 Cor. vii. 21-23; Gal. iii. 28; Eph. vi. 5-9; Col. iii. 22-25; Phm. 10-17. His general teaching is that, since the Christian's true freedom, and also his true servitude, are constituted by his relationship to Christ, he need not attach too much importance to his social position in the world. Whatever that may be, he must be aware that in Christ there is neither bond nor free in the ordinary sense of these words. Hence he made no attempt to alter the institution of slavery, but was quick to emphasize that the ties of brotherly love uniting a Christian master and his slave transcended the very different relative standing assigned them by society.

This, so far as space allows, is the attitude revealed by the present passage; if the emphasis seems mainly on the duty of obedience, the underlying premiss is the brotherly love uniting Christians. Many have found it surprising, not to say disturbing, that the Church did not from the very start launch an out-and-out attack on an institution so degrading and so contrary to its fundamental teaching. We must remember, however, (a) that in the apostolic age Christians were not greatly interested in the reform of social institutions since they looked forward to the speedy coming of the Lord; (b) that in any case their chief concern was to focus attention on something much more important than social organization, viz. the new and blessed life which was open to the individual through fellowship with Christ; (c) the idea of service was not in itself so repellent to them as to modern people because of their vivid awareness that the Lord had assumed the role of a servant; and (d) that although slavery as an institution was to continue for centuries, Christianity at once succeeded in modifying the relations of master and slave.

The expression **under the yoke as slaves** is, of course, 1 tautologous, since the very status of a slave implies his being, metaphorically, under a yoke. It is needlessly subtle, however, to read out of it the innuendo either that the slaves of heathen masters have to bear a double yoke, or·alternatively that there is nothing peculiar in the condition of slavery since all men are in some kind of bondage. This first verse deals with Christian slaves in general, irrespective of whether their masters are Christians or not. The motive suggested for treating these with **complete respect** is to prevent **the name of God and the Christian teaching** (lit. 'the teaching': see on iv. 6) from being **exposed to scandal**. The language recalls Is. lii. 5 (LXX: cf. Rom. ii. 24): 'because of you my name is exposed to scandal among the nations'. As usual (see on iii. 7 above) Paul is painfully aware of the disastrous come-back which would ensue if Christian slaves abused their new-found liberty in Christ to behave insolently towards their masters.

In the next verse he considers a second case, viz. **Slaves** 2a **who have believing masters.** These obviously constitute a special problem, for they might well be tempted to assume that, since all are **brothers** in the fellowship of Christ, they are entitled to **take liberties with them.** The verb (Gk. *kataphronein*) is the one used at iv. 12, where the translation is, 'Let no one underrate you'. It does not signify 'despise' (AV), but rather to treat without the full consideration due to the other man's station. On the contrary, Paul points out, they **should be all the better slaves** precisely because the masters they are serving **are believers and beloved,** i.e. Christians. We recall Paul's advice in Gal. v. 13: 'Be slaves to one another in love'. The description of the work the slaves perform as **good service** (Gk. *euergesia*) elaborates the same point by reminding the masters that they are beneficiaries and the slaves that the tasks they think so toilsome are really only forms of the mutual service Christians should render one another.

14. THE DANGERS OF FALSE TEACHING.
vi. 2b-10

These are the things you should teach and preach. (3) Anyone who teaches differently and does not give his mind to the wholesome message, that of our Lord Jesus Christ, and the teaching which accords with sound religion (4) is a swollen-headed person, possessing no real knowledge but morbidly taken up with idle speculations and verbal quibbles which give rise to jealousy, quarrelling, slanders, base suspicions, (5) and persistent wranglings between people whose minds are corrupted and who have lost their hold of the truth, who regard religion as a source of profit. (6) Religion is indeed a great source of profit, for the man with a contented spirit. (7) For we brought nothing into the world, since we can take nothing out either. (8) If we have food and clothing, we shall be content with that. (9) Those who want to be rich fall into temptation and a snare and a mass of irrational, pernicious desires, which submerge men in ruin and destruction. (10) For evils of every kind are rooted in the love of money; and there are people who, through making this their objective, have been led astray from the faith and have got themselves spiked with many pangs.

Paul has now finished his advice to particular groups. In this concluding section he renews his attack on perverters of orthodoxy, tracing their attitude to pride and cupidity.

Scholars have debated whether **These are the things you** 2b **should teach and preach** should be taken closely with the preceding section about slaves, or be regarded as introducing a new paragraph. The latter is preferable, since a contrast is clearly intended between Timothy as a teacher and the false teachers mentioned in the next sentence. If so, **These . . . things** probably cover all the subjects treated and instructions given in the letter. So, in the following verse, **Anyone who** 3 **teaches differently** does not refer to heterodoxy in general, but to the specific issues on which the errorists were leading people astray. For the verb (Gk. *heterodidaskalein*), cf. i. 3. Later it came to mean 'to teach heresy'; the fact that, while carrying a pejorative flavour, it still retains its original significa-tion is evidence for the early date of the letter.

The Apostle then lays his finger on what he considers the root cause of the errorists' deviation; they do not **give** their **mind** (or perhaps, 'agree with') to the gospel and the Church's teaching founded on it. The words rendered **the wholesome message, that of our Lord Jesus Christ** could be more liter-ally translated, 'wholesome words, those of our Lord J. C.' If this is correct, the reference must be to the words actually spoken by our Lord, and the passage will provide interesting confirmation of the early collection of these. Many prefer this rendering, and find in it an expression of the Apostle's con-viction that Christ and his teaching constitute the supreme authority for Christians and that to swerve from them spells disaster. They point to the fact that Paul elsewhere (e.g. 1 Cor. vii. 10) evinces an interest in our Lord's sayings, treating them as a norm of Christian behaviour.

While this is an attractive exegesis, there are important con-siderations which weigh against it. (*a*) There is no definite article in the Greek before 'wholesome words', and we should have expected one if the meaning were 'the sayings of Jesus'. Further, if this had been the meaning, it is odd that Paul did not simply write, 'the wholesome words of our Lord J. C.', but instead added 'those of our Lord J. C.' as a kind of qualification of 'wholesome words'. (*b*) The recorded utterances of Jesus have at best an indirect bearing on the problems discussed in the Pastorals. (c) The description of them as **wholesome** is distinctly condescending, whether we regard the writer as Paul or a later Paulinist. For these reasons it seems more satisfactory to take 'wholesome words' as denoting the sound Christian message and broadly equivalent to **the teaching which accords with,** etc. Paul then defines this **message** as **that of our Lord Jesus Christ** to bring out that its ultimate source is Christ himself and that he is its theme. For a similar use of the genitive, cf. 'the word of the Lord' (1 Thess. i. 8; 2 Thess. iii. 1) and 'the word of the cross' (1 Cor. i. 18).

The adjective **wholesome** is a favourite one of Paul's in this connexion; see on i. 10. As usual, it denotes that the gospel, in contrast to the false teachers' morbid speculations, is healthy in itself and also imparts spiritual well-being to anyone who founds his faith upon it.

By **the teaching which accords with sound religion** (Gk. *eusebeia*—another favourite word: see note on ii. 2) Paul means the orthodox faith as held by himself and Timothy. It is divinely guaranteed, being rooted in the gospel of Christ. Consequently anyone who rejects it in favour of some private doctrine of his 4 own can only be **a swollen-headed person** (for the Greek verb *tetuphōtai*, see on iii. 6). So far from **possessing** superior religious and theological insight, he in fact has **no real knowledge**—we may compare Paul's observation in 1 Cor. viii. 1 that pretensions to esoteric knowledge are liable to foster conceit. The subjects with which he is **morbidly taken up** (the Greek participle *noson* literally means 'being sick', and contrasts pointedly with **wholesome** in the previous verse) amount to no more than **idle speculations and verbal quibbles,** which not only lead to no profitable conclusion (how could they, since they do not look to the saving gospel as their ultimate authority?), but only provoke unedifying and profoundly un-Christian wrangling, backbiting, and mutual suspicion.

As in 2 Tim. ii. 23; Tit. iii. 9, the word translated **idle speculations** (Gk. *zētēseis*: cf. *ekzētēseis* in i. 4) covers much more than 'disputes' or 'controversies', and denotes the sectaries' preoccupation with pseudo-intellectual theorizings. Paul has already criticized this in i. 4. He now further stigmatizes it as a sham battle about words (Gk. *logomachia*: a N.T. hapax), and paints in lurid colours the pride from which it springs, the spirit of anti-social bitterness and suspicion which it sows in the church, and the moral degeneracy which it eventually produces. The picture is a savage one, and although some of the details may be borrowed from conventional catalogues of vices, it suggests a concrete situation which excited Paul's distress and indignation.

He now describes the moral degradation of the sectaries themselves. First, as is evident from their **persistent wrang-** 5 **lings** (this seems to be the sense of the Greek hapax *diapara-tribai*), they have become **people whose minds are corrupted** or depraved. The word 'mind' (Gk. *nous*) is here used to denote their whole mental and moral attitude or way of thinking (cf. Rom. i. 28), not just their reasoning powers as such. Secondly, as a direct consequence of this, they **have lost their hold of the truth.** By this Paul means, not so much that they have lost their capacity to apprehend the truth in general, but, more specifically, that they have become blind to the true content of the Christian revelation. For this sense of **the truth,** see on ii. 4: cf. also 2 Tim. ii. 25; iii. 7; Tit. i. 1; 14.

This leads directly to the third, and most shocking, stage of degradation: they have come to **regard religion as a source of profit.** As in 3, the Greek word for **religion,** here and in the next verse, is *eusebeia.* It has been disputed whether the charge is that they used their show of piety as a lever for material advancement, or that they exacted fees for the esoteric religious instruction they gave to their adherents. The latter is almost certainly correct, for it coheres better with what follows, and also (if we are justified in regarding it as a parallel) with the picture of their strenuous propagandist methods given in Tit. i. 11. Further, it is inconceivable that the profession of Christianity was materially advantageous at any of the times which have been seriously proposed for the composition of the Pastorals. As we have seen (v. 17 f.: cf. 2 Tim. ii. 6), Paul has no objection to church officials, least of all teachers, receiving emoluments. His complaint against the sectaries seems to be that they make money their prime objective and set a specific price upon their wares.

With a fine touch of irony, therefore, he takes up and reinterprets in a Christian way their blasphemous claim. **Religion is** 6

indeed a great source of profit, he agrees, recalling perhaps his statement at iv. 8 that 'sound religion is beneficial all the way'. The benefits it bestows, however, have nothing to do with material riches, for what it offers to the believer is 'the promise of life here and now and of life to come'. An essential condition of this is that, so far from yielding to covetousness, a man should have **a contented spirit,** i.e. a spirit which accepts gratefully the gifts God has bestowed and is satisfied. The word thus translated is *autarkeia*, or 'self-sufficiency'. This was a technical term in Greek philosophy, particularly favoured in the Cynic-Stoic tradition, which used it to denote the wise man's independence of circumstances. We find Paul employing it in 2 Cor. ix. 8 with the sense of 'sufficiency', 'adequate means'; but the deeper, more characteristically Christian meaning which it has here is illustrated by Phil. iv. 11, where he claims, 'I have learned to be content (Gk. *autarkēs*: the related adjective), whatever my situation'.

The next verse gives a sound practical reason for the religious man's contented attitude; he knows that, from the point of view of eternity, none of the things people covet has any permanency.
7 The words, **For we brought nothing into the world,** etc., express a commonplace as familiar in Jewish as in Graeco-Roman thought: cf. Job i. 21; Eccl. v. 15; Wis. vii. 6; Philo, *Spec. leg.* i. 294 f.; Seneca, *Ep.* cii. 24 f. For Christian parallels, cf. Lk. xii. 16-21; Hermas, *Sim.* i. 6. The Greek original contains an awkwardness of construction which the translation hardly masks, for the two clauses are connected by the conjunction *hoti*, which must mean either 'because' or 'that'. A number of MSS insert either 'it is plain' or 'it is true' before *hoti*, making the text read, 'For we brought nothing into the world; it is plain (*al.* true) that we can take nothing out either'. These and other variants, however, are clearly attempts to iron out a difficult, and therefore intrinsically more probable, reading. If *hoti* is given its full value (it must be **since,** as in the translation), the general sense will be that the reason why we brought nothing into the world is because we are not going to be able to take anything out; but this seems intolerably banal. The most satisfactory solution is to suppose either that *hoti* has lost its full causal force and has the weakened sense of 'as' or even 'and',

or that Paul is expressing himself confusedly because he is con-
flating proverbial clichés.

After all, the basic necessities of life are in fact quite few and **8**
simple, and can be summed up as **food and clothing** (the
latter word, Gk. *skepasmata*, may include shelter as well, but
the dictionary evidence is on the whole against this). These are
frequently lumped together as minimum requirements both in
the Bible (e.g. Deut. x. 18; Is. iii. 7; Mt. vi. 25) and, still more,
in popular Stoic-Cynic teaching (e.g. Musonius, xviii-xix, ed.
Hense; Diogenes Laertius, vi. 104; x. 131). Hence some think
a Stoic maxim is being quoted. The future **we shall be content**
is unexpected, for an admonitory construction such as 'we
should be content' would seem more in place. It may be that
Paul is incorporating a proverbial tag without troubling to
modify it. Alternatively, and more probably, the future may be
a Hebraism with the force of an imperative.

These thoughts prompt the Apostle to contemplate the disastrous effects of the inordinate love of money on the soul. It
is not the rich as such whom he castigates; there were such in
the Ephesian church (cf. 17 below), and while he has advice for
them, he does not condemn their possessions as intrinsically
wrong. His warning is for **Those who want to be rich,** i.e. **9**
those who have fixed their desires on material wealth and made
it their overriding motive; again he is probably thinking of the
sectaries and their view of religion as a profitable enterprise.
Like animals lured from the safe track, the would-be rich **fall
into temptation and a snare.** Presumably their moral sense
becomes blurred as a result of their overmastering passion, and
they become the prey of **a mass of irrational, pernicious
desires,** of the kind **which submerge men in ruin and
destruction.** The verb for **submerge** (Gk. *buthizein*) is a vivid
one which conjures up the image of drowning someone in the
sea, while the two nouns **ruin** and **destruction,** if they are to
be differentiated, may signify material and spiritual disaster
respectively.

To justify his strong language Paul cites what is evidently a
current proverb, **For evils of every kind are rooted in the 10
love of money.** This was a popular theme of Jewish and pagan
popular ethics: for the former, cf. Ecclus. xxvii. 1 f.; Philo, *Spec.*

leg. iv. 65; *Test. xii patr.*, *Jud.* 19. The translation adopted is perhaps more satisfactory than the usual 'the love of money is the root of all evils', for there is no definite article before 'root' in the original Greek, and it is extravagant to assert that love of money is the root-cause of all sins.

In the second half of the verse, after citing the popular proverb, Paul reveals that his polemic is directly aimed at the sectaries and their commercialization of religion. He reminds Timothy that **there are people who, through making this their objective, have been led astray from the faith,** not necessarily apostatizing in the strict sense, but leading lives out of accord with the gospel. By **this** he means money-making; in the Greek the word strictly agrees with **the love of money,** but the bodily insertion of the popular adage accounts for the loose connexion. For **the faith,** see on iii. 9. With **people** (Gk. *tines* ='some', 'certain') he makes a pointed reference to certain individuals who are doubtless as familiar to Timothy and the Ephesian church as to himself. These unhappy souls, he adds, **have got themselves spiked with many pangs**—a graphic metaphor describing the thorns of remorse and disillusionment which now lacerate them.

6-10 have often been represented as a block of mainly Hellenistic material, without any specifically Christian motive and only loosely connected with the polemic which precedes. This is, however, a complete misreading of the passage. There are plenty of parallels to its ideas, as the notes have indicated, in popular pagan moralizing, and some of the former may be direct echoes of the latter. But it should be observed (*a*) that the Biblical and Jewish parallels are equally impressive, (*b*) that the attitude to riches revealed coincides with that of Jesus, and (*c*) that even 8, described by B. S. Easton as 'the very essence of Stoicism', reflects the advice Jesus gave his disciples (cf. Mk. vi. 7 ff. and parr.; Mt. vi. 25-33 = Lk. xii. 22-31). The little homily dovetails neatly with the Apostle's criticism of the heretics' money-grubbing propensities in 6, and if he seems to pass almost at once into general reflections, that is natural enough; he soon comes back to the painful actualities of the Ephesian church.

15. A PERSONAL CHARGE TO TIMOTHY.
vi. 11-16

(11) But you, man of God, shun these things. Aim at integrity, piety, faith, steadfastness, gentleness. (12) Play your part in the noble contest of faith; possess yourself of eternal life, to which you were called and made the noble confession in the presence of many witnesses. (13) I charge you, in the presence of God, who gives life to all things, and of Christ Jesus, who bore witness to the same noble confession in Pontius Pilate's time, (14) to keep your commission spotless and free from reproach until the manifestation of our Lord Jesus Christ, (15) which HE will make visible at the appropriate time, the blessed and unique Sovereign, the King of kings and Lord of lords, (16) who alone has immortality, dwelling in unapproachable light, whom no human being has seen or can see. To him be honour and eternal power. Amen.

As his letter draws to a close, Paul addresses a direct appeal to Timothy himself. The strongly personal note in it is unmistakable; it is putting too great a strain on the passage to construe it as an exhortation to the typical pastor, and a still greater strain if we regard 'Timothy' as standing for the Christian disciple in general.

The opening words, **But you,** are emphatic; they stand in 11 sharp antithesis to **there are people** in the preceding verse, perhaps also to **Anyone** in 3. Timothy's conduct, and the principles on which he bases it, must be precisely the opposite of those of the moral bankrupts who have just been described. The title **man of God** is applied to him deliberately. It connotes one who is in God's service, represents God and speaks in his name, and admirably fits one who is a pastor (cf. 2 Tim. iii. 17). An attempt has been made, with the aid of parallels from Philo, the Hermetic literature, and the *Epistle of Aristeas*, to give the expression a semi-mystical meaning, as if 'God's man' signified the baptized Christian in general. Such subtleties, however, are unnecessary and artificial, for 'man of God' is regularly used in the O.T. to designate God's servants and agents: cf. Deut. xxxiii. 1 and Josh. xiv. 6 (Moses); 1 Sam. ix. 6 f. (Samuel); 1 Kings xvii. 18 (Elijah); 2 Kings iv. 7 (Elisha); Neh. xii. 24 (David).

Consecrated as he is to God's service, Timothy must **shun these things,** i.e. primarily the love of money and the evils of which it is root-cause, but also no doubt all the false, disastrous courses which the sectaries encourage. Instead he should **Aim at** (lit. 'pursue', a thoroughly Pauline usage: cf. Rom. ix. 30; xii. 13; xiv. 19; 1 Cor. xiv. 1; Phil. iii. 12; 14) **integrity, piety, faith, love, steadfastness, gentleness.** The list of qualities is chosen with an eye to Timothy's needs in his pastoral office. We find **integrity** and **piety** coupled together, in the form of adverbs, in Tit. ii. 12. The Greek word for the former (*dikaio-sunē*) stands neither for 'righteousness' in the characteristic Pauline sense nor, more narrowly, for strict justice, as opposed to the greed and cupidity of the sectaries. It is a general word for conduct which is absolutely upright and impartial in relation to all the members of the community: cf. 2 Tim. ii. 22; iii. 16. By **piety** (again his favourite word *eusebeia*) Paul means a devout, entirely correct religious attitude: see on ii. 2.

The triad **faith, love, steadfastness** recurs in Tit. ii. 2; it is also found in 1 Thess. i. 3. The first two represent, of course, the supreme Christian graces; having regard to Timothy's special position, as defender of the faith against error and also as apostolic delegate, it is most appropriate that **steadfastness** and **gentleness** should be added. The former is frequently used by Paul with the sense of patient endeavour; the latter (Gk. *praüpathia*) is a N.T. hapax, but the Apostle was familiar with its cognate *praütēs* (e.g. 2 Cor. x. 1; Gal. v. 22).

It is sometimes argued (see Introduction, pp. 18; 20) that the treatment here of **faith** and **love,** which for the Apostle were all-inclusive, as particular virtues which can be catalogued along with others, is a blatantly un-Pauline trait. But we should observe that both of them figure, without any indication of precedence, in the miscellaneous list of 'fruits of the Spirit' in Gal. v. 22. The objection that 'to Paul these are God's gifts, not man's achievements' (F. D. Gealy) is equally superficial. If one must be literal, Paul himself counselled the Corinthians, in identical language, 'Aim at love' (1 Cor. xiv. 1). More generally, the doctrine of the primacy of grace does not exclude all advice and exhortation.

The challenging words which follow, **Play your part in the 12 noble contest of faith,** conjure up the picture of a wrestling match or other athletic event; as the translation attempts to bring out, the metaphor is drawn from sport, not warfare. For Paul's use of analogies from sport, see on iv. 7: cf. also 1 Cor. ix. 24 ff.; Phil. ii. 16; iii. 12-14; 2 Tim. iv. 7. Paul calls it **the . . . contest of faith** either because it is the struggle which the true faith undertakes against error (in which case RSV's 'the faith' is to be preferred), or, more probably, because he has in mind 'the personal warfare with evil to which every Christian is called' (J. H. Bernard). The imperative is purposely in the present, indicating that the struggle will be a continuous process. On the other hand, the aorist imperative **possess yourself** suggests that Timothy can lay hold on **eternal life** (here conceived of as the prize for the athletic event) immediately, in a single act. Thus it is something which the Christian who takes the demands of his faith seriously can in some measure enjoy here and now. There is no contradiction between this and Paul's teaching elsewhere. If in Rom. vi. 22 and Gal. vi. 8 he speaks of eternal life as a blessing which the faithful Christian reaps at the end, there are other passages (e.g. Rom. vi. 4; 2 Cor. iv. 10-12; Col. iii. 3 f.) in which he conceives of the new life in Christ as a present reality.

Two compelling reasons why Timothy should engage in this lifelong struggle are (*a*) that God has **called** him to eternal life, and (*b*) that he has publicly acknowledged and accepted that call. For God's call, cf. 1 Cor. i. 9; 2 Thess. ii. 14. The occasion when Timothy accepted it was when he **made the noble confession in the presence of many witnesses.** This has sometimes been explained as a reference either to his ordination or to his brave confession of Christ when persecuted and haled before the civil magistrates (cf. Heb. xiii. 23 for a mention of his imprisonment). The former is not particularly suitable to the context, which is concerned with Timothy's call as a Christian (that is surely the meaning of being called to eternal life), not as a minister of God. In any case we have no reason to suppose that

a solemn confession of faith in Christ was demanded at a
minister's ordination; no hint of one appears in early accounts
of the rite. The latter explanation seems even less appropriate,
for an appearance before a magistrate can scarcely be called a
summons to eternal life. Further, if Timothy had suffered in
this way, and had made a courageous showing, we should have
expected some more direct allusion to the affair in the letters,
especially in view of their tendency to dwell on his timidity.
Almost the only point in favour of this exegesis is the parallelism
with 13, which possibly (but see below) recalls Christ's trial
before the Roman governor. While this suggests, however, that
the two confessions are parallel, it is unnecessary to seek a strict
parallelism in the situations too.

Much more plausible than either of these is the interpretation
which identifies Timothy's **noble confession** with the profession of faith which he made at his baptism. This above all
was the occasion on which a Christian could be said to have
accepted the call to eternal life, and in the primitive Church
the sacrament was administered publicly before the assembled
congregation, i.e. **in the presence of many witnesses.** From
earliest times its climax was a solemn affirmation of faith by
the candidate, and Paul is almost certainly quoting such an
affirmation, or an excerpt from one, when he writes (Rom. x. 9),
'If you confess [the verb he uses, Gk. *homologein*, is the cognate
of the noun *homologia* rendered **confession** here] with your
mouth Jesus as Lord, and believe in your heart that God has
raised him from the dead, you will be saved'. No argument can
be brought against this exegesis from 2 Tim. iii. 15, for while
this discloses that Timothy had been early instructed in Scripture, it does not in the least imply that he was baptized in
infancy, which in any event is exceedingly unlikely. The fact
that Paul places the definite article before **noble confession**
confirms that he is speaking of a formula which has a recognized,
official character.

His reference to Timothy's baptismal profession moves him,
as he builds up his admonition, to make a final solemn appeal to
him in language consciously reminiscent of that very profession.
13 **I charge you,** he writes, **in the presence of God, who gives
life to all things, and of Christ Jesus, who bore witness to**

the same noble confession in Pontius Pilate's time. These
two clauses reproduce the substance of a primitive baptismal
creed. If we can judge by the practice of only a few generations
later, the candidate for initiation, as he stood in the water, was
first asked whether he believed in God the Father almighty (or
words to that effect), where 'Father' denoted the life-giving
source of all reality. This question is here represented by **God,
who gives life to all things,** the motive for the particular
wording chosen being to suggest that God is not only the
original creator, but also in baptism bestows the new, blessed
life in Christ to which Timothy has been called. Having
answered this first question in the affirmative, the candidate
was then asked whether he believed in Christ Jesus, who had
suffered and risen again. Very often, as we know from the
primitive Roman creed which underlies the present Apostles'
Creed, this interrogation included a mention of Pontius Pilate,
and this was also a feature of schematic summaries of the
apostolic preaching from earliest times: cf. Acts iii. 13; iv. 27;
xiii. 28; Ignatius, *Magn.* xi. 1; *Trall.* ix. 1; *Smyrn.* i. 2; Justin,
1 *Apol.* xiii. 3; lxi. 13. In these early credal formulae, where the
form used was, as here, *epi Pontiou Pilatou*, the meaning was
'in the time of Pontius Pilate', the intention being to fix the
passion at a definite date in history, and that is almost certainly
the force of the words here too.

Many scholars have preferred the translation 'before Pontius
Pilate' (the Greek preposition *epi* can bear either sense). This
has seemed to them to provide a neat antithesis to **in the
presence of many witnesses** in 12, and also to agree well
with **bore witness,** etc., in the present verse, which they interpret as referring to Christ's admission (Mk. xv. 5 and parr.)
that he was King of the Jews. The parallel, however, between
Timothy's confession and Christ's cannot be pressed in detail,
and it is definitely awkward to have **in the presence of God,**
etc., and 'before Pontius Pilate' so closely juxtaposed. It is
further doubtful whether his **noble confession** would naturally, in the absence of explanation, suggest to a reader the
acknowledgment of his status (in any case a very guarded one)
which Christ made at his examination before Pilate; and the
practical certainty that the passage echoes a primitive baptismal

creed makes it extremely probable that the words refer to the
Lord's crucifixion. If so, **in Pontius Pilate's time** must be the
correct translation.

The resulting sense is excellent. Timothy is adjured, in the
sight of God his creator, who also gives him eternal life, and of
Christ Jesus who died for him, to be loyal to his commission;
and the appeal is reinforced by a vivid reminder both of the
solemn engagement he himself undertook at his baptism and of
the still more awful witness which the Saviour bore on the cross.
The words **bore witness to the same noble confession** are
not to be pressed too literally, for Paul has deliberately adapted
his language to the wording of 12. The point he wishes to impress on Timothy is that, while he identified himself with faith
in Christ when he accepted baptism, Christ himself had, as it
were, attested the same confession in deed (one might almost
say, enacted it) when he died and rose again. The moral is that
the disciple should exhibit the same steadfastness and unflinch-
ing courage as his master.

14 There has been much discussion about what Paul has in mind
in charging Timothy to **keep** his **commission** (lit. 'the commandment') **spotless and free from reproach.** He may be
thinking either of the specific injunctions with which the paragraph opens (11 f.) or of the teaching of the letter as a whole,
but neither of these seems comprehensive enough in view of the
heightened tone of the passage. Those who interpret 12 as referring to Timothy's ordination naturally take the verse as an
encouragement to him to be faithful to his ordination vows. As
the reference there, however, is probably baptismal, it is much
more attractive to understand by 'the commandment' the whole
law of Christ, the rule of faith and life enjoined by the gospel, to
which Timothy has pledged himself at his baptism and of which
as an apostolic leader he is a trustee. It is interesting to note that
Cyril of Jerusalem, when quoting the verse (*Cat.* v. 13), substitutes 'the faith delivered to you', i.e. the creed summarizing
the rule of faith, for 'the commandment'.

The adjectives **spotless** and **free from reproach** have also
caused difficulty, some making them qualify Timothy and
others 'the commandment'. The former is grammatically possible, for the Greek contains 'you' in the accusative as the

subject of the infinitive **keep,** but the fact that the two adjectives are separated from 'you' by 'the commandment' makes it extremely unlikely that they agree with it. On the other hand, if taken with 'the commandment' they yield an admirable sense and one entirely in harmony with the concern of the letter for strict orthodoxy. In itself, of course, the faith of the gospel, which is what Timothy's commission amounts to, is **spotless and free from reproach,** but Paul now reminds him that it is his bounden duty to preserve it so, immune from the contaminations of heresy or vain speculations.

The words **until the manifestation of our Lord Jesus Christ** contain a reminder that Christ himself will judge his servants at his coming. Although Paul fixes no definite date for this (see note on 15 below), he seems to hint that it may happen in Timothy's lifetime. The importance of a Christian's being found blameless on the day of the Lord's coming is a thoroughly Pauline idea: cf. 1 Thess. iii. 13; v. 23; 1 Cor. i. 8; Phil. ii. 15 f.

The word **manifestation** (Gk. *epiphaneia*) was a technical term in the language of contemporary Hellenistic religion for the self-disclosure of a god or semi-divine being (e.g. a king, or, in the imperial cult, emperor). It could refer to the god's birthday, or some occasion when he miraculously displayed himself or his divine power, or to the anniversary of a king's coronation, or to his homecoming from a journey abroad. In the Pastorals it denotes in 2 Tim. i. 10 Christ's first coming or incarnation, but here and elsewhere (2 Tim. iv. 1; 8; Tit. ii. 13) his expected eschatological return. Its occurrence here, instead of the common N.T. *parousia*, has been pointed to as a suspiciously un-Pauline trait. As a matter of fact, Paul uses it of the second coming (in conjunction with *parousia*) in 2 Thess. ii. 8, and only employs *parousia* with this sense in 1 Cor. xv. 23; 1 Thess. ii. 19; iii. 13; iv. 15; v. 23; 2 Thess. ii. 1; 8; 9. Apart from it he has a variety of expressions for the second coming, such as 'the day of the Lord' (1 Thess. v. 2; 1 Cor. i. 8; v. 5), or 'the revelation of the Lord Jesus' (2 Thess. i. 7; 1 Cor. i. 7). The choice of the word here is in harmony with Paul's practice in the Pastorals of borrowing his vocabulary from that of Hellenistic religion.

In his early days Paul had anticipated that he himself would live to witness Christ's glorious return (1 Thess. ii. 19; iii. 13;

v. 23; etc.). The present passage confirms that in old age he came to realize that, so far as he himself was concerned, its date lay in the indefinite future; it would come about exactly when 15 God would judge it fit to manifest his Son. Thus **HE** (i.e. God himself) **will make it visible at the appropriate time,** i.e. at his own good time: see note on ii. 6.

This and the following verse form a solemn and splendid doxology, quite in the manner of Paul, although the formula itself is longer and more hymn-like than his usually are. Thoroughly Jewish in tone, it extols the unique sovereignty of God as against every human authority. It may well be a gem from the devotional treasury of the Hellenistic synagogue which converts had naturalized in the Christian Church. As applied to God, **the blessed and unique Sovereign** has parallels in 2 Macc. i. 24 ('the unique king'); xii. 15 ('the great sovereign of the universe'); Ecclus. xlvi. 5 ('the lofty sovereign'). We have already come across **blessed** used as a predicate of the Godhead in i. 11, where its Hellenistic flavour was stressed: see note. The titles **King of kings** and **Lord of lords** are attributed to Yahweh in the O.T. (Deut. x. 17; Ps. cxxxvi. 3; 2 Macc. xiii. 4), and together to Christ in the N.T. (Rev. xvii. 14; xix. 16). In their use, both by Jews and by Christians, a conscious rebuttal of the claims of earthly potentates—in the present context, probably, of emperor worship—was implied.

The same critique of the imperial cult can probably be de-16 tected in the emphatic **who alone has immortality,** since in the first century the practice of treating the deceased emperor as immortal was becoming fashionable. God was defined as immortal in i. 17; the statement here, with its more elaborate wording, is not intended to deny immortality to other beings, but to bring out that it belongs inherently and by right only to God, as the very source of life.

The description of God as **dwelling in unapproachable light** recalls Ps. civ. 2, where he is said to cover himself with light as with a garment, and also Paul's reference in Col. i. 12 to 'the saints in light', i.e. who dwell in God's realm of light. The underlying idea is that of the divine glory, which in Hebrew idiom indicated the pure spirituality and transcendence of his nature. It was this blinding radiance which made him **un-**

approachable to men. Ex. xxxiii. 17-23, which describes how God allowed Moses to look upon his glory, is in the mind of the author of the doxology, as comes out in **whom no human being has seen, or can see** (cf. Yahweh's warning to Moses, 'No man shall see me and live': also Jn. i. 18; vi. 46).

The doxology terminates with **To him be honour and eternal power. Amen.** The form is customary, but one would normally have expected 'honour and glory', as in i. 17. The substitution of **power** is suggested by the general theme, which stresses God's role as a potentate supreme over all would-be rivals, and to which **power** is clearly more appropriate.

16. POSITIVE ADVICE FOR THE RICH. vi. 17-19

(17) Instruct people who are rich so far as the present world goes not to be haughty or fix their hopes on anything so unstable as riches, but rather on God, who richly provides us with everything for our enjoyment, (18) and to do good, to be rich in deeds of kindness, and to be open-handed and generous, (19) thus storing up for themselves a good foundation for the future, so that they may possess themselves of the life which is life indeed.

After the magnificent doxology of the preceding section, these three verses bring one down from the heights with a jolt. Because they are so flat in themselves and introduce such a prosaic note into the climax which the Apostle is building up, commentators have been tempted to regard them either as displaced from their true position (some argue after 2, others after 10) or as interpolated at a time when well-off Christians were becoming a problem in the church. Such a dislocation, however, is in itself extremely unlikely, and a later editor would have surely chosen a more appropriate place for inserting new material of this kind. Actually the three verses are not so much out of place as these critics suppose, for it is the doxology and the exalted appeal leading up to it which are the real digression. Paul has been carried away, in a manner quite typical of him, by his own exhortation to Timothy. Now he returns to complete his advice about riches, realizing that something constructive should be added about their use in order to balance his negative remarks in 9 f.

His opening words underline the truth that material wealth
17 is only wealth **so far as the present world goes.** For the expression, cf. 2 Tim. iv. 10; Tit. ii. 12; also Rom. xii. 2; 1 Cor. ii. 6; 2 Cor. iv. 4 (the wording is slightly different in these three passages). The contrast implied between the present age and the age to come is, of course, thoroughly Jewish. The thought recalls the warning in Lk. xii. 21 about the man who piles up wealth for himself and is not rich 'unto God'. The attitude Paul here displays to wealth is moderate, and he does not condemn it in itself, contenting himself with pointing out the temptations to which rich people are exposed. These are, first, **to be haughty,** i.e. to throw their weight about and use their affluence to get the better of people who are less well off, and, secondly, to **fix their hopes** on their material possessions, which in the nature of things are fickle and 'make themselves wings' (Prov. xxiii. 5). The second infinitive is in the perfect; for the force of this, see note on v. 5.

The warning, with its positive suggestion that the rich would be better advised to found their hopes **rather on God,** strikingly recalls the Psalmist's, 'Lo, this is the man who would not make God his refuge, but trusted in the abundance of his riches' (Ps. lii. 7); but the thought is commonplace in the O.T. Reliance is to be placed on God rather than riches precisely because he **richly provides us with everything for our enjoyment.** The last words are probably emphatic; Paul rounds off his acknowledgment of God's fatherly beneficence with a fresh hint to the sectaries that their excessive asceticism runs counter to the divine intention.

The thought of God's generosity leads him to a constructive exposition of the duty of comfortably-off people. They are to
18 employ their wealth **to do good,** and thus **to be rich in deeds of kindness;** this is a form of wealth which will really please God. In fact, they are **to be open-handed and generous,** just as he is. For the store set by practical kindness in the Pastorals, see note on ii. 10.

If they conduct their lives on these principles, rich people will not really be making themselves any poorer, but, on the contrary, will be **storing up for themselves a good founda-** 19 **tion for the future.** The accent here is on **themselves;** they may well imagine that they will only be helping others, but in fact they will be piling up great benefits for themselves. The language of the clause is awkward, for **storing up** (the Gk. verb is *apothēsaurizein*: lit. 'to amass a treasure') and **foundation** represent two quite different ideas (although the Greek word for the latter, *themelion*, can also, in a transferred sense, mean 'fund'). But Paul not infrequently mixes his metaphors, and his thought is clear. Our Lord had himself pointed out that a man could lay up treasure in heaven by giving alms (Lk. xii. 33: cf. xviii. 22; Mt. vi. 20), and it is not unlikely that the Apostle has these *logia* in mind.

The concluding clause, **so that they may possess themselves of the life which is life indeed,** defines the nature of this heavenly treasure. It is nothing less than the 'eternal life' which Paul advised Timothy to lay hold on in 12. In contrast to life as it is commonly lived, it is not transitory, and knows no vicissitude; it alone has the quality which merits the description 'life'. Again Paul is recalling sayings of our Lord, who had declared (Lk. xii. 15) that a man's 'life' does not consist in the abundance of his possessions, and in the parable of the Rich Fool (*ib.* xii. 21) had portrayed the quick downfall of the man 'who lays up wealth for himself and is not rich for God'. These echoes of the gospel (quite apart from the insistence in 2 Tim. i. 9 that our holy calling does not depend on our own 'good works') should exclude any suspicion that the Pastorals are concerned to sponsor a post-Pauline moralism based on human merit.

17. FINAL EXHORTATION. vi. 20-21

(20) Timothy, keep safe the trust committed to you, steering clear of the profane chatter and counter-affirmations of what is falsely called knowledge. (21) Certain people who lay claim to it have missed the mark as regards the faith.—May grace be with you.

In this brief finale the Apostle gathers together in one pregnant sentence all his concern for the integrity of the gospel and all his horror of deviation from it. The language he uses does not suggest a generalized picture of heresy, but seems to envisage a specific brand which has already had disastrous consequences which are plain for all to see. The strongly personal tone may be a sign that, in his usual manner, Paul added these closing lines in his own hand.

20   By **the trust committed to you,** which he begs Timothy to **keep . . . safe,** Paul means, not simply the specific instructions given him for the performance of his charge, but, as the context confirms, the pure faith of the gospel, with the guardianship of which he, as apostolic delegate, has been entrusted. In the second century this traditional teaching based on the kerygma was to be known as 'the rule of faith' or 'the canon of the truth', but as early as Paul's time it was beginning to assume a definite shape and pattern, as is shown by the catechetical and traditional material embodied in or clearly underlying his letters. The noun translated **trust** (Gk. *parathēkē*) is found only here and in 2 Tim. i. 12; 14. It is a legal term connoting something which is placed on trust in another man's keeping. The suggestion is that the Christian message ('the faith' or 'the truth', as it is so often called in these letters) is not something which the church's minister works out for himself or is entitled to add to; it is a divine revelation which has been committed to his care, and which it is his bounden duty to pass on unimpaired to others.

In sharpest contrast to this stands **the profane chatter** (Gk. *kenophōniai*: lit. 'empty sounds') of the sectaries, which Timothy is pointedly advised to eschew. Exactly the same phrase recurs in 2 Tim. ii. 16; it is of a piece with Paul's scathing descriptions elsewhere (e.g. i. 6; iv. 7 where see note on **profane**) of the heretics' propaganda. Evidently they made a great parade of their pseudo-theological jargon. They also laid claim, as the present passage indicates, to a special **knowledge,** which the Apostle contemptuously describes as **falsely called** (Gk. *pseudōnumos*: a N.T. hapax). Their claim, and their use of the technical term **knowledge** (Gk. *gnōsis*), reinforce the conclusion that their teaching had at any rate some kinship with the general religious attitude later designated Gnosticism.

vi. 20 FINAL EXHORTATION

Though tempting, it is unnecessary and mistaken to press this kinship more closely than the evidence warrants. The special 'knowledge', or *gnōsis*, claimed by the great Gnostic systems of the second century consisted essentially of an esoteric grasp of the mystery of the upper world and of man's attainment of salvation by finding a passage back to it. There is little or no hint of this in the letters, nor, in all probability (see note on i. 4), of the complex families of aeons by which the Gnostics bridged the chasm between the material order and the ultimate unknowable God. The heretics' **knowledge,** or allegedly superior insight, is probably to be understood in terms of their 'endless fables and genealogies', their asceticism in food and sex, and their dualism involving the denial of the resurrection (see Introduction, pp. 11 f.). It is worth recalling that, while in Paul's acknowledged letters Christianity itself is treated as a form of 'knowledge' (e.g. 2 Cor. ii. 14; iv. 6; Phil. iii. 8; Col. ii. 3) and Christians are in a sense 'gnostics' (e.g. 1 Cor. i. 5; 2 Cor. viii. 7), the Apostle is already on his guard against the misguided presumption of knowledge, divorced from charity, which is itself puffed up and only causes scandal to the brethren (1 Cor. viii. 1; 7; 10; 11). It is this kind of pretentious pseudo-science that he seems to be criticizing here rather than an elaborate theosophical metaphysic of the type later known as Gnosticism.

Much speculation has gathered round the term **counter-affirmations** (Gk. *antitheseis*) which he uses in connexion with the deviationist *gnōsis*. Strictly it was a technical term in rhetoric meaning a counter-proposition (its literal meaning is 'contrary thesis') advanced in debate or argument. In the middle of the second century the famous heretic Marcion, who tried to free Christianity from its O.T. heritage and background, wrote a book bearing this very name as its title, *Antitheses*. In this he seems to have set out *seriatim* the contradictions, as he took them to be, 140 in all, between the O.T. and the gospel of Christ. It has therefore often been claimed that in this verse we have an allusion to his treatise, and that in consequence the letter must belong to the second half of the second century.

This daring identification has little, if anything, to recommend it except the coincidence of words. Marcion was not really a Gnostic, as the language of the text would make him out to be

if this exegesis were accepted; in any case he was violently anti-
Jewish, whereas the error of the heretics is a distinctly Jewish
form of *gnōsis*. More generally, there is nothing to show that
they professed any of Marcion's characteristic doctrines. Thus
much the most plausible interpretation of **counter-affirmations** is the simple and natural one. The heretics, according to
Paul, from their vantage-point of presumed superior knowledge,
develop their propositions systematically in opposition to, and
contradiction of, those advanced by sound Christian teachers.
Thus they build up and propagate a body of pseudo-beliefs
which amount to a denial of the gospel. Little wonder that
21 **Certain people who lay claim to** this esoteric knowledge
have missed the mark (for the verb, see note on i. 6) **as
regards the faith.**

The letter closes with a brief blessing, **May grace be with
you.** Paul's usual formula in his earlier letters was of the type,
'The grace of our Lord Jesus Christ . . .', but the closing words
of Colossians are identical with these. The final word **you** is in
the plural; we have precisely the same form in 2 Tim. iv. 22
and Tit. iii. 15. Many critics profess to be puzzled by this, since
all three letters claim to be addressed to individuals, and one
would therefore expect the singular. Some have suggested that
the pseudonymous author may have forgotten the setting of his
letter and simply taken over the stock Pauline plural form, but
this (*a*) raises the question why then he did not employ Paul's
normal formula ('the grace of our Lord Jesus Christ, etc.'), and
(*b*) presupposes a degree of carelessness which passes belief.
Others have discerned a subtler motive; though to all appear-
ances addressed to 'Timothy', the letter was really intended for
all Christian teachers in positions of pastoral responsibility.
This is even more far-fetched and improbable; we are left
wondering why the author should have decided to drop his
skilfully contrived illusion at the last moment. On the assumption that the letter is a piece of real correspondence, the change
from singular to plural is easily accounted for; though addressing
it to the chief pastor of the Ephesian church, Paul expected him
to have it read out to the assembled congregation, to which he
sent his blessing in this final sentence.

THE SECOND EPISTLE
TO TIMOTHY

1. ADDRESS AND GREETING. i. 1-2

(1) Paul, an apostle of Christ Jesus by the will of God, according to the promise of life in Christ Jesus, (2) to Timothy, my beloved son: grace, mercy and peace from God the Father and Christ Jesus our Lord.

Like its predecessor, the second of the letters to Timothy opens with a brief formula of salutation of the customary pattern. In Paul's usual manner it is emphasized that he is **an apostle of Christ Jesus** (not, that is, merely the repre- I sentative of a local church), and that his appointment is **by the will of God.** The latter expression contrasts with 'commissioned by God our Saviour and Christ Jesus our hope' in 1 Tim. i. 1 and reproduces the normal Pauline form (1 Cor. i. 1; 2 Cor. i. 1; Eph. i. 1; Col. i. 1). It has been objected, as at 1 Tim. i. 1, that these are stiff and formal reassurances which a collaborator so intimate as Timothy can scarcely have needed. But this plea overlooks the fact that, like 1 Timothy, this letter is not simply a piece of private correspondence; Paul may well desire to leave the congregation, to whom he expects it to be read out, in no doubt about his status and authority.

The words **according to the promise of life in Christ Jesus** (a literal rendering) are at first sight obscure. They go closely with **an apostle of Christ Jesus,** not with **by the will of God.** The preposition **according to,** i.e. 'in reference to', (Gk. *kata*) defines the aim and purpose of Paul's apostleship, while **promise** denotes the promise of eternal life which, according to the Christian understanding of the O.T., God has from the beginning held out to those who have faith (cf. Tit. i. 2). Thus what is claimed is that Paul's mission is to make known that this promise receives fulfilment through fellowship with Christ.

In Col. iii. 4 Christ is described as 'our life', while in Phil.
ii. 16 the gospel message is 'the word of life'. Paul's teaching
(which anticipates Jn. iii. 15) is that Christ bestows newness of
life, and that anyone who through faith 'puts on' Christ (Gal.
iii. 27) can share this life. In the light of this exegesis we are
entitled to give **in Christ Jesus** in this passage the full force
which **in Christ** regularly has in Paul's letters. It stands for the
mystical union with Christ which the believer enjoys as the fruit
of his faith. Some critics (e.g. B. S. Easton) prefer the weakened
sense 'given by Christ'. They argue (see on 1 Tim. i. 14; iii. 13)
that, where the phrase carries the mystical sense, it is almost invariably used of persons, and that since this is never the case in
the Pastorals, its meaning there must be 'given by Christ' or
'by the fact of Christ's existence' or, simply, 'Christian'. Their
theory receives no support from a passage like this, where the
mystical sense 'in union with Christ' is fully in place and the
alternatives proposed are strained and unnatural.

2   For the description of Timothy as **my beloved son,** and
also for the triad **grace, mercy, peace,** and the structure of
the greeting as a whole, see notes on 1 Tim. i. 1 f.

2. THANKSGIVING. i. 3-5

**(3) I give thanks to God, whom from my forbears I serve
with a clean conscience, whenever I mention you (as I
do incessantly, night and day) in my prayers (4)—for I
long to see you, recalling as I do your tears, so that I may
be filled with happiness—(5) being reminded of your
sincere faith, a faith which dwelt first in your grandmother Lois and your mother Eunice, and which dwells,
I am convinced, in you too.**

Ancient letters commonly opened, immediately after the
greeting, with a polite assurance of prayer, or alternatively an
expression of thanks, for the recipient's health and prosperity.
Paul followed this procedure, adapting the sentiments to his
Christian idiom, in most of his letters (e.g. Romans, 1 and 2

Corinthians, Philippians), but not in Galatians, where it did
not suit his mood, or in 1 Timothy or Titus. He reverts to it
here, and the deep emotion and spontaneous affection which his
words radiate prove that it was for him no merely conventional
formula. The sentence is a long and involved one, but its drift
becomes clear if we remember that 4 is a warmly emotional
parenthesis. His purpose is to brace Timothy to remain loyal
to the faith and to be ready to suffer for it. To reinforce this he
reminds him, with thanks to God, of the sincere piety he has
inherited from his family.

As in 1 Tim. i. 12 (where see note), Paul uses the construction
charin echō for **I give thanks** instead of his usual *eucharistō*. 3
Scholars have noted other deviations from his normal usage:
(*a*) there is no object phrase 'for you (all)' after **I give thanks;**
(*b*) **incessantly** is represented by the adjective *adialeiptos* instead of the adverb (Rom. i. 9; 1 Thess. i. 2; ii. 13); (*c*) *mneian
echō* is used for **I mention** instead of *mneian poioumai*, and *en
tais deēsesin mou* for **in my prayers** instead of *epi tōn pros-
euchōn mou*. These may be due either to the development of
the Apostle's vocabulary, or (more probably) to a change of
amanuensis. Critics who are sceptical of Pauline authorship
naturally find support for their case in them. On the other hand,
it should be noted that the structure of the passage strikingly
resembles that of the normal Pauline thanksgiving, including in
4 a participial clause followed by a final clause.

The Apostle stresses that the worship he offers God not only
springs from **a clean conscience** (for 'conscience', see note
on 1 Tim. i. 5), but has been traditional in his family. In making
the former point he has more in mind than the purity of intention indispensable in all worthwhile worship. As in the whole
of this letter, he is painfully conscious of his position as a
prisoner on a criminal charge, and is by implication protesting
his innocence (cf. Acts xxiii. 1). The reference to his **forbears**
deliberately prepares the way for 5, where he pointedly underlines the excellent family background which Timothy himself
has had. There is nothing incongruous in the pride Paul takes
here in his Jewish religious upbringing. The same pride breaks
out in Rom. ix. 3-5 and Phil. iii. 4-6, and it is clear that, while
in one sense his acceptance of Christ as his Saviour represented

a complete break with his ancestral piety, in another sense it was its proper development and flowering. Even the law, which he was so firmly convinced was superseded, had served its purpose in bringing him to Christ (Gal. iii. 24).

Paul mentions Timothy **incessantly, night and day,** in his prayers, just as he intercedes constantly for the Romans (Rom. i. 9), the Philippians (Phil. i. 3), the Colossians (Col. i. 3), and doubtless all the communities which he had evangelized. The words **night and day** (the usual Jewish order: see on 1 Tim. v. 5) are connected by many authorities (e.g. RV, RSV, Moffatt) with the following clause, being made to qualify the participle 'longing'. Though possible, this is unlikely, for (*a*) **night and day** is a cliché regularly associated with prayer, and (*b*) while it was conventional to speak of uninterrupted prayer, the picture of the Apostle longing twenty-four hours in the day to see Timothy seems unnatural.

4   Paul's pent-up affection breaks out in the parenthesis, **—for I long to see you,** etc. Similar expressions occur in 1 Thess. iii. 6; Phil. i. 8; Rom. i. 11, but the intensity of feeling is more urgent and personal here. In **recalling as I do your tears** Paul is harking back to his final parting from the young man, who seems to have broken down with the uninhibited emotion natural in the East. Some editors think that the reference, if historical at all, must be to the farewell scene at Miletus, when the whole company is reported (Acts xx. 37) to have dissolved in tears, but that took place several years previously and Paul must have seen Timothy in the interval. On the assumption that the theory of a second imprisonment is correct, it is natural to infer that Paul is thinking of the occasion, evidently still fresh in his memory, when, having been again arrested, he took his last leave of Timothy, presumably at Ephesus, before being carried off to Rome.

The Apostle wants to see Timothy so that he **may be filled with happiness,** and the same eager desire runs through the whole letter. 'Come to see me quickly', he pleads in iv. 9, and in iv. 21 he repeats with renewed urgency, 'Come before winter'. The time of his execution is approaching, and his keenness to see his young and uniquely devoted assistant is understandable. The juxtaposition of sorrow and joy is effective, and is also a characteristically Pauline touch (cf. 2 Cor. vii. 8 f.; Phil. ii. 17).

Paul now comes to the object of his thanksgiving, Timothy's **sincere faith,** of which he is **reminded** whenever he recalls 5 the young man. Because the participle **being reminded** is in the aorist ('having received a reminder of'), some have con-jectured that the reference must be to some more specific re-minder, such as the receipt of a letter or of some news about Timothy. For the expression **sincere faith,** cf. 1 Tim. i. 5 (where see note). It has been argued that, as in that passage, **faith** must here have the weakened sense of religious feeling because 'the question of sincerity cannot arise in that inner relation of the soul to God which Paul usually defines as faith' (E. F. Scott). In theory that may be true, but there can be no doubt that Paul is thinking here specifically of Timothy's atti-tude to Christ. It may be suggested that faith in the strictly Pauline sense has an external as well as an interior aspect, and that the profession of it can be unreal. By his stress on sincerity, Paul is emphasizing that there can be no question of that in Timothy's case. The passage may perhaps be illustrated by 1 Thess. iii. 5 ff., where we find the Apostle inquiring about the quality of his correspondents' faith.

We are now told that this **faith . . . dwelt first** in Timothy's **grandmother Lois and** his **mother Eunice.** Paul's point is that, just as his own religious life had powerful family roots, so Timothy's was grounded in that of his mother and grandmother. It has been argued that he must be referring to the devout Jewish upbringing which the two women gave the young man in boyhood, but the context makes it clear that **faith** means faith in Christ. If so, the sentence suggests either that Lois was converted to Christianity first, being followed by Eunice, or simply (and more probably) that the two women were the first Christians in Timothy's family. According to Acts xvi. 1, his mother was 'a believing Jewess', an expression which can only mean a convert to Christianity, while his father was a pagan—a fact which explains the absence of any mention of him here.

A passage like this, so lifelike and with its delicately personal note, creates special difficulties for supporters of the theory of pseudonymity. Some of them are prepared to admit that the writer must have been drawing on genuinely Pauline material.

On the other hand, the suggestion that, in dwelling on Timothy's religious antecedents, his real object was to impress on his readers his 'great confidence and joy in third-generation Christian ministers, and the security he feels in the case of those who in the home have been rooted and grounded in the received (Pauline) form of Christianity' (F. D. Gealy) is an example of the artificial interpretations to which they are sometimes driven.

3. A CHALLENGE TO COURAGEOUS WITNESS.
i. 6-14

(6) For this reason I remind you to rekindle the gift of God which is in you as a result of the laying on of my hands. (7) For the spirit which God gave us is not a spirit of cowardice, but one of power, of love, and of self-discipline. (8) So do not be ashamed of testifying to our Lord, or of me, his prisoner; but join with me in suffering for the gospel in the power of God, (9) who has saved us and called us with a holy calling, not in virtue of anything we have done, but in virtue of his own purpose and grace, which was bestowed on us ages ago in Christ Jesus, (10) and has now been revealed through the manifestation of our Saviour Christ Jesus, who has destroyed death and brought life and immortality to light through the gospel (11)—for which gospel I have been appointed a herald, an apostle, and a teacher. (12) This is the reason why I undergo these sufferings; but I am not ashamed, for I know whom I have believed, and I am confident that he is able to keep what has been entrusted to me safe against that day. (13) Take as your model the sound teaching you have heard from me, in faith and love in Christ Jesus. (14) Keep safe your splendid trust with the help of the Holy Spirit who dwells in us.

After the brief thanksgiving Paul sets about trying to brace the resolution of his young disciple, and in particular encourages him to be ready to endure suffering for the gospel's sake. The

note of anxiety which pervades the passage springs partly from
the Apostle's awareness that Timothy's inexperience and natural
timidity need stiffening, but even more from his consciousness of
the weighty responsibilities which must shortly devolve upon
him. Even so he is able to point to the divine commission given
in ordination, to the example of his own endurance, and to the
new life bestowed on men through Christ, as compelling motives
for courageous exertion.

The transition from the preceding section is easy and natural.
It is **For this reason,** i.e. because he knows Timothy is a man 6
of solidly established faith, that Paul does not hesitate to exhort
him **to rekindle the gift of God which is in** him and which
he received at his ordination. There is a reference to Timothy's
ordination in 1 Tim. iv. 14, where Paul also speaks of it as
having imparted a 'special gift' (the same word as here: Gk.
charisma) to him. Here the **gift** is compared to a fire (cf. 1 Thess.
v. 19: 'Do not extinguish the Spirit'), the suggestion of **rekindle** being not so much that it has gone out as that the
embers need constant stirring (the verb is in the present infinitive). We notice that, if ordination is already regarded as
imparting a positive grace, the idea that this grace operates
automatically is excluded. The Christian minister must be con-
tinuously on the alert to revitalize it.

Paul recalls that the **gift** was bestowed **as a result of the
laying on of my hands.** For the significance of this, see note
on 1 Tim. iv. 14, where the important question whether the
ordination was carried out by Paul himself or by a board of
elders presided over by him is also discussed. The language
here is just possibly consistent with the latter view, but as
straightforwardly interpreted favours the former.

The grace Timothy then received, Paul proceeds to point out,
has a direct relevance to his present situation, for **the spirit 7
which God gave us** has provided exactly the equipment he
needs for it. He is not referring, as some have deduced from the
plural **us,** to God's gift of the Holy Spirit to Christians generally, whether at Pentecost or in baptism. The aorist **gave** (this
reflects the sense of the original better than 'has given') recalls
the ordination service which he has mentioned, while by **us** he
means Timothy and himself. He could equally well, and with

more pointed effect, have written 'you', but a kindly tact prevented him. He is obliquely chiding Timothy for his timidity, but softens the blow by lumping himself with him. The **spirit** they both received at their commissioning was not **a spirit of cowardice** (for the expression, cf. Rom. viii. 15), such as might make them falter when faced with challenging responsibilities, dangers, etc. Rather it was **one of power** (cf. 1 Cor. ii. 4), enabling them to dominate any situation with moral authority; **of love,** i.e. of self-sacrificing, affectionate service to the brethren; and **of self-discipline,** as a result of which they should possess that restraint and self-control which every Christian leader requires.

The last of these three qualities (Gk. *sōphronismos*) is mentioned only here in the N.T., but cf. 1 Tim. ii 9; 15 for the related noun *sōphrosunē, ib.* iii. 2; Tit. i. 8; ii. 2; 5 for the adjective *sōphrōn,* Tit. ii. 12 for the adverb *sōphronōs,* Tit. ii. 4 for the verb *sōphronizō,* and Tit. ii. 6 for the verb *sōphronein.* All these words express the idea of 'temperance', 'self-control'. In his acknowledged letters Paul uses *sōphronein* twice (Rom. xii. 3; 2 Cor. v. 13), but the predilection of the Pastorals for the whole group is another token of their Hellenized idiom. Yet it should be noted that **self-discipline** here is not regarded, any more than **power** or **love,** as either a natural endowment or the fruit of painstaking efforts. All three are aspects of a divinely bestowed *charisma,* for while **spirit** in this context does not directly denote the Holy Spirit, it defines specific graces which he mediates.

Paul develops his plea. Thus fortified Timothy has no need 8 to **be ashamed of testifying to our Lord.** For the idea of being ashamed of the gospel, cf. Rom. i. 16. The Greek (lit. 'testimony of our Lord') could mean either 'testimony borne by Christ' or 'testimony about Christ'. If the former is accepted, the sense is that of 1 Tim. vi. 13, the reference being to the testimony which Christ sealed by his sacrificial death. The latter, however, is on the whole preferable, agreeing as it does with the parallel phrase (Gk. *to marturion tou Christou*) in 1 Cor. i. 6. It also suits the context better, the point of which is to brace Timothy to be a fearless evangelist. We know from 1 Cor. i. 23 that the gospel of a crucified Saviour struck Jews as blasphemous and pagans as plain nonsense, and it is understandable that a faint-hearted person like Timothy (for this trait in his character, cf. 1 Cor. xvi. 10) should shrink from incurring the inevitable scorn and odium.

Equally he should not be **ashamed,** as he might well be tempted to be, of associating with Paul himself, in spite of his being chained (the word translated **prisoner,** Gk. *desmios,* implies this) like a common felon. As elsewhere (Eph. iii. 1; Phm. 1), the Apostle treats what outsiders might judge a disgraceful situation as a source of humble pride. Though he might appear the emperor's **prisoner,** he is in fact **his,** i.e. Christ's. The underlying thought is, not just that men have imprisoned him as a follower of Christ, but that Christ has made him his prisoner for purposes of his own.

So far from being ashamed of Paul's humiliations and sufferings, Timothy should pluck up his courage and take his own share in them. If he does so, it will redound to the advantage of the gospel—**for the gospel** (a dative of interest). The verb 'suffer . . . with' (Gk. *sunkakopathein*) has been coined by Paul, who has a liking for compounds with *sun* ('with'). Its meaning here is 'suffer with me on behalf of the gospel', rather than 'suffer with the gospel' (Vulgate) or 'be thou partaker of the afflictions of the gospel' (AV). Paul reinforces his appeal by assuring him that, if he steels himself to suffer, it will be **in the power of God,** i.e. God's power (cf. 'spirit of power' in 7) will sustain him.

The next two verses set out, in moving terms, the reasons why Timothy, and indeed any Christian in any age, can rely on God's power to carry him through suffering and disaster triumphant. It comes from One whose saving purpose, based wholly on grace and not on men's achievements, has been at work since before the foundation of the world and has done what they could never have accomplished for themselves, redeeming them and in the historical mission of Christ breaking the hold of death and bestowing immortal life. In the view of many scholars these verses, which seem to them to have the air of a parenthesis, are an extract from some primitive hymn or liturgical piece, and they point to their careful antitheses, compact wording, and elevated tone. They may possibly be right, but against their suggestion we should note: (*a*) the passage does not, like the other citations in the Pastorals, stand on its own feet, but is subordinated syntactically to the preceding clause; (*b*) the ideas and the language are Pauline, and also characteristic of the Pastorals. A more likely explanation would seem to be that, while Paul is drawing on semi-stereotyped catechetical material, he is moulding it freely to his purposes and impressing his own stamp upon it.

Paul's first point is that Timothy, in facing suffering, can 9 rely on divine assistance because God **has** already **saved us.** The title 'Saviour' is applied to God six times in the Pastorals (see note on 1 Tim. i. 1); for the use of the verb as here, cf. 1 Cor. i. 21. This salvation, involving deliverance from sin and death, is something which Christians enjoy here and now. Its other side is expressed in the statement that God has **called us with a holy calling.** In Pauline language the verb 'call' denotes the first stage in the process of salvation (Rom. viii. 30; 1 Tim. vi. 12), and the sense of the clause is that God, who himself is holy, has called Christians out of the world to a new life of consecration. They are 'called to be saints' (1 Cor. i. 2), or 'called to holiness' (1 Thess. iv. 7). The suggestion, advanced in the interests of the view that the passage is post-Pauline and probably second-century, that **calling** here has the technical sense of the Christian ministry is far-fetched in the extreme. Not only does the word (Gk. *klēsis*) never have this narrowed down meaning in the N.T. (1 Cor. vii. 20 is no parallel, for it there signifies a man's station in life generally), but the context requires that the reference should be to God's call to holiness.

Paul's second point is to emphasize (it is the heart of his gospel) that the divine call does not come to us **in virtue of anything we have done** (lit. 'our works'), but solely **in virtue of his own purpose and grace.** If it depended on our merits, our position would be at best precarious, and on a realistic estimate hopeless; but since it depends wholly on God, our confidence can be unshaken. For the same rejection of 'works', cf. Tit. iii. 5.

For God's saving **purpose,** cf. Rom. viii. 28; ix. 11; Eph. i. 11; iii. 11. Naturally it has existed from all eternity, but here the Apostle (or the catechetical tag he is quoting) affirms that his freely given **grace . . . was bestowed on us ages ago** (lit. 'before eternal times') **in Christ Jesus.** The thought is related to that of Eph. i. 4, where it is stated that '. . . he chose us in him [i.e. in Christ] before the foundation of the world'. Both passages presuppose the idea of Christ's pre-existence, and also imply that he is the unique mediator through union with whom men have the grace of God imparted to them.

God's gracious purpose, determined before the creation of the world, has **now been revealed,** i.e. made visible, even actualized, in the historical process (cf. Rom. iii. 21; Col. i. 26), **through the manifestation of our Saviour Christ Jesus.** For **manifestation** (Gk. *epiphaneia*), see note on 1 Tim. vi. 14. Elsewhere the term denotes Christ's return in glory, but here (for the use of the cognate verb with the same sense, cf. Tit. ii. 11; iii. 4) his appearance on earth in the incarnation. It does not necessarily imply his pre-existence, but in view of the teaching of the previous verse probably does. Christ has been revealed as **our Saviour** because he embodies, and thus makes visible and effective, God's purpose to save.

In 1 Tim. i. 1 (where see note); ii. 3; iv. 10; Tit. i. 4; ii. 10; iii. 4 the description **Saviour** (Gk. *sōtēr*) is applied to God, but here and in Tit. ii. 13; iii. 6 to Christ. It had a wide currency in popular Hellenistic religion, being used as a title for the many redeemer gods of paganism, and also for the emperor in the state cult. It is noteworthy that Jesus himself never claimed it, and that the Messiah is never called 'Saviour' in the O.T. These facts, combined with its Hellenistic associations, probably explain why the title is never used of Christ in the primitive strata of the N.T. which took their rise on Palestinian soil. Outside the Pastorals we see the usage beginning in Phil. iii. 20 and Eph. v. 23; after that it rapidly established itself and became normal. There can be little doubt that one of the main motives behind this growing, and increasingly confident, readiness to hail Christ as Saviour was conscious reaction against the pretentions of the numerous pagan 'saviours' and of the imperial cult, with its solemn acclamation *Kaisar Sōtēr*, in particular.

Christ's saving work is now briefly summarized: he **has destroyed death and brought life and immortality to light through the gospel.** Paul uses the same verb 'destroy' in 1 Cor.

xv. 26, speaking of death as 'the enemy that will be destroyed last'. The text does not imply that Christians are exempt from death, but that for them it has lost its sting (1 Cor. xv. 55). The verb translated **brought . . . to light** (Gk. *phōtizein*) originally means 'illuminate', 'flood with light'. Here it is used metaphorically (cf. 1 Cor. iv. 5; Eph. iii. 9) to suggest that by his resurrection Christ has revealed to men the nature of the risen **life** which can now be theirs. It is a **life** characterized by **immortality** (Gk. *aphtharsia*, i.e. 'incorruptibility'). The word is regularly employed by Paul of the resurrection body (1 Cor. xv. 42; 50; 53; 54); it denotes for him something which God alone can bestow (Rom. ii. 7).

To some the conception of salvation sketched in this passage has seemed akin to the Gnostic one, with its stress on knowledge; others have found the language (cf. 'life', 'immortality', and especially 'light') reminiscent of the mysteries. As regards the latter suggestion, it should be clear that the vocabulary and ideas are thoroughly Pauline. The former is refuted by the final clause, in which Paul affirms that this disclosure has been made **through the gospel,** by which he means not just the Christian message, but the entire revelation of God in Christ which forms its content.

At the mention of the gospel, a note almost of exaltation 11 comes into Paul's writing. It is **for** this **gospel** that he, even he (in the Greek **I** is very emphatic), whose humiliating imprisonment has just been recalled, has **been appointed a herald, an apostle, and a teacher.** The language closely resembles that of 1 Tim. ii. 7, where the verb **appointed** (Gk. *etethēn*: cf. 1 Cor. xii. 28) is also used to underline his divine commission. Some have questioned whether, if the writer was Paul himself, he would have needed to convince Timothy of his right to preach the gospel. This is, however, to miss the point. Paul is not so much trying to impress Timothy as marvelling that God should have singled him out for such responsibilities. In so far as the words are addressed to Timothy at all, they are intended to hint that he too will find, when the Apostle's mantle descends upon him, that the privilege of testifying to Christ entails suffering.

If fine distinctions are to be drawn between **herald, apostle,** and **teacher,** the first word stresses the boldness and publicity with which the evangelist must proclaim his message, the second brings out his special commission, while the third draws attention to his pastoral obligations.

This is the reason, i.e. because he has been appointed a 12 preacher of the gospel, **why** Paul has to **undergo these sufferings.** Some have argued that this is a deliberately vague expression which is intended to enable every 'Timothy' to relate his own sufferings to his role as a minister of the gospel. It is more natural to interpret it as a precise reference to the wretched plight he finds himself in at the moment of writing. In spite of it, he exclaims, **I am not ashamed;** on the contrary, it is an honour to suffer for Christ. The verb is the one he used in his appeal to Timothy in 8; its repetition contains a hint that, if Paul finds no occasion for shame in his sufferings, there can be no reason why others should in theirs.

The Apostle then gives the reason for his confidence: **I know whom I have believed.** It is difficult to determine whether he has God or Christ in mind; either is possible, but in view of the stress on the power of God in 8 the former seems more likely. His point is that the Christian knows, on the basis of personal experience as well as the facts of the gospel, that God will never let him down. Characteristically, the faith he appeals to here is not faith in a creed but in a Person.

As a result he can be **confident that he,** i.e. God, **is able to keep what has been entrusted to** him, i.e. Paul, **safe against that day.** The key-word here (Gk. *parathēkē*) occurs also in 14 below and 1 Tim. vi. 20 (where see note); it is a legal term connoting something which one person places on trust in another's keeping. It is ambiguous in the present passage and could be translated 'what I have entrusted to him'. If this rendering is preferred, Paul will be asserting that he has placed himself (perhaps also his work, even his converts) in God's hands and is confident that, whatever disasters ensue, he will watch over him.

The main objection to this interpretation is that it clashes with 1 Tim. vi. 20 and, above all, with 14 immediately below, where *parathēkē* clearly denotes something which God has entrusted to Timothy's keeping. A minor one is that a concern for his own welfare seems out of keeping with the Apostle's general tone. It seems better, therefore, to understand by the word, as in 1 Tim. vi. 20, the gospel message regarded as a precious trust of the Church; this has the further advantage of harmonizing well with the instructions given in ii. 2 below. By **that day** is obviously meant the great day when 'we shall all stand before God's judgment seat' (Rom. xiv. 10). The expression (cf. i. 18; iv. 8) is frequent in the LXX; Paul uses it in an O.T. citation in 2 Thess. i. 10, but normally prefers some other form (e.g. 'the day of the Lord'). The passage as a whole thus expresses his supreme assurance that, whatever misfortunes overwhelm his ministers, God will himself preserve the faith entrusted to them from corruption, so as to enable them, as it were, to hand back their charge to him intact at the final judgment.

In 9-12 Paul has been carried away by his exposition of God's redeeming power. He now resumes the advice he was giving Timothy in 6-8, urging him to base his teaching on his own. Although the construction of the Greek is not free from diffi-
13 culty, this is the plain meaning of the sentence translated, **Take as your model the sound teaching you have heard from me.** An alternative rendering might be, 'As a model of sound teaching keep before you what you have heard from me'. Paul is not saying that Timothy should reproduce his teaching word for word, still less has he in mind some fixed credal formula which he wants him to recite without deviation. The word translated **model** (Gk. *hupotupōsis*: cf. 1 Tim. i. 16) denotes an outline sketch or ground-plan used by an artist or, in literature, a rough draft forming the basis of a fuller exposition. The suggestion contained in it, therefore, is that, while Timothy should be unswervingly loyal to Paul's message, regarding it as his pattern, he should be free to interpret or expound it in his own way. For **sound,** or 'wholesome', **teaching** (lit. 'words'), a favourite expression in the Pastorals, see note on 1 Tim. i. 10.

Further, in modelling his teaching on his master's, Timothy must do so **in faith and love in Christ Jesus.** For all their proximity to the verb **you have heard,** these words yield an intolerably weak sense if taken with it. It is much more satisfactory, and syntactically possible, to link them with **Take as your model** and to understand them as defining the spirit

166

which should characterize Timothy's orthodoxy. In expounding it to others he must himself display 'the faith and love which are ours in Christ Jesus' (NEB). As this paraphrase shows, the formula **in Christ Jesus** is much richer in meaning than 'Christian' (B. S. Easton: see note on i. 1). It expresses the truth that the Christian man's faith and love are the fruits of his union with Christ (see note on 1 Tim. i. 14).

It is precisely this teaching of Paul's which is now identified as the **splendid trust** (against the Gk. *parathēkē*) which has 14 been committed to Timothy, and which he is exhorted to **Keep safe,** i.e. preserve from distortion and corruption at the hands of the sectaries. The clear implication is that the Apostle regards him as his successor and legatee.

In carrying out this duty Timothy should rely, not on resources of his own, but on **the help of the Holy Spirit who dwells in us.** This clause recalls Rom. viii. 9, where Paul speaks of the Holy Spirit dwelling in Christians and directing their lives. Many consider that the meaning here, but in view of the prominence given to the spiritual equipment of ministers in 6 f. it seems certain that Paul's primary thought is of that. In using the pronoun **us,** therefore, he really means, not Christians generally, but 'you and me'. It was his view, of course (cf. 1 Cor. xii. 4 ff.), that every ministerial function in the community had its appropriate endowment of the Spirit, and it was natural that, as the need for preventing heretics from tampering with the gospel became more pressing and obvious, he should extend this to the special responsibilities of men like Timothy and himself in this regard. Very shortly (we already find it clearly delineated in 1 *Clem.* xlii. 2-4; xliv. 2) the doctrine was to be elaborated that the hierarchy of the Church forms an orderly succession of teachers charged with preserving the apostolic tradition and specially sustained in this by the Holy Spirit. Some scholars find this teaching in the present passage, and, since they hold that the apostolic Church was 'creative' and 'prophetic' rather than 'transmissional' and 'priestly', conclude that it is a symptom of the post-Pauline, probably second-century date of the letters. Two comments may be made in criticism of this. (*a*) While the germ from which the later doctrine (legitimately or illegitimately) developed is undoubtedly to be detected here, it is only the germ. There is no trace of theory, no conscious theology, in the text under discussion; it suggests a much more elementary, and presumably more primitive, situation than is presupposed by the elaborate and well-articulated doctrine put forward even by so early a writer as Clement. (*b*) The distinction between the 'creative' and the 'transmissional' stages in the first-century Church is entirely misleading, for the emphasis on tradition was prominent from the very start. Any careful analysis of Paul's acknowledged letters will reveal how packed with traditional material they are, and it is understandable that in his later years his concern for the preservation of the tradition should become increasingly evident.

4. THE EXAMPLE OF PAUL'S ASSOCIATES.
i. 15-18

(15) You must be aware that all in Asia Minor deserted me, including Phygelos and Hermogenes. (16) May the Lord show mercy to Onesiphorus's household, for he has often cheered my spirits, and he was not ashamed of my chain, (17) but when he arrived in Rome searched for me eagerly, and found me. (18) May the Lord grant him to find mercy from the Lord on that day. You know as well as anyone all the services he rendered at Ephesus.

These personal reminiscences have a closer connexion with the preceding verses than might at first sight appear. Timothy is being exhorted to show steadfastness and courage, and so Paul points to warning examples of good Christian friends who have left him in the lurch, as well as to a more comforting example of outstanding loyalty. It is notes like these which create in 2 Timothy a particularly vivid impression of authenticity, and also special difficulties for any theory of pseudonymity.

Paul begins by appealing to Timothy's knowledge of the shabby treatment he has had from Asiatic Christians, from whom he might have expected something better in view of his long residence at Ephesus. The translation **You must be** 15 **aware** is an attempt to reproduce the emphatic tone of the Greek, which literally means, 'This you know, that . . .' **Asia Minor** (Gk. *Asia*) is the Roman province officially called 'Asia', which comprised the west parts (including Mysia, Lydia, Caria, large parts of Phrygia, and the off-shore islands) of the great land-mass now known by the same name; Ephesus (see note on 1 Tim. i. 3) was its capital.

As head of the Ephesian church Timothy was well placed to have first-hand knowledge of the Asian Christians' conduct towards Paul. It is unnecessary to press **all in Asia** too literally, as if he were complaining of widespread disaffection, or even a complete falling-away from his teaching. He is writing with the exaggeration natural in depression. Apparently all the key-friends on whom he thought he could count **deserted** him. Though used of doctrinal apostasy in Tit. i. 14, the verb (lit. 'turned away from') here denotes their abandonment of the Apostle personally. We are given no clue to the circumstances, although it is natural to think of the time of his arrest. Alternatively it has been proposed that Paul is expressing disappointment at the failure of Asian Christians in Rome to rally to his support, but this is not so likely. It would involve taking **all in Asia** as a Hebraism for 'all from Asia', which is difficult, and seems further ruled out by the special reference below to Onesiphorus's visit to Rome.

Nothing else is known of **Phygelos and Hermogenes,** although we may infer from Paul's having singled them out for mention that he found their defection particularly distressing. By contrast he is able to point to another comrade whose loyalty rose to his fullest expectations and provides Timothy with an inspiring example. **Onesiphorus** is mentioned again 16 in iv. 19, where we learn that his family lived at Ephesus. According to the second-century *Acts of Paul and Thecla* (ed. M. R. James, *Apocryphal New Testament*, pp. 272 f.), he had earlier been a citizen of Iconium who, along with his wife Lectra, entertained the Apostle on his first missionary journey, and was converted by him. Paul's insistence on speaking of **Onesiphorus's household** (so also at iv. 19) and the tone of the prayer for him in 18, not to mention the lack of any personal

greetings for him at the end, make it practically certain that he
was already dead.

The expression **May the Lord show mercy** occurs only
here in the N.T. So too **cheered my spirits** translates a verb
(Gk. *anapsūchein*: lit. 'refresh') found nowhere else in the N.T.
(but cf. Acts iii. 20 for the related noun *anapsūxis*). The meaning
is, not that Onesiphorus helped the Apostle at Ephesus materially or with practical services, but that he braced his morale
with his fellowship.

What he found particularly comforting was that Onesiphorus
was not ashamed of my chain. The statement conjures up a
graphic picture at once of the humiliation of Paul's position and
the embarrassment it caused him, and of the cowardly behaviour
17 of many of his friends. In contrast to them Onesiphorus, **when
he arrived in Rome,** went to the trouble of tracking down (cf.
searched . . . eagerly) Paul's prison, and eventually **found**
him. On the assumption that the correspondence is genuine, the
occasion was his second captivity, during which the Christian
community in Rome seems to have lost touch with him. Had
it been the earlier captivity, as several editors suppose, Onesiphorus's task should not have been at all difficult, since the
Apostle was then enjoying relative liberty (Acts xxviii. 30 f.) and
his whereabouts must have been known to all Christians.

18   In the prayer which follows **find** consciously echoes **found**
(the identical verb in Greek) in 17. The sentence, with its repeated **the Lord,** reads awkwardly, especially in English, in
which the absence of the definite article before the second **the
Lord** cannot be brought out. The construction may be a
Hebraism (cf. LXX Gen. xix. 24), **the Lord** denoting God in
both cases. More probably, however, **May the Lord . . .** refers
to Christ, this being in harmony with the usage of the Pastorals
(e.g. 2, 8, 16 above), and **from the Lord** to God, whom Paul
elsewhere (e.g. Rom. ii. 6; iii. 6) represents as exercising judgment, and who in the Pastorals is regularly described as Saviour.
This is supported by the LXX practice of using 'Lord' (Gk.
Kurios) without the article of God. It may well be (so J.
Jeremias) that two formulae ('May the Lord grant him to
find mercy', and 'May he find mercy from the Lord') have been
conflated.

By **on that day** (see note on 12) is meant the day of judgment. On the assumption, which must be correct, that Onesiphorus was dead when the words were written, we have here an example, unique in the N.T., of Christian prayer for the departed. The prayer in question, it should be noted, is an exceedingly general one, amounting only to the commendation of the dead man to the divine mercy. There is nothing surprising in Paul's use of such a prayer, for intercession for the dead had been sanctioned in Pharisaic circles at any rate since the date of 2 Macc. xii. 43-45 (middle of first century B.C.?). Inscriptions in the Roman catacombs and elsewhere prove that the practice established itself among Christians from very early times.

In the final sentence Paul turns from the personal help he has received from Onesiphorus to **all the services he rendered at Ephesus,** i.e. the solid work he did for the community as a whole (AV's 'unto me' has poor MS support, and is an obvious intruder), and which Timothy is bound to **know as well as anyone.** The last four words represent the Gk. *beltion* (lit. 'better'). This is not a true comparative ('better than I', though preferred by most editors, does not yield a natural sense, since Paul is perfectly familiar with his friend's service), but is the elative use intensifying the force of the positive.

5. FRESH ENCOURAGEMENT TO SERVICE AND SUFFERING. ii. 1-13

(1) It is for you, then, my son, to be strong in the grace which is in Christ Jesus, (2) and to entrust what you have heard from me with many witnesses to reliable persons, who will be able to instruct others also. (3) Take your share of rough treatment like a brave soldier of Christ Jesus. (4) No one on active service gets involved in the preoccupations of civilian life, so that he may satisfy the officer who enlisted him. (5) An athlete, again, is not crowned unless he competes according to the rules. (6) It is the farmer who works hard who has the first claim on the crop. (7) Think out my meaning, for the Lord will

give you understanding in everything. (8) Bear in mind
—Jesus Christ, risen from the dead, of David's stock.
Such is my gospel, (9) in preaching which I put up with
rough treatment, to the point of being chained as a
criminal—not that God's word is chained! (10) It is with
this object that I bear everything patiently, for the sake of
God's chosen, that they too may obtain salvation in
Christ Jesus, with eternal glory. (11) It is a trustworthy
saying, 'For if we have died with him, we shall also live
with him; (12) if we bear patiently, we shall also reign
with him; if we disown him, he will also disown us; (13)
if we prove faithless, he remains faithful, for he cannot
deny himself.'

    Paul now applies the moral of the preceding exhortation to
1 Timothy. The translation **It is for you, then** . . . is intended to
bring out the emphatic tone of the Greek (lit. 'You, then . . .').
The young disciple has been reminded of his ordination, of the
Apostle's own devotion to the gospel, and of the glittering example of Onesiphorus. It is now up to him to show his mettle
and **be strong in the grace which is in Christ Jesus.** The
verb is typically Pauline: cf. Rom. iv. 20; Eph. vi. 10; Phil. iv. 13.
The force of **in** with **grace** is probably instrumental: 'by means
of', or 'in the power of'. The addition of **in Christ Jesus**
suggests that, while Paul doubtless has the special gift bestowed
at ordination in mind (cf. i. 6 f.), his real thought is of grace in
the widest Christian sense. The whole expression (see notes on
i. 1; 13) can be paraphrased as 'the grace of which we are recipients through fellowship with Christ Jesus'. Timothy is to
show manly resolution, but the real strength of his efforts will
come from the grace Christ freely gives.

2   In addition, he is to take steps **to entrust what** he has
heard from Paul to other reliable teachers. The verb (Gk.
paratithesthai) is related to the noun (Gk. *parathēkē*) used in i. 12
and 14 (also 1 Tim. vi. 20) of the orthodox Christian message
which is committed to Paul and Timothy as a sacred trust.
Hence **what you have heard from me** does not denote
general instruction in the Christian faith, but the apostolic
gospel itself.

If Paul's general drift is clear, it is not so easy to determine exactly what he means by **with** (Gk. *dia*: lit. 'through') **many witnesses**. The majority of editors take **with** as equivalent to 'in the presence of'. Paul is thus making the point that, when he preached to Timothy or (this seems more probable) delivered the gospel message to him, it had been in the presence of numerous bystanders. Thus the solemnity of the charge was enhanced or, alternatively, the people present served to corroborate the soundness of his doctrine. If this is accepted, it is natural to interpret the verse as referring to some specific occasion, such as Timothy's baptism or (better still) ordination, when the Apostle may be presumed to have publicly impressed upon him an outline of the faith.

This is probably the best explanation of the text; it also agrees well, if the reference is to Timothy's formal commissioning, with the emphasis on his ordination in i. 6 and 14. Other editors, however, argue that it does not do justice to the role of the witnesses, and so prefer to give **with** the meaning 'with the attestation of'. On this exegesis two alternatives are open. (*a*) Paul is reminding Timothy of his habit of citing authorities for his teaching (e.g. the prophets, the Lord's disciples: cf. 1 Cor. xv. 3-11), especially when it concerned matters of which he had not had direct experience. But if this were his meaning, **what you have heard** would not be the natural way of expressing it; we should have expected something like, 'What I imparted to you'. Paul's point, therefore, must rather be (*b*) that Timothy has been able to check the version of the gospel he received from his master by independent testimony, and therefore can be doubly sure of its authenticity. The **many witnesses** will include Barnabas, his own grandmother and mother, and numerous other persons of weight and authority.

All these difficulties, it has been claimed (B. S. Easton), vanish if we recognize that it is really a second-century Pastor who, in the guise of Paul, is addressing a neophyte in the ministry who has himself never seen or known the Apostle. We can then give *dia* its original meaning; it is 'through' many intermediaries, including the Pastor himself, that the latter receives the Pauline tradition. Though highly ingenious, it is doubtful if this proposal is admissible even if the general theory of which it is a part could be accepted. If this had been his meaning, we may be sure that the writer would not have said **you have heard from me,** which even granting the fiction can only imply that the recipient has been personally a pupil of Paul's; nor is 'witnesses' a natural description, in second-century idiom, for a succession of accredited teachers. It is noticeable that in I Tim. vi. 12 it has its original meaning of bystanders who in some way witness or attest. No special credit can be made out of 'the original meaning' of *dia*, for the technical use 'in the presence of' is well supported. Finally, it seems incredible that, after so skilfully constructing his façade of verisimilitude, the pseudonymous author should suddenly decide to shatter it.

Paul's advice to Timothy to pass on the apostolic gospel **to reliable persons, who will be able to instruct others also** is of immense interest as containing, in embryonic form, the twin, closely related ideas of the tradition of the original revelation and of a succession of authorized persons charged with the responsibility of passing it on intact: see note on i. 14. Essentially the same ideas, though less explicitly set out, appear in Paul's earlier letters, e.g. I Cor. xi. 23; xv. 1 ff. From the beginning the conception of tradition, or the handing down of the original revelation, was integral to Christianity. In this passage, where the stress is on the gospel transmitted, we are clearly at a primitive stage; in contrast, for example, to I *Clem.* xlii. 2-4; xliv. 2 (often cited as a parallel), no theory of apostolical succession is expounded. There is no suggestion of apostles as such passing on the faith to bishops and deacons, but we simply have Paul himself charging Timothy, and his interest is in the reliability rather than the status of the men Timothy will select.

3 Paul now urges Timothy to **Take** his **share of rough treatment.** The lot of a Christian evangelist and leader is to be full of hardships, a fair sample being provided by his own present plight. The same verb is used as at i. 8. As illustrations the Apostle then points to the experience of the soldier, the sportsman, and the peasant. All three—the first with his detachment, the second with his strict training, the third with his unremitting toil—reflect different aspects of the life of anyone who gives himself to Christ's service. These were stock examples in the

popular diatribe of the time; Paul himself had earlier used all
three in the space of a single chapter (1 Cor. ix. 7; 24).

So Timothy is bidden behave, despite his natural shyness and
timidity, **like a brave soldier of Christ Jesus.** In addition to
being tough in the most trying conditions, there are two specially relevant characteristics which belong to a man **on active 4
service.** First, he does not let himself get **involved in the
preoccupations of civilian life;** and, secondly, he is domin-
ated by the single-minded desire to **satisfy the officer who
enlisted him.** Not only is the soldier relieved by his profession
of the need, and indeed the possibility, of making a living in
the ordinary way, but the demands of his service necessitate his
giving undivided attention to carrying out his commanding
officer's plans.

The second clause, **so that he may satisfy . . .,** connects
rather clumsily with the main clause, but the meaning is clear.
The conclusion has sometimes been drawn that ordained ministers should not engage in business or commerce, or indeed in
matrimony, and that in the writer's view there is something
wrong, or at all events second-rate, in the pursuits of ordinary
life. This is, however, a pedantic misreading of his intention,
which is simply to insist that Timothy, and presumably Christian leaders in analogous positions, should cut out of their lives
anything, however good in itself, which is liable to deflect them
from total service to Christ. He indicates in 1 Tim. iii. 2; 12;
Tit. i. 6 his acceptance of the fact that overseers and deacons
would be married.

Paul draws his second illustration from the professional athlete
who took part in the games which were such a prominent
feature of the contemporary Graeco-Roman scene. For his use
of sporting metaphors, see notes on 1 Tim. iv. 7; vi. 12. **An 5
athlete,** he points out, **is not crowned,** i.e. cannot win the
prize in his particular event, **unless he competes according
to the rules.** There has been much argument whether these
rules (the Greek has the adverb *nomimōs*, i.e. 'lawfully': cf. 1
Tim. i. 8) are (*a*) the particular rules of the game in question,
or (*b*) the official regulations imposed on athletes taking part in
public games, which in order to maintain high standards included prescriptions about training. As an example of the latter,

competitors at the Olympic Games had to swear an oath before
the statue of Zeus that they had been in strict training for ten
months (Pausanias, *Graec. descr.* v. 24. 9). Either is possible,
but since cheating is not relevant to Paul's theme whereas
arduous self-discipline is, (*b*) seems much more plausible
than (*a*).

Paul's thought has begun to move from the hardships involved in devoted Christian service to the reward which will
crown it. This idea becomes more prominent in his third illus-
6 tration, drawn from **the farmer who works hard.** The accent
is on the verb, Paul's point being that it is the peasant who has
really exerted himself in the field **who has the first claim on
the crop,** i.e. has the priority over those who have either done
nothing or been thoroughly idle. The analogy is not, as some
editors suggest, far-fetched, dragged in because the writer
noticed its occurrence in 1 Cor. ix. 10 f. Paul's mind has been
turned naturally to rewards by his mention of the athlete's
chaplet. For some reason he thinks it appropriate to remind
Timothy of the special blessing which God will bestow on the
ministry of a hard-working, faithful evangelist. But he has also
in mind, no less than in 1 Cor. ix. 10 f., the material support
which the apostolic leader is entitled to expect from the community in which he has laboured (cf. 1 Tim. v. 17 f.). It should
be noted that the verb translated **works hard** (Gk. *kopiān*) is
peculiarly apt, being almost a technical term in Paul's vocabulary for ministerial work (see note on 1 Tim. v. 17).

7   In the next verse, **Think out my meaning,** i.e. 'work out
what I am getting at', is a better rendering of the Greek (*noei
ho legō*) than 'Think over what I say' of RSV and others. With
a fine tact Paul leaves it to Timothy to discover for himself the
deeper implications of his three parables, particularly, perhaps,
the allusion to his honorarium from the community. This
exegesis is confirmed by the encouragement which he adds, **the
Lord will give you understanding in everything,** i.e. in
matters like these no less than in weightier ones. For the en-
lightenment which God gives the spiritual man, cf. 1 Cor. ii.
10; 15.

7 was almost a parenthesis; Paul now resumes his theme,
representing Christ as the supreme inspiration of Christian

service. The disciple should **Bear in mind** the Messiah him- 8
self, who, though he now reigns in glory, is **risen from the
dead.** The innuendo probably is that even he had to walk the
way of the cross and taste death before being exalted. The
Apostle makes his reminder all the more impressive by clothing
it in a fragment of semi-stereotyped credal material which
Timothy probably knew by heart. The order **Jesus Christ,**
unprecedented in 2 Timothy, and the addition of **of David's
stock,** which is irrelevant in the context, as well as the structure,
confirm that the tag is a quotation. The formula is a primitive
one, probably of Jewish Christian origin, and resembles the one
cited by Paul in Rom. i. 3 f. These are the only two such credal
tags in the N.T. which stress the Saviour's Davidic descent; for
later examples, cf. Ignatius, *Eph.* xviii. 2; *Trall.* ix. 1; *Rom.* vii.
3; *Smyrn.* i. 1.

  Such, Paul claims, **is my gospel;** the sentence paraphrases
the typically Pauline (cf. Rom. ii. 16; xvi. 25; 1 Tim. i. 11)
'according to my gospel'. In other words, the truth enshrined
in the credal fragment just cited is the heart of the message with
which Paul has been entrusted, and **in preaching which** (lit.
'in which', indicating the gospel as the sphere of his sufferings)
he has to **put up with rough treatment, to the point of** 9
being chained as a criminal. Paul comes back, as so often in
this letter, to himself as an example for Timothy. The word
criminal (Gk. *kakourgos*) is a strong one, and in the N.T. is
only used elsewhere of the brigands who were crucified alongside Jesus (Lk. xxiii. 32; 33; 39). In technical legal parlance it
was reserved for burglars, murderers, traitors, and the like. Its
use here suggests the conditions of the Neronian pogrom rather
than the relatively mild imprisonment of Acts xxviii.

  This passage contains yet another indication of the shame
and resentment Paul felt at his confinement. All the more ex-
ultantly, therefore, sounds his triumphant interjection, **not
that God's word is chained!** As in 1 Thess. ii. 13; 2 Thess.
iii. 1, **God's word,** here equivalent to **my gospel** above, is
almost personified. Notwithstanding the restrictions placed on
its preacher, it continues to spread, winning men to God. We
are reminded of Phil. i. 12-18, where he notes that his imprisonment (his earlier one), so far from hindering the gospel, has

given his fellow-Christians the confidence to preach the word
of God with exceptional fearlessness.

But he is not thinking primarily, in this passage, of preaching
done by others. The idea he wants to get across to Timothy
is that the very sufferings he is deploring have a positive,
10 evangelistic significance. So he states, **It is with this object**
(lit. 'Because of this': the words point forward to **for the sake
of . . .** and **that . . .**) **that I bear everything patiently, for
the sake of God's chosen, that they too may obtain
salvation in Christ Jesus.** Here **God's chosen** (lit. 'the elect')
denotes those whom God's eternal predestination has chosen to
receive salvation (Rom. viii. 33; Col. iii. 12; Tit. i. 1), but who
have not yet responded to his call. What Paul is saying is, not
simply that the example of his endurance will be an inspiration
to others, but that the deeper motive of his patient acceptance
of hardships is the conviction that he is thereby actually making
it easier for them to attain salvation. His presupposition here,
as in Col. i. 24 (a passage which should be carefully compared
with this), is that there is a predetermined amount of suffering
which the Messianic community, the body of Christ, must
undergo before the End can come. For the tribulations which,
according to primitive Christian thought, must precede the end,
cf. Mt. xxiv. 6 ff.; Mk. xiii. 7 ff.; Lk. xxi. 9 ff. (esp. 24); 2 Thess.
ii. 1-12. The more Paul himself, therefore, suffers now, the
less his brethren who are also 'in Christ' will have to suffer
themselves, and so he will hasten the coming of the End.

In this way his anguish and martyrdom definitely pave the
way for others, so **that they too may obtain salvation in
Christ Jesus.** The Apostle's assurance of his own salvation is
brought out strikingly by **too.** The words **salvation in Christ
Jesus** (lit. 'the salvation which is in Christ Jesus') convey much
more than that the Christian's salvation comes from Christ.
As in i. 1; 9; 13; ii. 1 (where see notes), they contain the essence
of Paul's gospel, which is that the believer is a new creature as
a result of being united with Christ (cf. 2 Cor. v. 17).

And the concomitant of this **salvation** will be **eternal
glory.** This is illustrated by Rom. v. 2, where Paul describes
how Christians exult in the hope of the divine glory which is to
be theirs. He means that reflected glory of God with which

Adam was clothed in the Garden of Eden, but of which men
have since been deprived as a result of the Fall (*ib.* iii. 23). It is
this glory which will be revealed in and for us at the End (*ib.*
viii. 18), and which in 2 Cor. iv. 17 the Apostle represents as
'an eternal weight of glory beyond all comparison', which will
put any afflictions we suffer at the moment into the shade.

Paul rounds off the section with another **trustworthy say-** 11
ing. For this expression, a cliché in the Pastorals, cf. 1 Tim. i.
15; iii. 1; iv. 9; Tit. iii. 8. Some commentators, following John
Chrysostom, identify the **saying** with what precedes, or at any
rate with some part of it (e.g. 8); they back this with the plea
that the following verses cannot be intended since they open
with the particle **For.** But they are clearly mistaken. 8 is separated by a gap of two verses, and there is nothing aphoristic or
at all resembling a quotation in the rest of Paul's remarks;
whereas the following lines (11b-13) have precisely this character. The obvious explanation of **For** is that the extract cited
is an incomplete one; Paul begins it at a point relevant to his
subject, disregarding the abrupt opening.

It seems certain, then, that 11b-13 constitute the **trustworthy saying.** Their parallel structure and rhythmic character
make it likely that they are an extract from a liturgical hymn,
probably familiar to Timothy and the community (cf. 1 Tim.
iii. 16 for the similar use of a hymn); the last line (**for he
cannot . . .**), which breaks away from the pattern, may be a
gloss added by Paul himself. The hymn seems of Jewish
Christian provenance, its first strophe being reminiscent of
Rom. vi. 8 and its third of the Lord's saying reported in Mt. x.
33. It has been described as an encouragement to Christians
facing persecution, but the rite of baptism (see notes below) has
a much stronger claim to be its source. It is, however, useless
now to hope to identify its original setting too precisely. All we
can be sure of is that Paul's motive in quoting it was to press
home the connexion between the Christian's fellowship with
Christ in suffering and in glory.

A baptismal context is certainly suggested by **For if we have
died with him, we shall also live with him.** This dying
with Christ is not primarily, as has often been proposed, death
through suffering martyrdom for him, but rather the death to

sin and self which every Christian undergoes in baptism. Paul expounds his mystical doctrine of this in Rom. vi. 2-23, where he also develops the thought (see esp. 8, with which this line is almost identical) that being joined with Christ in his death entails also being joined with him in his resurrection and sharing his glorified life. Cf. also Col. iii. 3. But the Christian's death with Christ in baptism is only a first instalment. It is his vocation, being mystically united with the Crucified, to embrace a life of trials and hardships. Nevertheless he has his reward, for

12 **if we bear patiently, we shall also reign with him.** The line crystallizes the primitive Christian hope that, when Christ returns in glory to reign (1 Cor. xv. 24 f.), the saints who have endured will sit on thrones like kings alongside him (Rev. i. 6; iii. 21; v. 10; xx. 4).

The implied call to endurance also fits in with the baptismal setting. Mark's Gospel, written only a few years later, shows how deep was the conviction of the Church that hardship was of the essence of discipleship. But what **if we** actually **disown him?** The stern answer, based on Christ's own warning (Mt. x. 33), is that **he will also disown us.** The reference is again to the Last Judgment, when the Lord will refuse to recognize those who have denied him.

13   The hymn then envisages a further possibility—**if we prove faithless.** Some interpret this (Gk. *apistoumen*) as equivalent to 'if we abandon faith in him', i.e. apostatize. But this is to repeat the thought of the preceding sentence; it also ignores the fact that the verb is in the present (of continuous action?), not in the future, like **disown.** Hence the paraphrase 'if we fail to live up to our profession', or 'if we sin and prove unstable in trials and temptations', seems to bring out the meaning better. The rejoinder which in strict logic we expect is, 'he too will be faithless', but the paradox of the divine love does not permit that. Triumphantly the truth comes out: **he remains faithful.**

This does not mean, 'God keeps his word both for reward and for punishment' (W. Lock), i.e. relentlessly exacts the penalty due to our backsliding. The great affirmation of the hymn is that, however wayward and faithless men may be, God's love continues unalterable and he remains true to his promises. As Paul expressed it in Rom. iii. 3 f., the faithlessness of men only serves to show up the faithfulness of God; after all, he has saved us, 'not in virtue of anything we have done, but in virtue of his own purpose and grace' (i. 9 above). And the explanation, of course, is that **he cannot deny himself.** To be faithful through everything, in spite of the worst that men can do, is the essence of his nature. As suggested above, the final clause may be an explicative comment of the Apostle's himself, but many hold that it is fully in the spirit of the hymn and is necessary to complete the thought. On either interpretation the aim of this fourth strophe is not, of course, to open the door to backsliding and apostasy, but rather to provide a balm for troubled consciences.

6. A SUMMONS TO AVOID FALSE TEACHING.
ii. 14-21

(14) Keep reminding people of these things, adjuring them in God's sight not to dispute about words—no good comes of it; it only demoralizes the listeners. (15) Do your best to show yourself worthy of God's approval, a workman who has no need to be ashamed, dispensing the word of truth in the right way. (16) But keep clear of profane chatter, for those who indulge in it will advance more and more in ungodliness, (17) and their talk will eat its way like gangrene. Among them are Hymenaeus and Philetus, (18) who have shot wide of the truth, saying that the resurrection has already taken place, and are undermining people's faith. (19) Nevertheless God's solid foundation stands firm, with this seal on it, 'The Lord knows his own', and, 'Everyone who names the Lord's name must turn his back on wickedness'. (20) In a large house, admittedly, there are not only gold and silver utensils, but also ones of wood and earthenware; but while the former are for honourable, the latter are for ignominious purposes. (21) Anyone who keeps himself clean from these will be a utensil for honourable purposes, consecrated, serviceable to the householder, ready for any good work.

Having done his best to fire Timothy with courage to face suffering in the spirit of Christ, Paul passes on to specific instructions about his preaching, with a special eye to the growing menace of heresy. He has already stressed the importance of sound teaching modelled on his own (i. 12-14; ii. 1 f.), and now
14 he bids him **Keep on reminding people of these things,** i.e. in the first instance the profound gospel truth summarized in 11-13, but also, more generally, the Christian message as he had learned it from the Apostle (ii. 2). The verb (Gk. *hupomimnēske*: lit. 'remind') is in the present imperative, indicating that this is to be his regular practice; hence the translation **Keep on . . .**

It is particularly important, Paul stresses, to warn people solemnly (for **adjuring them in God's sight,** cf. 1 Tim. v. 21) **not to dispute about words.** This translation seems preferable to Moffatt's 'not to bandy arguments', which implies that the Apostle is discouraging public debates with the heretics. This does not give a very plausible picture in itself; and in any case the related noun 'disputing about words' (Gk. *logomachia*) is found in 1 Tim. vi. 4, where it undoubtedly has the meaning of verbal quibbling. What Paul is underlining here is the danger of getting involved in that kind of theological discussion which is in the end purely verbal, having nothing to do with the realities of the Christian religion. Although his strictures have a general bearing, they are primarily aimed at particular individuals at Ephesus. Whatever the content of their teaching (unfortunately Paul only gives us the most fragmentary hints of it), he is satisfied that the discussion to which it gives rise is so much profitless word-splitting, the kind of argumentation from which **no good comes,** and which **only demoralizes the listeners.**

The constructive line for Timothy to take is to give proof of his own qualities as an efficient, absolutely trustworthy purveyor
15 of sound doctrine. **Do your best,** Paul therefore exhorts him, **to show yourself worthy of God's approval, a workman who has no need to be ashamed.** A more literal translation of the first half of this would be, 'to present yourself to God [for the verb, Gk. *parastēsai*, cf. Rom. vi. 13; 1 Cor. viii. 8] as tested and approved' (the Greek adjective *dokimos* contains both

ideas). The image in **workman** is that of an agricultural labourer (cf. Mt. xx. 1; 8). The adjective which accompanies it (Gk. *anepaischuntos*) could mean 'who is not ashamed of his job', thus taking up and repeating the thought of i. 8 (cf. Rom. i. 16; Heb. ii. 11; xi. 16). But this sense is alien to the context, which draws the picture of a workman who has done his job well and can therefore submit it to his employer without qualms or embarrassment.

The next clause contains the weight of Paul's charge. Timothy will accomplish his task efficiently, and thus enable himself to face God without shame, by **dispensing the word of truth in the right way.** By **word of truth** some have understood Scripture, but both the context and Paul's use of the same expression elsewhere (Eph. i. 13; Col. i. 5) confirm that it stands for the gospel, the Christian message as a whole.

The remaining words are an attempt to render the rare Greek verb *orthotomein* (lit. 'cut straight'), found only here and in Prov. iii. 6; xi. 5. Some argue, on the basis of its literal meaning, that Paul's image must be that of a mason cutting a stone (here **the word of truth**) to the correct pattern (i.e. the gospel standard). Others, noting that the workman is an agriculturist, follow John Chrysostom in supposing that it is that of a plough driving a straight furrow. On the other hand, in both the Proverbs passages the verb is used with *hodous* (='roads') and plainly means 'to cut a straight road', or 'to drive a road in a straight direction'; there are also many instances of the verb 'cut' being used of making roads. A possible interpretation, therefore, is that Paul is admonishing Timothy, in preaching the gospel, to follow a straight path, without being turned aside by disputes about mere words or impious talk. The debate, however, is probably fruitless (an example of the *logomachia* which Paul deplores!), for the broad sense is clear enough and the underlying image, whatever it is, has lost all its freshness and force.

If positively his task is to preach the gospel in its purity, negatively Timothy should **keep clear of profane chatter.** 16 Paul is again hitting at the teaching of the sectaries, in language identical with that he used in 1 Tim. vi. 20. The noun under-lines its futility, while the adjective hints that it is materialistic in bias, substituting human speculation for divine revelation. Little wonder that **those who indulge in it** are doomed to **advance more and more in ungodliness.** The construction is clumsy in the original, for no subject for the third-person plural **will advance** is expressed. The context, however, especially **their** in 17, establishes that the errorists are intended. Evidently they claimed to be 'advanced', i.e. go-ahead and intellectually alive, Christians (for the verb *prokoptein* = 'advance' in the sense of making progress, cf. Rom. xiii. 12; Gal. i. 14: also 1 Tim. iv. 15 for the related noun *prokopē*). Hence the deliberate irony in Paul's comment that the only real progress they are likely to make is in the direction of **ungodliness.**

Equally disastrous will be their influence on other members 17 of the church, for **their talk will eat its way** (lit. 'will have pasture') **like gangrene.** The translation 'cancer' has sometimes been preferred (e.g. AV), but **gangrene** suits both the Greek (*gaggraina*) and the sense of the passage better. It is not just the dangers of false teaching to its adherents that worry Paul, but its insidious tendency to spread and infect other people, just as gangrene spreads to and eats up the neighbouring tissues.

Two of the false teachers are now mentioned by name. **Philetus** is not heard of elsewhere, but **Hymenaeus** is referred to in 1 Tim. i. 20, where were are told that Paul had excommunicated him. In spite of this he seems to have continued his activities successfully, since he appears here as one of the errorist leaders. Some have found this surprising, and have concluded that 2 Timothy must have been written before 1 Timothy. The inference, however, is quite unnecessary; we cannot assume that the Apostle's ban was instantaneously effective in silencing a heretic, and indeed the fact that Hymenaeus could apparently ignore it illustrates the difficult situation in the Ephesian church.

18   Paul states that these two **have shot wide of the truth.** For the verb (Gk. *astochein*: lit. 'miss the mark'), cf. 1 Tim. i. 6; vi. 21. Their error, he continues, consists in **saying that the resurrection has already taken place.** This is a most valuable pointer, the only really precise and concrete one in the letters, to the actual theological tenets of the deviationists.

Although much is obscure, the most likely interpretation is that they chose to identify the resurrection, not with the raising of the body on the last day, but with the mystical dying and rising again which the Christian experiences in his baptismal initiation. That this is the correct account of their teaching, which thus in effect denied the resurrection of the body, is borne out by Irenaeus's report (*Haer.* i. 23. 5) that the Samaritan Gnostic Menander, who was a disciple of Simon Magus (Acts viii. 9 ff.), taught his followers that, as a result of having been baptized by himself, they had already undergone the resurrection and would never grow old and die. Cf. *Acts of Paul and Thecla* xiv.

The belief that the physical body will rise from the grave was, of course, integral to Christianity from the beginning. Side by side with it was the doctrine, which we have no reason to suppose was confined to Paul (for his version of it, cf. Rom. vi. 1-11; Eph. ii. 6; v. 14; Col. ii. 13; iii. 1-4), that the Christian undergoes a mystical death and resurrection with Christ in baptism. The Greek mind, however, with its conception of the soul as immortal and of release from the body, its prison, as its true happiness, felt an instinctive repugnance for the idea of physical resurrection. Thus in Hellenistic circles Paul early found it necessary (cf. 1 Cor. xv; Acts xvii. 32) to combat complete scepticism about it. It is understandable that people of this way of thinking would find the idea of sacramental resurrection in baptism much more congenial, and would confine their teaching about the resurrection to it. Tendencies like these had a special appeal wherever Gnosticism was establishing a hold, and the present passage is evidence of the Gnostic leanings of the sectaries.

By teaching such distortions, Paul claims, they **are undermining people's faith.** Inevitably so, since belief in the bodily resurrection is the keystone of Christianity; without it, as he had assured the Corinthians (1 Cor. xv. 17), 'Your faith is vain, and you are still in your sins'. The danger was all the greater where (as almost certainly in the present case) the denial sprang from a depreciation of the body, which opened the door on the one hand to the idea of self-salvation by means of ascetic practices (cf. 1 Tim. iv. 3), and on the other to moral indifference (cf. 1 Cor. vi. 12 ff.).

19 **Nevertheless** (Gk. *mentoi*: an emphatic word), in contrast to these weaker brethren who are dislodged like ill-fastened stones from the church's structure, **God's foundation stands firm.** Depressed as he is by the effects of the heretics' campaign, Paul gratefully recognizes the immovability of the main building. Various interpretations have been proposed for the **solid foundation**: Christ and his Apostles (cf. Eph. ii. 19 f.), the truth of the gospel, the church as a whole (cf. 1 Tim. iii. 15), or the unshakeable core of genuine Christians at Ephesus. It almost certainly stands for the last, or at any rate for the Ephesian church considered as part of the great Church, since the Apostle is clearly contrasting the **solid foundation** with the unstable few whose faith has been undermined. This is confirmed by the content of the two inscriptions which the **solid foundation** has engraved on it, and which both refer to God's elect and faithful people.

In **this seal** we have an allusion to the practice of placing on a building, or its foundation stone, an inscription or other sign to indicate its owner or purpose (cf. Rev. xxi. 14). So the community of God's faithful people at Ephesus is stamped with two mottoes. The first, **'The Lord knows his own'**, is an almost literal citation from LXX Num. xvi. 5, consisting of words of stern reproof uttered by Moses on the occasion of the rebellion of Korah, Dathan, and Abiram. Some have conjectured that it is an excerpt from an early Christian poem, but there is nothing particularly poetic about it. Much more probably it was a proverbial tag whose associations were familiar to Christians of the time. As we know from Jude 11, Korah soon became the stock type of the apostate teacher. In any case Paul's object in citing it was to give encouragement to Timothy, and others who were worried by backsliding in the community, by reminding them that God can be relied upon to discriminate between his loyal and disloyal servants.

The second motto, **'Everyone who names the Lord's name must turn his back on wickedness'**, is packed with Scriptural reminiscences. For the first part, cf. LXX Lev. xxiv. 16; Josh. xxiii. 7; Is. xxvi. 13: for the second, cf. Ps. vi. 8; Is. lii. 11; Mt. vii. 23; Lk. xiii. 27. Again it is a proverbial slogan which Paul assumes will be recognized by his readers. It reinforces the first by defining who the Lord's true servants are; they reveal that they are **his own** by forsaking **wickedness,** i.e., in the present instance, erroneous teaching which, according to the Apostle, inevitably brings moral corruption in its train.

Yet the fact remains that, in spite of the real stability of the community and the confident mottoes it bears, there are un-satisfactory elements in it, as events are tragically showing, and the question might be asked why this should be. Paul attempts to deal with the problem by comparing the church to **a large 20 house,** a simile which occurs frequently in these letters (e.g. 1 Tim. iii. 5; 15) and which links up naturally with his language about **God's solid foundation.** In such a dwelling no one is surprised to find **not only gold and silver utensils, but also ones of wood and earthenware.** Equally no one should be taken aback that the church should contain both good and bad Christians. The point is that the different kinds of utensils, and so by analogy the different types of Christians, serve entirely different, indeed opposite, functions: **while the former are for honourable, the latter are for ignominious purposes.**

The imagery, and also the manner, of the verse are inescap-ably Pauline, and many have argued that this is because it is modelled on such passages as 1 Cor. iii. 12; xii. 23 f.; Rom. ix. 21. But the resemblances are remote and verbal, and the setting totally different. Moreover, if a Pauline imitator had been basing himself on Rom. ix. 21, he would surely have been prompted to include some reference to the ultimate fate of the false teachers. As a matter of fact the awkward and incomplete way in which the comparison is worked out is a token of the genuineness of the passage; Paul frequently gets into precisely such difficulties with his similes. Logically we should expect him to draw the inference that unworthy Christians, like earthenware utensils, have their necessary, though subordinate, function in the church; but this is, of course, far from his thoughts, and in any case he is already moving on to a quite different conclusion.

This is that, so far from resting content with what, according to the analogy, might seem to be the natural order of things, the sound, orthodox Christian should rigorously eschew his un-worthy brethren. As he expresses it, striving to keep up his picture of a house with its pots and pans, **Anyone who keeps 21**

himself clean (lit. 'cleanses himself') **from these will be a utensil for honourable purposes, consecrated, serviceable to the householder, ready for any good work.** The meaning of **these** can only be 'these latter utensils', i.e. those for ignominious purposes. Admittedly this is very awkward, for one utensil is not cleansed from another, but from the impurities besmirching it, and because of this some have interpreted **these** as referring back to **profane chatter** in 16. But Paul's awkward way of expressing himself has parallels elsewhere and is in itself no reason for rejecting the obvious exegesis; further, it is unnatural to connect **these** with so remote an antecedent as **profane chatter**.

Stripped of metaphor, Paul's advice to Timothy is that he should sternly separate himself from teachers like Philetus and Hymenaeus. In this way he will prove of real use to his Master, and will be in a state of readiness to carry out **any good work** (for the stress on works of charity in the Pastorals, see on 1 Tim. ii. 10) to which he may be calling him (cf. Eph. ii. 10).

7. TIMOTHY'S CONDUCT AS A TEACHER.
ii. 22-26

(22) So avoid youthful passions, and aim at integrity, faith, charity, and peace with those who call on the Lord out of a pure heart. (23) Have nothing to do with foolish, undisciplined speculations, for you know that they breed quarrels. (24) But the Lord's servant should not be quarrelsome, but kindly to everybody, an understanding teacher, forbearing, (25) correcting his opponents with gentleness in case God should grant them a change of attitude leading to acknowledgement of the truth, (26) and they should return to their senses from the devil's snare, having been made captive by him in subjection to his will.

Paul now resumes the personal note which his outburst against the deviationists in 16 ff. had interrupted. The advice 22 to **avoid youthful passions** reminds us that Timothy is still a young man by ancient standards: see on 1 Tim. iv. 12. The sequel, with its reference to **integrity,** etc., suggests that the Apostle is not thinking so much of sensual temptations as of certain faults of character which headstrong young men are liable to display. He wants Timothy to wean himself of partiality, intolerance, quickness of temper, self-assertion, and the like, and thus to attain moral maturity. He had set the ideal of **integrity, faith, charity** before him in 1 Tim. vi. 11, where see note. Now he adds, as essential to his conduct as a minister, that he should cultivate **peace with those who call upon the Lord out of a pure heart.**

Some connect the words **with . . .** closely with **aim,** translating it 'in company with' in order to bring out the meaning more effectively. If this is correct, Paul's point is that fellowship with other Christians provides the milieu in which these virtues will develop. What he is really thinking about, however, is the brotherly concord which should flourish among Christian people (cf. Rom. xii. 18). These are designated, we observe, **those who call upon the Lord,** a phrase which (often with the addition of 'the name of') in the O.T. denotes the worship of Yahweh, but in the N.T. the act of invoking Christ in prayer. To be effective this should be done **out of a pure heart,** i.e. in complete sincerity. For the expression, which is essentially Semitic, see note on 1 Tim. i. 5.

In addition Timothy, in his capacity as a church leader, should **Have nothing to do with foolish, undisciplined 23 speculations.** The last word (Gk. *zētēseis*) has often been interpreted more broadly as 'disputes', 'controversies'. If this is its true meaning, Timothy is being counselled against futile theological wrangling which not only gets one nowhere but raises tempers. It seems preferable, however, to detect here, as in 1 Tim. vi. 4 (where see note), an allusion to the fanciful ideas mooted by the sectaries, and this is borne out by the Apostle's description of them as **foolish** and **undisciplined** (the latter adjective probably underlines their deviation from the traditional faith). It is not theological argument as such that he finds objectionable in these letters, but rather the controversial raising of recondite questions which draw men away from the apostolic witness.

24 Such pseudo-questions, he reminds Timothy, only **breed quarrels.** On the other hand, **the Lord's servant,** i.e. the Christian pastor, **should not be quarrelsome** (lit. 'should not fight'). Every Christian is of course a servant of the Lord, but the phrase is here used almost technically of the Christian leader or minister. The more usual N.T. formula is 'servant of Christ' or 'servant of God'. It has been suggested with much plausibility that the wording here, as indeed the whole picture of meekness and gentleness which is conjured up, has been inspired by the Servant passages in Is. xlii. 1-3; liii.

When controversy arises, even when heresy is afoot, the good pastor should be **kindly to everybody,** as Paul himself had been among the Thessalonians (1 Thess. ii. 7), exercising his pastoral authority with constructive gentleness. In harmony with this he should be **an understanding teacher,** the emphasis in the word (Gk. *didaktikos*: cf. 1 Tim. iii. 2) being not so much on his knowledge as on his ability to bring the best out of his charges, and at the same time **forbearing,** i.e. ready, when the argument waxes violent and tempers are becoming frayed, to listen patiently without answering back heatedly. The adjective used (Gk. *anexikakos*) literally means 'ready to put up with evil'.

25 Similarly, when **correcting his opponents,** the overseer of truly Christian character will do so **with gentleness** (cf. 2 Thess. iii. 15). The participle might be rendered 'chastising', but Paul has in mind the constructive re-education of misguided Christian brethren. The English **gentleness** hardly brings out the full force of the original (Gk. *praütēs*), which includes humility or meekness as well. It is in this spirit, which is Christ's own spirit, that the Christian leader will set to work, always on the look-out **in case God should grant them a change of attitude** (Gk. *metanoia*: the same word as for 'repentance') enabling them to arrive at an **acknowledgement of the truth** (for this phrase, characteristic of the Pastorals, see on 1 Tim. ii. 4). This will be wholly God's work; but while love will open a door to his grace, violence can only obstruct it by exasperating those who desperately need it.

The next verse defines what is involved in this conversion; it 26 is that they **should return to their senses** and escape **from**

the devil's snare. As the translation indicates, Paul is mixing his metaphors incongruously, but his words vividly delineate the tragic condition in which the false teachers have landed themselves and their followers. In effect it is equivalent to being drunk and besotted, for the verb (Gk. *ananēphein*) literally means 'return to sobriety'. Actually it is the result of the machinations of Satan, who has trapped them in his **snare** (for the same picture, cf. 1 Tim. iii. 7).

The language of the second half of the verse is so slipshod that its exact meaning is obscure. The translation printed above interprets it as elaborating the idea of captivity suggested by **snare.** The false teachers have **been made captive** (the Greek verb *zōgrein* means 'capture alive', a different image from that contained in **snare**) **by him,** i.e. the devil, and as a result are **in subjection to his** (i.e. the devil's) **will.** This yields a perfectly acceptable sense and, in spite of the change of metaphor, fits the context admirably. But it is exposed to the objection, completely concealed in an English translation, that **by him** and **his,** which in the Greek are only separated by the preposition 'to' and the definite article, are there represented by two totally different pronouns, *autou* and *ekeinou* respectively. In classical Greek they would be bound, placed so close to each other, to refer to different subjects.

Of the various alternative exegeses which have been proposed it will be sufficient to mention two. The first (RV) takes **by him** as referring to **the Lord's servant** in 24 above, and **his** to **God** mentioned in 25. Paul will then in effect be saying that the restored backsliders exchange **the devil's snare** for captivity at the hands of their pastor or overseer, thus finding themselves brought back to obedience to God. This is excellent so far as the sense goes, but extremely difficult grammatically in view of the awkwardness of referring **by him** to an antecedent so distant as **the Lord's servant,** especially after two other subjects have been mentioned. Further, in spite of the parallels alleged (e.g. 2 Cor. x. 5), being captured alive by their overseer does not seem a natural description of the reconversion which is envisaged.

The second proposal (RVm, RSVm) is that, while **by him** refers to the devil, as indeed the position of the word makes practically certain, **his will** relates to God, and the whole

clause should be translated '. . . and they should recover their
senses from the devil's snare (having been made captive by him),
thus returning to subjection to God's will'. This again makes
excellent sense, but is stylistically intolerable because of the gap
of several words, including a participial phrase, between the
main verb **return to their senses** and 'to subjection to his
will', which must be construed with it. Thus on balance the
rendering printed in the text, in spite of its difficulties, remains
the least objectionable. Its acceptance is made easier if we recall
that the originally sharp distinction between *autos* ('he') and
ekeinos ('that one') had broken down in the *koinē*. An almost
exact parallel, with the two different pronouns referring in one
short sentence to one and the same subject, can be cited from
Wis. i. 16.

8. DISASTERS OF THE LAST DAYS. iii. 1-9

**(1) Take note of this, however, that in the last days
troublesome times are to set in. (2) For men will be self-
loving, money-loving, boastful, haughty, abusive, disobedient to parents, ungrateful, irreverent, (3) unloving,
implacable, slanderous, profligate, savage, hating what
is good, (4) treacherous, reckless, swollen with conceit,
pleasure-loving rather than God-loving, (5) keeping up
the outward form of religion but denying its power.
Keep clear of such people. (6) For they are the sort who
worm their way into households and get silly women
into their power who are weighed down with their sins
and pulled about by all kinds of lusts, (7) always learning
but incapable of reaching a knowledge of the truth. (8)
Just as Jannes and Jambres withstood Moses, so these
withstand the truth, men perverted in mind whose faith
has failed the test. (9) However, they will get no further;
for their senselessness will be exposed for all to see, as
was that of those two also.**

As in 1 Tim. iv. 1 ff. (where see notes), Paul now reminds
1 Timothy (**Take note of this**) of the primitive Christian con-

viction that the period preceding Christ's return would be one
of agonizing crisis, involving a collapse of moral standards.
Since he is availing himself of prophetic material current in the
Church, he naturally uses the future tense, but it soon becomes
plain that his gaze is fixed on the present, in which those pre-
dictions are being only too accurately realized. His point is that,
so far from being discouraged, Timothy should be put on his
guard, and in a sense even braced, by the evidences around him
of misconduct and unsatisfactory religious faith, which the
Apostle brackets together, since they are all part of the pattern
of events that has been foretold.

For the expression **in the last days**, cf. Acts ii. 17, Jas. v. 3;
2 Pet. iii. 3; Jud. 18. Not found in the acknowledged Paulines
(but cf. 1 Tim. iv. 1: 'in the last times'), it denotes the period
just before the Parousia and the end of the present age. The
apostolic Church believed that Christ himself had predicted
that these events would be ushered in by a crisis of evil, including the emergence of religious impostors and a general
apostasy (Mt. xxiv; Mk. xiii; Lk. xxi), and Jewish apocalyptic
foresaw a complete breakdown of morality before the coming of
Messiah. So Paul can take it as an accepted truth (cf. 2 Thess.
ii. 3-12) that **troublesome times are to set in,** i.e. trying and
dangerous for God's true servants, and the deplorable situation
at Ephesus seems to provide empirical confirmation of it.

In order to describe the moral breakdown of **the last days**
Paul introduces (2-5) a catalogue of vices of the kind that occurs
frequently in his acknowledged letters: see on 1 Tim. i. 9. This
particular list bears a remarkable resemblance, in content as
well as rhetorical construction and use of assonance, to the one
in Rom. i. 29-31, but there are also differences which make the
hypothesis of direct borrowing implausible. The fact that the
most striking parallels of style and vocabulary are to be found
in Philo (see C. Spicq, pp. 381 f.) suggests that the ultimate
source of the material embodied in it is Jewish traditional
teaching rather than the Hellenistic diatribe.

Paul opens with the sweeping statement that **men will be** 2
vile in various ways. He is not at first thinking of particular
groups, but is voicing the apocalyptic foreboding of a general
repudiation of law, decency, and natural affection. The epithets

which follow seem to be grouped in pairs, being in several cases linked by assonance. Thus the adjectives **self-loving** and **money-loving** both have the prefix *phil-* in Greek. It is noticeable that the catalogue closes with a similarly constructed pair, **pleasure-loving** and **God-loving.** These provide the clue to the rest, since complete moral corruption is liable to ensue when men abandon God for absorption in self and material satisfactions. For the view of money as a root-cause of evil, cf. 1 Tim. vi. 10.

The second pair, **boastful, haughty,** express different but related aspects of the pride which springs from self-centredness. The former has to do with words, gestures, and outward behaviour, and the latter with inward feelings. The two are coupled together in Rom. i. 30. The third pair, **abusive, disobedient to parents,** cover unnatural conduct in relation to other people and one's own family respectively. The latter vice figures also in Rom. i. 30.

The two members of the fourth pair, **ungrateful, irreverent,**
3 both have the adversative prefix *a-* in the original, as have **unloving, implacable.** The adjective **unloving** (Gk. *astorgos*) connotes lack of all natural affection; it is found only here and in Rom. i. 31 in the N.T. The Greek word rendered **implacable** (*aspondos*) derives from *spondē* (='truce'), and thus denotes a man who cannot bring himself to come to terms with other people.

The next epithets, **slanderous, profligate, savage, hating what is good,** paint a terrible picture of men who, while sunk to the animal level of instinct, remain sufficiently human to recognize truth and goodness and to be animated by hatred towards them. The latter two both have the adversative prefix
4 in Greek, and thus form a pair. So do **treacherous, reckless,** which both have the same Greek prefix *pro-*. It is possible that **treacherous** hints at the sectaries' readiness to betray, perhaps even inform against, their brethren; but we do not hear elsewhere of trouble between the church and the civil authority, and it is not necessary that every item in the catalogue, which is largely conventional, should have an exact reference. A man who is **reckless** stops at nothing to gain his ends.

With **swollen with conceit** (for this, see note on 1 Tim. iii.

6; vi. 4), **pleasure-loving rather than God-loving,** the list might seem complete, but the Apostle thrusts in, by way of a climax, the stinging clause, **keeping up the outward form of 5 religion but denying its power.** Clearly he has now descended from the generalizations of the conventional catalogue, and is fastening on the actual conduct and attitude of the Ephesian errorists. His charge against them is more than one of simple hypocrisy. They make a great parade of Christianity, and are active in preaching and practising what they conceive to be the true faith. But whereas the authentic gospel is a regenerative force, the disordered quality of their lives proves that they have to all intents and purposes rejected it. For a similar charge, cf. Tit. i. 16. The word here rendered **outward form** (Gk. *morphōsis*) is used by Paul in Rom. ii. 20 (he may be borrowing it from a Rabbinical context) with the rather different sense of 'visible embodiment'.

Little wonder Timothy is admonished to **Keep clear of such people.** The setting of apocalyptic prediction is now completely abandoned, and Paul does not conceal the fact that he is speaking of the sectaries. The verb (Gk. *apotrepesthai*) is a strong one, implying that Timothy is to avoid them with horror. The reference is not so much to his personal relations with them (he has already been told in ii. 24 f. to be kindly to everyone) as to his official attitude.

People like these, Paul continues, **are the sort who worm 6 their way into households and get silly women into their power.** For all his biting sarcasm, he is drawing a life-like picture of the tactics of religious propaganda. Since women in antiquity were largely confined to the home, it was by methods not dissimilar to these that orthodox Christianity fastened its hold on pagan society in the Graeco-Roman world; it was only unfortunate that they could be exploited with at least equal success by its counterfeit forms. The mention of **silly women** (Gk. *gunaikaria*: a scornful diminutive) is also a vivid touch. Paul doubtless has concrete instances in mind, and this explains his contemptuous tone; but it remains a fact that women, with their more intuitive and receptive approach, are in all ages peculiarly susceptible to proselytism, bad as well as good.

With true psychological insight Paul observes that these

worthless creatures, as he represents them to be, fall easy victims to the false teachers' wiles when they are **weighed down with their sins and pulled about by all kinds of lusts.** Although his immediate object is to castigate the short-comings of particular individuals, it is a truism that women, and of course men too, are most ready to embrace the gospel, in its authentic but also, alas, its perverted form, when they are most conscious of the squalor and futility of their lives. The women in question, however, suffer in addition from the in-stability which often accompanies religious dilettantism. They 7 are, Paul alleges, **always learning,** i.e. avidly, and perhaps morbidly, curious about religion and prepared to fall for any novel theory put before them, **but,** since they lack serious purpose and are simply attracted by novelty as such, they prove **incapable of reaching a knowledge of the truth** (for this latter phrase, cf. ii. 25, and see note on 1 Tim. ii. 4).

With the mention of **the truth,** which in his usage stands for the authentic gospel, Paul reverts to the false teachers, claiming 8 that they in fact **withstand the truth,** and do so exactly as **Jannes and Jambres withstood Moses.** These personages were two of Pharaoh's magicians who tried to demonstrate that they were as effective as Moses at working miracles (Ex. vii. 11; ix. 11). Their names do not occur in the O.T., nor are they mentioned by Philo or Josephus, but there are references to them in the Qumran documents as well as in late Jewish, pagan, and early Christian literature. The legend about Moses under-went great elaboration in late Judaism, and its details were evi-dently widely familiar in first-century Christian circles (e.g. Acts vii. 22 f.; 53; 1 Cor. x. 2; 4; Gal. iii. 19; Heb. ii. 2; Jude 9). Thus Paul's comparison of the Ephesian heretics to the two ill-fated sorcerers was probably a telling shaft. It also coheres with the typological treatment of the O.T. which he shared with other Christians of the first century, according to which the experiences of Israel in Egypt and the desert were a kind of divinely ordered anticipation of those of the Church.

It is possible, though probably mistaken, to detect behind Paul's comparison an insinuation that the sectaries were guilty of magical practices. The sum of their condition, he adds by way of finale, is that they are **men perverted in mind, whose**

faith has failed the test (lit. 'disqualified in the faith'). For the first half of this description, cf. 1 Tim. vi. 5. In the second half **faith** has the definite article, and therefore probably connotes, as so often in these letters (see on 1 Tim. iii. 9), the content of belief.

Paul's pessimistic diatribe ends on a more confident note. The false teachers, he is satisfied, **will get no further** (for the 9 verb, Gk. *prokoptein* = 'make progress', cf. ii. 16 above). Their attempts to impose on people may have been successful so far, but a halt will soon be called to them. Alternatively we can ignore the comparative force of the words translated **further** (Gk. *epi pleion*) and render 'will not get very far'; but of the two possible versions the former seems more pointed. The dénouement will come when **their senselessness,** i.e. the hollowness and indeed sheer folly of their doctrines (cf. **perverted in mind** in 8) **will be exposed for all to see.** The Apostle is convinced that this must happen, since **those two** (lit. 'of those'), i.e. Jannes and Jambres, who were their types, had their impostures shown up. Their exposure is briefly touched on in Ex. vii. 12 f.; ix. 12, but was probably described in elaborate detail in the Moses legend.

9. AN EXHORTATION TO STEADFASTNESS.
iii. 10-17

(10) You, however, have closely followed my teaching, my manner of life, my purpose, my faith, my patience, my love, my steadfastness, (11) my persecutions, my sufferings—all that befell me at Antioch, at Iconium, and at Lystra, all the persecutions I had to put up with; yet the Lord rescued me from them all. (12) Indeed all who wish to lead a godly life in Christ Jesus will be persecuted, (13) but wicked men and impostors will advance from bad to worse, deceivers and deceived. (14) But as for you, stand by the things you have learned and have been convinced of, realizing from whom you learned them, (15) and that from a child you have been familiar

with the sacred writings which can give you the wisdom which leads to salvation through faith in Christ Jesus. (16) Every Scripture is inspired by God and is profitable for instruction, for reproof, for correction, and for training in uprightness, (17) so that the man of God may be complete and completely equipped for every good work.

From the sombre picture he has painted of the last days, and of the demoralized Christians whose character and conduct provide a foretaste of them, the Apostle turns with relief to Timothy, confident that he at any rate, by modelling himself on his master, has laid a sure foundation for his ministry. Even so, the anxiety which his lieutenant's timorous and irresolute nature inspires in him comes out in his renewed exhortation to him to hold fast to the traditional faith and, above all, to make Scripture his sheet-anchor.

10   **You, however,** he remarks, pointedly contrasting Timothy with the teachers of alien doctrines, **have closely followed my teaching, my manner of life, my purpose, my faith, my patience, my love, my steadfastness** ... The verb used (Gk. *parakolouthein*) literally means 'follow' in the sense of accompanying, but although Timothy has been Paul's constant companion this meaning is in the background here. It is also a technical term defining the relation of a disciple to his master, and can be paraphrased 'study at close quarters', 'follow in spirit', 'carefully note with a view to reproducing', and so 'take as an example'. This is the sense which suits the present context, for ever since his conversion Timothy has been the Apostle's intimate associate, and as such must have assimilated, and learned to model himself upon, his **teaching** and **manner of life.** Long ago Paul had told the Corinthians (1 Cor. iv. 17) that he was dispatching 'Timothy ... who will remind you of my ways in Christ, as I teach them everywhere in every church'. In the same way he must have come to appreciate his **purpose,** i.e. the guiding motive of his life and work (Gk. *prothesis*: used elsewhere by Paul exclusively of God), and **faith,** or conviction (cf. ii. 22).

The qualities so far singled out are the ones immediately relevant to the antithesis Paul is making between Timothy and the false teachers. But by a natural, if not very logical, transition he is led on to mention others which he himself had been called upon to display and which he knows will be necessary to Timothy as a Christian leader. His disciple had witnessed at first hand his master's **patience, love,** and **steadfastness,** and should now derive inspiration from them for his own struggle.

These naturally suggest to his mind his **persecutions** and 11 **sufferings,** and in fact all that **befell** him long ago **at Antioch, at Iconium, and at Lystra.** On his first missionary journey he had been hustled unceremoniously out of Pisidian Antioch (Acts xiii. 50), at Iconium had narrowly escaped being assaulted and stoned (*ib.* xiv. 5 f.), and at Lystra had been stoned and dragged as dead out of the town (*ib.* xiv. 19). Some commentators find it odd that Paul should have selected these early examples of ill-treatment, which happened to him in any case before he met Timothy, rather than the more recent hardships they must have endured together on several occasions. The difficulty vanishes, they argue, if we assume that a pseudonymous author has uncritically borrowed these illustrations from Acts without troubling about their chronological incongruity.

Against this it can be urged that it is precisely a seeming incongruity of this kind that such a writer, especially if he belonged to a circle which admired Paul and was acquainted with his life-story, would have been careful to avoid. There were certainly much more obvious examples available (cf., e.g., Acts xvi-xvii), and we should have expected him to choose them. On the other hand, if the Apostle himself is the author, it is easy to conjecture special personal reasons for his preferring to mention these particular incidents. His motive, for example, may well have been to concentrate on sufferings which occurred just before Timothy's conversion, and which he knew had left an indelible impression on the young man's imagination. The verb **closely followed,** as has been pointed out above, does not necessarily imply that Timothy had been personally present at them.

The ejaculation which follows—**yet the Lord rescued me from them all**—expresses Paul's spontaneous gratitude as he looks back on his career; it is also intended as an encouragement to Timothy, who can rely on similar help. The words them-

selves echo LXX Ps. xxxiii. 18 ('The Lord . . . rescued them
from all their troubles'). The reassurance they contain is all
the more apposite because, as Paul now impresses on Timothy,
12 persecution such as he has had to endure is to be the lot of **all
who wish to lead a godly life in Christ Jesus.** Christ himself
had taught his followers to expect to bear the cross, and Paul's
lifelong experience (cf., e.g. 2 Cor. xi. 23-29) convinced him
that this was an inescapable ingredient of the Christian vocation
(cf. esp. 1 Thess. iii. 4). Fellowship with Christ in suffering is
indeed part and parcel of the Christian's mystical union with
him. The formula **in Christ Jesus** therefore carries the normal
Pauline implication of incorporation into Christ (see note on i. 2:
also 1 Tim. i. 14), and it is arbitrary to give it a watered down
sense. For 'life in Christ Jesus', cf. Rom. vi. 11; 23.

There are, of course, others, the Apostle proceeds with
characteristic bitter irony, whose lot will be different; these are
13 **wicked men and impostors.** He has returned to his attack
on the sectaries, and the terms in which he describes them
(**impostors** = Gk. *goētes*: lit. 'magicians') are intended to link
them with Jannes and Jambres (cf. 8 f.). Again, as in 8, there is
conceivably an allusion to their dabbling in magic arts. Paul
declares that they **will advance** (for the verb, Gk. *prokoptein*,
cf. ii. 16; iii. 9), and we expect him to complete the clause by
some reference to the 'progress' they will make. Instead he
turns the idea upside down and lashes out with the ironical
from bad to worse. For all its apparent freedom from dis-
comfort and distress, their lot will really be a pitiable one, since
they are at once **deceivers and deceived** (a proverbial tag).

Paul now prescribes the sovereign remedy against being
taken in by such charlatans, viz. loyal adhesion to the gospel
14 message as opposed to the fanciful novelties (cf. ii. 16) which
they hawk around. **But as for you,** he says, contrasting Timothy
with the specious deceivers just mentioned, **stand by the
things you have learned and have been convinced of.**
His confidence in these truths should have a twofold basis. First,
he knows **from whom** (the pronoun is plural in the Greek) he
has **learned them.** These truths of the Christian tradition have
been imparted to him, not by clever individualist adventurers
whom nobody can vouch for but themselves, but by people like

his mother and grandmother (cf. i. 5), the Apostle himself, and
other witnesses of proved reliability; and he has given his firm
assent to them.

The second motive for his confidence should be his sure 15
grounding in Scripture; **from a child,** as he knows full well,
he has **been familiar with the sacred writings.** Jewish
parents were expected to teach their children the Law from the
age of five onwards. The expression **sacred writings** (Gk.
hiera grammata) is found only here in the Bible, in which the
noun denoting Scripture is normally *graphē* (singular or plural).
Commentators have exerted themselves needlessly to think out
reasons for its choice in the present passage, much the least
plausible theory being that the plural covers specifically Christian writings, including the letters of Paul himself, as well as
the O.T. Those who take this view believe that the writer
belonged to the second quarter of the second century, and that
therefore a reference to authoritative Christian literature is to
be expected. Even on this assumption, however, (*a*) there is
nothing in the sentence which in the least suggests Christian
writings, and (*b*) it is incredible that the writer, who is presumably doing his best to represent the Apostle as reminding
Timothy of his youthful education, should fall into such a
clumsy anachronism.

Actually by **sacred writings** Paul means, of course, the O.T.;
there is abundant evidence that this was a stock designation for
it in Greek-speaking Judaism (cf. Philo and Josephus). The
absence of the definite article in the Greek confirms that it is
used technically. His use of the phrase, in place of the more
usual *graphē*, is of a piece with his (or his amanuensis's) predilection in these letters for a more rabbinical idiom. The O.T. was
the only canonical Scripture for Christians as well as Jews in
the apostolic age and for several generations after it. Irenaeus
(*c*. 180) was the first writer to speak unequivocally of a 'New
Testament'; but as early as 2 Pet. iii. 15 f. Paul's letters were
being ranked with 'other Scriptures', while for Ignatius (*c*. 110)
'the gospel' was an equivalent authority to 'the prophets' (e.g.
Smyrn. v. 1; vii. 2).

The reason why the O.T. books are so precious is that they
can give you the wisdom which leads to salvation. In

other words, they convey, not simply facts or even sacred
history, but a revelation of God's saving purpose. The **wisdom**
referred to (the Greek has the verb: 'make you wise') is the
profound insight or grasp which the believer possesses, and is
contrasted with the **senselessness** of the errorists stigmatized
in 9. And this apprehension comes **through faith in Christ
Jesus.** The key to Scripture is Christ, and it can say nothing
to men until they have accepted him as Saviour and Lord. This
is on the whole the most likely sense of the concluding words,
although many prefer to take them closely with **salvation.** On
this view Paul will be emphasizing that the **salvation** in which
the O.T. instructs men can only be obtained through a living
faith in Christ.

Paul develops his doctrine of the value of the O.T. in a
sentence which commentators have found bafflingly ambiguous.
16 **Every Scripture,** he states, **is inspired by God and profitable . . .** There need be no hesitation about the noun (Gk.
graphē), at any rate so far as its broad reference is concerned.
While it literally means 'writing' or 'book' and could conceivably cover writings or books in general, both the context
and N.T. usage require that it should have the narrowed-down
sense of **Scripture,** i.e. the O.T. Much more difficult is the
total expression (Gk. *pasa graphē*) here rendered **Every Scripture.** In the singular *graphē* can denote (*a*) a book of Scripture,
(*b*) Scripture as a whole (e.g. Gal. iii. 8; 22; Rom. xi. 1: cf. also
1 Tim. v. 18), or (*c*) a particular passage of Scripture (e.g. Mk.
xii. 10; Jn. xix. 37; xx. 9; Acts viii. 35). The first usage, frequent
in Hellenistic Judaism, is entirely lacking from the N.T., and
we are probably justified in excluding it here. Many (e.g. AV,
RSV, Moffatt) prefer the second, and translate 'All Scripture',
and in favour of this is the fact that the Apostle is clearly thinking of the O.T. in its entirety. On the other hand, there is no
definite article in the Greek, and where *pas* (='all' or 'every')
is used with a noun in the singular without the article it usually
means 'every' rather than 'whole' or 'all'. The problem is
complicated by the fact that we cannot be sure how strictly this
dogma was observed in the first-century *koinē*, but the balance
of argument seems in favour of **Every Scripture.** Having
spoken generally of **the sacred writings,** Paul may now be

anxious to emphasize their usefulness in all the individual passages which make up the whole.

There has also been much discussion about the construction of the sentence, for there is no verb corresponding to **is** in the original. Since the particle translated **and** has the alternative meaning 'also', **inspired by God** can be construed either predicatively as above (so AV, RSV), or as a qualifying adjective (i.e. 'Every inspired Scripture is also useful . . .': so RV, NEB). Commentators who favour the latter argue that a direct affirmation of the inspiration of Scripture is out of place here, since Timothy had presumably never doubted it and Paul's object is to stress the *usefulness* of the O.T. Yet a reminder of its divine origin is perfectly appropriate in a passage intended to impress on his disciple its value both as authenticating the Christian message and as a pastoral instrument. A decision is not easy, but in support of the version adopted it can be argued (*a*) that it seems natural, in the absence of a verb, to construe the two adjectives in the same way; (*b*) that the construction of the sentence is exactly parallel to that of 1 Tim. iv. 4, where the two adjectives are predicative; (*c*) that if **inspired by God** were attributive, we should, in the circumstances, expect it to be placed before **Scripture,** while 'also' is pointless; and (*d*) that **Every inspired Scripture** seems to contain a hint that certain passages of Scripture are not inspired.

The adjective rendered **inspired by God** (Gk. *theopneustos*) occurs nowhere else in the Greek Bible, but is found four times in pre-Christian Greek literature and the Sibylline Oracles. Literally meaning 'breathed into by God', it accurately expresses the view of the inspiration of the O.T. prevalent among Jews of the first century (cf. Josephus, *C. Ap.* i. 37 ff.; Philo, *Spec. leg.* i. 65; iv. 49; *Quis rer. div.* 263 ff.). The Church took it over entire, as we see from the statement in 2 Pet. i. 21 that in prophecy 'men moved by the Holy Spirit spoke from God'.

Because God himself speaks through it, the O.T. is pastorally useful **for instruction,** i.e. as a positive source of Christian doctrine (cf. Paul's habit of constantly reinforcing his message with Scriptural citations); **for reproof,** i.e. for refuting error and rebuking sin; **for correction,** i.e. for convincing the misguided of their errors and setting them on the right path again;

and for training in uprightness, i.e. for constructive education in Christian life. The word translated **uprightness** means
literally 'righteousness' (Gk. *dikaiosunē*): for this sense, cf. ii. 22;
1 Tim. vi. 11—also Rom. xiv. 17; 2 Cor. vi. 14; xi. 15.

If Scripture is used in all these ways, it fulfils a definite
17 function, causing **the man of God** to **be complete and completely equipped for every good work.** The clause is introduced by **so that** (Gk. *hina*), which in classical Greek normally
expresses purpose, but which in the *koinē* was often used to
denote result. The latter seems preferable here. The phrase
man of God could designate Christians in general, but the
context and the deliberate use of the singular confirm that, as in
1 Tim. vi. 11 (where see note), Paul is thinking specifically of
the Christian leader. With the help of a sound Scriptural training he becomes perfectly adapted to his task and can face his
responsibilities squarely. The closing words repeat the emphasis
on charitable works which is so prominent a feature of these
letters: see note on 1 Tim. ii. 10; cf. also 1 Tim. v. 10; 2 Tim.
ii. 21; Tit. iii. 1; etc.

10. A FINAL APPEAL TO PREACH THE GOSPEL.
iv. 1-8

**(1) I adjure you, in the sight of God and of Christ Jesus,
who is going to judge living and dead, and by his manifestation and kingdom: (2) proclaim the message, keep
at it in season and out of season, refute, rebuke, exhort,
using every sort of forbearance and teaching. (3) For a
time is coming when people will not put up with wholesome teaching, but with their ears itching will amass
teachers to suit their own desires. (4) They will turn their
ears away from the truth, and will turn to fables. (5) You,
however, must keep your head in all circumstances,
endure hardship, carry out your job as an evangelist, and
discharge your ministry to the full. (6) For as for me, I
am already being poured out on the altar, and the hour
of my departure is at hand. (7) I have fought in the noble**

match, I have completed the race, I have been loyal to
my trust. (8) Now the garland of righteousness is in store
for me, and the Lord, the righteous judge, will award it
to me on that day—and not only to me, but to all who
have loved his manifestation.

As his letter draws to its close, Paul reiterates with solemn
earnestness the appeal which has been all through its main
theme (cf. i. 6; 8; 13; ii. 1-3; 8; 14; iii. 14). A heightened note is
imparted to it by his consciousness that his own martyrdom
cannot be long delayed and that, when he is gone, Timothy will
have to stand on his own feet and shoulder the responsibilities
of leadership as Paul's successor by himself.

As in 1 Tim. v. 21, he makes his appeal an entreaty, **I adjure 1
you,** this time calling as witnesses **God and Christ Jesus, who
is going to judge living and dead.** The reference to judgment
is specially appropriate, for it is Christ who at his second coming
will judge how far Timothy, and every other minister of the
gospel, has discharged his momentous obligations. The bini-
tarian formula, like that of 1 Tim. vi. 13, has a liturgical ring,
and is probably drawn from a primitive baptismal creed. Echoes
of credal material are frequent in Paul's writings, and 'judge of
living and dead' early became stereotyped (Acts x. 42; 1 Pet.
iv. 5).

Paul then varies the construction of his sentence, appealing
to Timothy **by,** i.e. in the name of, Christ's **manifestation
and kingdom,** articles of Christian hope and confidence which
should strengthen his resolution. While in i. 10 **manifestation** (Gk. *epiphaneia*) referred to Christ's first appearance on
the earth in the incarnation, here, as in 8 below, 1 Tim. vi. 14
(where see note), and Tit. ii. 13, it denotes his future return in
glory. His **kingdom** is naturally coupled with it, for after the
judgment he will consummate his **kingdom** for the elect (see
note on 18 below).

The next verse, with its insistent **proclaim the message 2**
(lit. 'the word': cf. Gal. vi. 6; Col. iv. 3), sums up what the
Apostle believes to be Timothy's urgent practical duty in the
present critical situation. He must **keep at it in season and
out of season.** The verb (Gk. *ephistanai*) can have the military

meaning 'be posted', 'stay at one's post', but there is no hint of that in the context; its more usual sense, 'stand by', 'be at hand', 'be at one's task' (here with reference to church leadership), brings out exactly what Paul wants to say. The two adverbs form a proverbial jingle (Gk. *eukairōs, akairōs*), and might be paraphrased, 'Whether the moment seems opportune or not'.

Though of course such an analysis was far from Paul's mind, the following three imperatives have often been taken to illustrate the preacher's threefold appeal to reason, conscience, and the will. Timothy must **refute** error by reasoned argument; and he must not hesitate to **rebuke** when censure is called for. More positively, he must **exhort** (this is a more suitable rendering than 'encourage', which some prefer), i.e. urge his flock to repentance and perseverance. In all these roles, however, he must deploy **every sort of forbearance and teaching** (lit. 'in all forbearance and teaching'). Whatever approach he is using (the words qualify all three preceding imperatives), he must never lose patience with people (cf. ii. 25; iii. 10; 1 Tim. i. 16), and must always show himself a sound and resourceful teacher of Christian truth.

Fearless teaching like this is all the more urgently necessary 3 because **a time is coming when people will not put up with wholesome teaching.** As elsewhere in the Pastorals (1 Tim. i. 10—where see note; vi. 3; 2 Tim. i. 13; Tit. i. 9; 13; ii. 8), the gospel message, in contrast to other doctrines and specifically those of the errorists, is described as 'healthy' or 'sound'. There is no need to suppose that a later writer is depicting the crisis of his own day by the transparent device of putting a prophecy into the historical Paul's mouth. Men and women are already, as the Apostle can only too painfully observe, finding the gospel unpalatable, and with his vivid sense of the growing tribulations of 'the last days' he can easily foresee that this is only a foretaste of still worse to follow.

For example, instead of being content with a single leader like Paul or Timothy, who preaches the gospel honestly, whether they like it or not, people **will amass teachers to suit their own desires,** i.e. who will tell them either things they want to hear or things calculated to excite their fancy or

whet their religious curiosity, irrespective in both cases of their
truth. They are the victims, Paul adds with a flash of insight
into morbid religious psychology, of having **their ears itching**
(lit. 'being tickled in their hearing'). Such will be their appetite
for the sensational that **They will turn their ears** (lit. 'their 4
hearing': the same noun as in the participial clause preceding)
away from the truth, and instead will find satisfaction in
fables. For these, see on 1 Tim. i. 4: Paul is making a dark
allusion to the errorists' teachings, and warning Timothy that
the diseases of the future, which he will have to cope with, will
be only an intensification of the present symptoms.

The sectaries, Paul implies (as already indicated, they are
very much in his mind, although he is looking to the future
when Timothy will be in sole charge), are in effect besotted by
their fantastic speculations, which have had the effect of strong
drink upon them. In contrast to them (**You, however,** is 5
deliberately emphatic), Timothy **must keep** his **head in all
circumstances.** The imperative used (Gk. *nēphe*) literally
means 'Be sober', the idea being, not that the Christian minister
should be calm and unflurried, or even always alert, but that he
should steer clear of the heady wine of heretical teaching.

His fidelity may mean that, like Paul himself, he has to
endure hardship; if so, he must be ready for it. His duty,
after all, is to **carry out** his **job as an evangelist,** i.e. to preach
the gospel he has been entrusted with as opposed to alien fables.
In the first-century Church 'evangelist' had already become a
title of office (cf. Acts xxi. 8; Eph. iv. 11), connoting according
to some a missionary, according to others an official who exercised the functions of an apostle without being accorded the
title. In this context, however, the idea of a special office is
quite inappropriate, and the word has its basic meaning of one
who teaches and expounds the gospel.

In fine, he must **discharge** his **ministry to the full.** The
admonition has a special urgency because he is about to become
the Apostle's successor. This comes to light in the next verse,
the opening words of which, **For as for me** (Gk. *Egō gar*), are 6
extremely emphatic, balancing **You, however** (Gk. *Su de*) in 5.
Paul himself can do no more, for he is **already being poured
out on the altar.** As in Phil. ii. 17, when the possibility of

death presented itself to him although he was in fact expecting release, he uses the Greek verb *spendein* (='pour out as a libation'). His vivid metaphor is probably drawn from the Jewish liturgical custom of pouring out, as the preliminary ritual of the daily offering in the Temple and of certain other sacrifices, a drink-offering of wine at the foot of the altar (Ex. xxix. 40; Num. xxviii. 7—in the LXX the same verb and the related noun *spondē* are used). Paul foresees that he will have to die, and thinks of his death as a sacrifice; behind his language lies the Jewish belief (cf. 4 Macc. vi. 28 f.; xvii. 21 f.) in the atoning value of the martyr's death. He is conscious that he is dying in God's service, and that the sacrificial action is now commencing; his blood, which has not yet been shed but which before long will be shed, is, as it were, a libation offered to God.

There is a note of pride and confidence in the solemn, quasi-hieratic language he uses, and this is carried over into the following clause, **and the hour of my departure is at hand** (not, as many misleadingly translate, 'has arrived'). The metaphor changes, for **departure** (Gk. *analusis*) evokes the picture of a ship weighing anchor or of a soldier or traveller striking camp. The verb is used in late Greek as a euphemism for death, the suggestion being that the deceased is going home. For the cognate verb *analusai*, cf. Phil. i. 23. The fact that the same pair of metaphors are found in similar contexts in two consecutive chapters of Philippians has led some critics to infer that these latter must be the quarry from which the present passage is derived. There is really nothing remarkable in the coincidence, however, especially as (*a*) 'to depart' was a common enough metaphor for dying, and (*b*) Paul was not likely to abandon the splendid imagery about being poured out like a libation once he had invented it.

7   As he looks back, the Apostle recalls with gratitude, **I have fought in the noble match.** As in 1 Tim. vi. 12 (where see note), the picture is not of warfare, but of an athletic contest, probably a wrestling-match. There is no note of arrogance as if he personally had distinguished himself. It is the game or sport, viz. his apostolic vocation and ministry, which is **noble**. The emphasis is on the verb, which is in the perfect tense: 'I have fought in the contest to the very end'. The same athletic imagery

is carried over into the next clause, **I have completed the race,** although the sport is varied.

Finally he sums up his achievement, **I have been loyal to my trust.** These words are often translated, 'I have kept the faith', i.e. the apostolic gospel. This fits in well with the stress in these letters on preserving the apostolic faith intact (cf. 1 Tim. vi. 20; 2 Tim. i. 12; 14), and may be correct. The present context, however, is general rather than particular, and a reference to one specific aspect of Paul's duty (however important) as a Christian leader comes in awkwardly between clauses heavily charged with metaphor. The formula employed (Gk. *tēn pistin tērein*) is also a stock expression meaning 'keep faith', 'be loyal to one's oath', etc. It therefore seems preferable to understand Paul as protesting his consistent loyalty throughout his ministry to his divine mandate. There is possibly a passing allusion to the pledges by which athletes competing in public games bound themselves to observe the rules (see note on ii. 5).

This possibility is strengthened by the Apostle's confident claim, **Now** (lit. 'for the rest': after the three perfect tenses one might paraphrase, 'all that now remains is to receive my reward') **the garland of righteousness is in store for me.** His mind is still filled with the imagery of sport, and **the garland** recalls the coveted laurel wreath of the athletic champion (cf. 1 Cor. ix. 25). Paul is assured that it is already prepared for him in heaven. The verb **is in store** (Gk. *apokeitai*), as numerous inscriptions prove, was a technical term employed by Oriental sovereigns when decreeing rewards for loyal service.

It is more difficult to decide what exactly **the garland of righteousness** connotes. On the analogy of 'the crown of life' in Jas. i. 12 and Rev. ii. 10, some take the genitive as appositional and paraphrase 'the crown consisting in righteousness'. If they are correct, Paul is treating perfect righteousness as the crowning blessedness of those who have striven faithfully. Cf. Gal. v. 5, where righteousness is regarded as a future gift to be hoped for. This is possible, but is open to the objections (*a*) that Paul's normal teaching is that the believer is already justified, and (*b*) that it is not easy to see how righteousness can be already prepared in heaven. There is therefore more to be said for the alternative, and more widely accepted, view that **the garland**

of righteousness stands for the crown, presumably eternal life, which is the fitting recompense for an upright life. For this sense of **righteousness,** see note on iii. 16.

Paul will receive his crown **on that day,** i.e. not on the completion of his great race, when his life is finally sacrificed, but on the glorious day of Christ's appearing. And it will be handed to him by **the Lord, the righteous judge.** The qualification (cf. Rom. ii. 5 f.) perhaps voices his confidence in the justice of Christ's tribunal as opposed to that of his trial in the emperor's court, when the true righteousness of his achievement will be overlooked.

These two verses, with their exalted and confident note, have been widely acclaimed as revealing the genuine Paul; where Pauline authorship has been questioned, they have been accepted as Pauline by supporters of the 'fragments hypothesis'. Others have doubted whether the Apostle himself would have dwelt exclusively on his own achievement, without mention either of his own weakness or of God's grace. But this is a very carping criticism, which takes no account of the brevity of the passage or of Paul's very special circumstances.

As a matter of fact, he is not exclusively taken up with himself, for he hastens to add that Christ will **award** the crown **not only to me, but to all who have loved his manifestation.** Paul seems anxious to avoid the impression of claiming any special privilege for himself. His chief object is to encourage Timothy with the reminder that anyone who sincerely yearns for (**have loved** here means 'have longed for') Christ's coming again will be eligible for the same prize. Christians are people whose true country is heaven, and whose distinctive mark is that they are always looking forward to the Lord's return in glory (Phil. iii. 20: cf. Tit. ii. 13, and the formula 'Marana tha' in 1 Cor. xvi. 22). For **manifestation** (Gk. *epiphaneia*) with the meaning, of Christ's Parousia, see 1 above.

11. PERSONAL REQUESTS AND A WARNING.
iv. 9-18

(9) Do your best to come to me quickly. (10) For Demas, in his love for the present world, has deserted me and

has gone off to Thessalonica, Crescens to Gaul, and Titus to Dalmatia. (11) The only one with me is Luke. Get hold of Mark and bring him, for I find him a useful assistant. (12) Tychicus I have despatched to Ephesus. (13) When you come, bring the cloak I left with Carpus at Troas; also my books, especially the parchment ones. (14) The copper-smith Alexander has done me much harm; the Lord will pay him back as his actions deserve. (15) You too should be on your guard against him, for he violently opposed what I said. (16) At my first defence no one gave me his support, but they all deserted me; may it not be laid to their account. (17) But the Lord stood by me and gave me strength, so that through me the preaching of the gospel might be brought to completion, and the whole pagan world might hear it. So I was rescued from the lion's mouth. (18) The Lord will rescue me from every evil contrivance and bring me safe to his heavenly kingdom. To him be glory for ever and ever. Amen.

The letter, save for some personal commissions, has virtually reached its end. Paul now comes, in a section which many who question the authenticity of the letters as a whole feel obliged to admit to be composed of genuinely Pauline fragments (see Introduction, p. 29), to what may well have been one of his main motives in writing it, viz. his eager desire for Timothy to pay him a visit in his dangerous isolation. **Do your best,** he pleads, **to come to me quickly.** The language suggests that the journey has already been agreed in principle; the emphasis is on **quickly,** and the same insistence on speed comes out in **before winter** in 21 below.

Some commentators find this appendix full of inconsistencies with the rest of the letter. In it, according to them, Paul has been bidding Timothy an elaborate farewell, in anticipation of his approaching execution, and has been handing over to him responsibility for the Ephesian church in its violent crisis. Here we find him inciting his lieutenant to leave heresy-ridden Ephesus and join him. While hitherto his death seemed imminent, he now makes a request which, with all the delays of post and travel, will take several months to fulfil. But this picture

overlooks certain facts and distorts the situation. In the opening
lines of his letter (i. 4) Paul has hinted at his hopes of seeing
Timothy, and the common description of it as a farewell
message is not borne out by its contents. While he has the
gloomiest forebodings of his likely fate, his formal trial (see
below, pp. 217 f.) has not yet taken place, and 6-8 should not be
read as implying that he is expecting his execution immediately.
It might well be delayed beyond the three or four months required for the letter to reach Timothy and for the latter to come
to Rome. Further, the Apostle's instructions to Timothy, while
coloured by the present situation, are addressed to him personally and are intended to equip him for a lengthy ministry. There
is nothing in them to indicate that the crisis at Ephesus was such
as to demand his uninterrupted presence there.

Paul's yearning to see Timothy is heightened by his present
10 isolation. For example, **Demas . . . has deserted** him. We
know that Demas (his name is Greek, possibly a shortened form
of Demetrius) was with the Apostle as a 'fellow-worker' during
his first Roman imprisonment (Phm. 24; Col. iv. 14). The
motive for his defection was not, apparently, apostasy in the
strict sense, but **love for the present world.** This presumably
means desire for ease and comfort, coupled with a disinclination
to share Paul's privations. The contrast between him and the
unnamed true Christians mentioned in 8 is brought out forcibly
by the use of the same verb 'love' (Gk. *agapān*) in both verses,
as well as by the antithesis between **the present world** and
Christ's glorious **manifestation.**

The presence of this contrast makes it likely, as against some
versions of the 'fragments hypothesis', that whoever wrote this
verse wrote the preceding paragraph also. A further small
pointer in favour of authenticity is the fact that Demas is represented in a different, more unfavourable light than in Philemon
and Colossians. In reply to this critics of Pauline authorship
urge that Demas must have become a renegade after the
Apostle's death, and the pseudonymous author is here bringing
his character, as it were, up to date. This seems most implausible, since (*a*) the present notice does not speak of Demas's
apostasy, but only of Paul's disappointment with him at a particular juncture, and (*b*) if it was a case of a real lapse on his

part after the Apostle's death, its date and circumstances were probably common knowledge in Pauline circles, and an imitator would have needlessly imperilled the verisimilitude of his letter by antedating it.

Demas **has gone off to Thessalonica**: we can only guess his object, but possibly it was to carry on Christian work in a region where a more friendly reception could be expected. Similarly **Crescens** has gone **to Gaul, Titus to Dalmatia.** We know nothing of the former, except that a later tradition makes him one of the founders of the church of Vienne, near Lyons. Most MSS read *Galatian*, but a few good ones *Gallian*. Until the second century the correct Greek name for Gaul was *Galatia*, the Galatia in Asia Minor being denoted by a periphrasis (e.g. 'Galatia in Asia'). *Galatian* is undoubtedly the true reading here, but the presence of *Gallian* in some MSS indicates that the region referred to was widely taken to be Gaul; and such in fact was the exegesis of several of the fathers (Eusebius, Epiphanius, Theodoret, Theodore). On the whole, if we believe the letter to have been written from Rome, it seems sensible to follow them, especially in view of Crescens's Latin name and the ancient tradition about his work in Gaul. The verse thus becomes an important witness to the expansion of the Church westwards.

Paul seems saddened by the departure of Crescens, but makes no complaint. It is even possible that he had himself despatched him on some missionary task. The same probably applies to Titus, who would appear to have left Crete. **Dalmatia** is the southern portion of the imperial province of Illyricum, on the western shores of the Adriatic (the present Yugoslavia). We learn from Rom. xv. 19 that Paul's missionary activity had extended there. This notice, too, supports the authenticity of the Pastorals, for an imitator would not have been likely to represent Titus as active in two such widely separated fields. On the other hand, if Paul wintered at Nicopolis and Titus joined him there (cf. Tit. iii. 12), the latter may well have moved north on missionary work.

Apparently **The only one** who is left at Paul's side **is Luke.** 11 This does not imply, as is often assumed, that the Apostle is literally alone, but that Luke is the only member of his intimate circle who is with him. He had also been with Paul during his earlier imprisonment, earning the title 'my well loved doctor' (Col. iv. 14: cf. Phm. 24). The motive of his staying, affection apart, can only be guessed at; it may have been because Paul needed medical attention, or assistance of some special kind.

His mention of Luke for some reason reminds him of another friend, and so he bids Timothy **Get hold of Mark and bring him** . . . Long ago, when setting out on his second missionary tour, he had refused to take Mark with him; he had lost confidence in him because of his reluctance to share the difficulties of his earlier tour (Acts xv. 38). This distrust, however, was now a thing of the past, for we find Mark with Paul during his first Roman imprisonment and even being commended by him to the Colossian church (Col. iv. 10). We must suppose that at the moment of writing he is at some spot on Timothy's proposed route. Paul explains why he wants him: **I find him a useful assistant.** A literal translation would give, 'for he is useful to me for ministry' (Gk. *diakonian*), where the last word means either personal service to Paul or public ministering. Either interpretation is possible, but the tone of the passage favours the former.

Paul's almost parenthetical reference to Mark has interrupted his account of how short-handed he is. He concludes his story 12 by recording, **Tychicus I have despatched to Ephesus.** This is the trusted disciple, Asian by birth, who had accompanied him on his final visit to Jerusalem (Acts xx. 4), and who had conveyed his letters to the Colossians and the Ephesians (Col. iv. 7-9; Eph. vi. 21 f.). From the wording **to Ephesus** some exegetes have deduced that Timothy cannot himself have been at Ephesus at the time, but this is quite unwarranted. On the assumption that he was there, how otherwise should Paul have expressed himself? Much more plausible are the conjectures either that Tychicus was to be the bearer of the letter (in which case **I have despatched**—Gk. *apesteila*—should be taken as an epistolary aorist), or that Paul intended him to act as Timothy's deputy during the latter's visit to the capital. If this second suggestion is correct, it is perhaps surprising that Paul has not been more explicit about it, but the matter may have been agreed in advance between Timothy and himself.

At this point Paul inserts a personal commission—**When** 13 **you come, bring the cloak I left with Carpus at Troas; also my books, especially the parchment ones.** Its simple realism and naturalness are so striking that even critics who doubt the authenticity of the letter as a whole are often prepared to concede that it must come from the Apostle himself. It is extremely unlikely that an imitator in the ancient world would have thought of inventing banal details like these. Troas was a city which Paul had visited on several occasions (Acts xvi. 8; xx. 6; 2 Cor. ii. 12), and through which he may have passed recently as he was being escorted under arrest to Rome. He apparently envisages Timothy as travelling via Troas through Macedonia and so across the Adriatic to Brindisi.

We know nothing of Carpus, except that the Apostle seems to have lodged in his house. A **cloak** (Gk. *phailonēs*: from the Latin *paenula*) was a large, sleeveless outer garment, made of a single piece of heavy material, with a hole in the middle through which the head was passed, like a chasuble or a bicycle-cape. It was used for protection against cold and rain. Commentators have suggested that Paul felt the need of it because winter was at hand (cf. 21) and his dungeon was cold.

By **my books** (Gk. *biblia*) Paul probably means papyrus rolls. We have, of course, no means of knowing what they contained. The phrase **especially the parchment ones** (lit. 'the parchments') has caused much needless trouble. The noun, a Greek transliteration of the Latin *membrana*, denotes in the singular a piece of skin or vellum prepared for writing purposes. Parchment of this kind, though more expensive than papyrus, had several advantages over it, such as the ability to be used over again. Many, preferring the translation 'the parchments', take the reference to be to Paul's personal documents, e.g. his certificate of citizenship. But (*a*) we have no evidence that the word was so used, or indeed that such certificates took this form in antiquity; and (*b*) even if they did, it is improbable that Paul would have let them out of his keeping at such a critical juncture. Even more unlikely is the conjecture that the expression means 'my stock of parchment'. The wording, particularly the absence of 'and' with **especially,** indicates that the Apostle is speaking of a particular kind of books, and this is brought out in the translation. As a matter of fact there is abundant evidence that the Latin *membrana* was a technical term, from the first century B.C., for a codex, or leaf-book, made of parchment. Such codices were widely used for note-books, account-books, memoranda, first drafts of literary works, and other writings not meant for the public; it is also likely that they were being used for literary purposes in the first century A.D. We must therefore infer that Paul's reference is to paged note-books of parchment which for some reason he particularly valued. Again we are in the dark about their contents, although the guess that they consisted of O.T. proof-texts is one among other possibilities.

The mention of Troas, or some association of ideas which
14 we cannot now fathom, reminds Paul of **The copper-smith Alexander.** He recalls that he **has done me much harm,** adding, **the Lord will pay him back as his actions deserve.** These words echo the thought of Ps. xxviii. 4; lxii. 12, and we should note that, since the verb is in the future, not the optative, they express a prediction rather than an imprecation. As he had himself advised the Roman church (Rom. xii. 19), Paul is prepared to leave the punishment of those who injure him to God. Nevertheless, since Timothy (as we may reasonably infer) is likely to be coming across Alexander in the near future, he
15 thinks it prudent to warn him in advance: **You too should be on your guard against him, for he violently opposed what I said** (lit. 'our words').

We are as ignorant who this Alexander was as of the precise nature of his opposition to Paul. It is far-fetched to identify him with the Alexander who was pushed to the front and made a defensive speech on the occasion of the riot stirred up by the Ephesian silver-workers during Paul's earlier stay in the city (Acts xix. 33). Whatever theory is held of the origin of these letters, that happened many years previously, and Alexander was one of the commonest names. It is more likely, though still far from certain, that he was the Alexander mentioned in 1 Tim. i. 20 as having been placed under a ban, for it seems odd that Paul should have come into conflict with two bearers of that name connected with Ephesus in a relatively short space of time. Accepting this, some have argued that it proves the present letter to be earlier than 1 Timothy, since there is no hint of formal excommunication here. The inference, however, is by no means necessary. I Tim. i. 20 makes it plain that Alexander's 'handing over to Satan' was a temporary measure, with a view to his repentance and rehabilitation, and in any case the reference here is to a specific act of personal hostility rather than to doctrinal irregularity.

Whatever his identity, Alexander was a **copper-smith,** although the word so translated (Gk. *chalkeus*) did not always bear this specialized sense in later Greek and may here mean no more than metal-worker in general. It is not easy to decide whether his offence consisted in contradicting the Apostle's teaching or in some more personal form of opposition. Paul's use of the aorist suggests that he has a specific occasion in mind, and many have inferred from the context that it was at Rome, during his imprisonment, that Alexander displayed his ill-will. Some have suspected that he may even have appeared as a witness for the prosecution.

The Apostle's mind now reverts to his **first defence** (Gk. 16 *prōtē . . . apologia*), when, he recalls, **no one gave me his support, but they all deserted me.** The chief problem, on the assumption of Pauline authorship of the letter, is to determine the situation envisaged. The fathers and the majority of pre-nineteenth-century commentators identified it with that earlier trial (**first** in contrast to the present legal proceedings) in which Paul's Roman imprisonment recorded in Acts xxviii culminated, the result of which must have been his acquittal. 17 would fit very well with this exegesis, the preaching there referred to being on this hypothesis the vigorous missionary campaign he undertook between his release and his second Roman captivity. But it is hard to believe that the Apostle was left entirely in the lurch at that earlier trial, or that Timothy would need information about events which happened so long ago. In any case the impression left by the passage is that the **first defence** is an incident in Paul's recent experience. An alternative explanation advanced by supporters of the 'fragments hypothesis' is that the reference is to Paul's appearance at Caesarea before Felix (Acts xxiv. 1-23), or possibly before the Sanhedrin (*ib.* xxiii. 1-10); the fact that he had a vision of the Lord encouraging him (*ib.* xxiii. 11) is cited as confirming

the latter view. Again, however, in addition to the inherent
difficulties of the theory, the Acts narrative gives us no hint of
Paul's being abandoned by his friends and indicates that at the
latter trial Pharisaic legal experts spoke out in his favour, while
the atmosphere of the former was markedly less harsh than his
language here implies.

In view of this it is preferable, with most present-day supporters of authenticity, to locate Paul's **first defence** in his
present, i.e. second, Roman captivity, and to understand by it,
not the trial proper (which of course was to issue in his condemnation), but what in Roman legal parlance was called the
prima actio, i.e. the preliminary investigation. This had apparently gone favourably for the accused, at least to the extent of
the judge not being able to resolve his doubts and thus pro-
nouncing the verdict '*Non liquet*', or '*Amplius*'. When this
happened, Roman legal practice required that a further investigation, or *secunda actio*, should take place, and this might
involve a considerable delay. Timothy may well have been
ignorant of the turn events had taken and may have needed
bringing up to date. It remains a mystery why no member of
the Roman church, with which his relations had been so close,
gave him **his support** (Gk. *paregeneto*: the verb is technical for
a witness or advocate standing forward in court on a prisoner's
behalf). Perhaps nothing more than fear or weakness of character was the cause of their defection; but some have detected
a hint here of deep-rooted personal tensions, even divisions, in
the community.

Whatever the reason, there is no bitterness in Paul's heart
and he adds the prayer, **may it not be laid to their account**
(for the idea, cf. 1 Cor. xiii. 5; 2 Cor. v. 19). Their desertion,
17 however, served only to highlight the divine succour, for **the
Lord stood by** him **and gave** him **strength.** He thus received
an access of courage and boldness, and the providential purpose
of this, as he views the matter, was **so that through** him **the
preaching of the gospel might be brought to completion
and the whole pagan world might hear it.** At first sight
this reads as if Paul were alluding to a renewed and more extensive preaching mission undertaken after his acquittal, and
so seems to support the theory (see note on previous verse) that

his **first defence** was his earlier trial at the end of his first Roman captivity. But his acquittal has not yet been mentioned, and when it is it seems to be the result of this crowning preaching effort. We should therefore interpret the clause as describing, in somewhat hyperbolical terms, how Paul exploited the preliminary investigation in order to proclaim the gospel. He had always used his previous trials for this purpose, and he now regards his appearance before the august tribunal of the capital as setting a crown on his career as a preacher.

The words **through me** are emphatic, and the verb used (Gk. *plērophorein*: cf. 5 above) does not mean 'make fully known' (AV), but 'carry out fully', 'complete'. His idea seems to be that the proclamation of the gospel reached a specially glorious climax when it was made in the capital, and he exults that he has been singled out to be the instrument of this. His mention of **the whole pagan world** (lit. 'all the nations') carries on and develops the same thought. It is possible that his meaning is that, having preached the gospel publicly in Rome, he has in a very real sense discharged his commission to proclaim it 'to all the nations' (Rom. i. 5). It is much more likely, however, that he is alluding to the cosmopolitan audience assembled in the imperial court before whom he delivered his message.

The result was an unexpected, if temporary, success, for he **was rescued from the lion's mouth.** The last three words are a proverbial expression for extreme danger (cf. Ps. vii. 2; xxii. 21; xxxv. 17; Dan. vi. 20 ff.; etc.). There is therefore no need to see in them a reference to the amphitheatre, with which there was no question of Paul's being threatened, or to Nero, with whom the Greek fathers liked to identify the lion, or to Satan. Paul's meaning simply is that, through God's marvellous intervention and as a result of the strength given him to proclaim the gospel, the judge or judges failed to reach a decision at his initial examination, and he was therefore saved from imminent death.

Paul is aware that, despite his good fortune at this first hearing, further proceedings await him, and their outcome is not likely to be favourable. Nevertheless, taking his cue from his own words about being **rescued from the lion's mouth,**

18 he exclaims triumphantly, **The Lord will rescue me from every evil contrivance and bring me safe to** (lit. 'save me into') **his heavenly kingdom.** Only an insensitive literalism could read these words as implying an expectation of further acquittal, in contradiction to the pessimism of 6-8. Paul is thinking of spiritual rather than physical protection, and is affirming his confidence that no assault of his enemies will undermine his faith or his courage, or cause him to lapse into disastrous sin. This interpretation is confirmed by the facts (*a*) that the sentence sounds like an echo of 'deliver us from evil' of the Lord's Prayer, and (*b*) that the climax of his deliverance is to be admission to God's **heavenly kingdom.** Christ himself had promised that 'anyone who loses his life for my sake will save it' (Lk. ix. 24). In a sense God's kingdom is a present reality, having been inaugurated in the person of Christ, but for Paul it is also the goal to which Christians look forward at the consummation of the age (cf. 1 Thess. ii. 12; 2 Thess. i. 4 f.; Gal. v. 21; 1 Cor. vi. 9 f.; xv. 50; Eph. v. 5).

It is habitual with Paul, after dwelling on God's power and grace, to break into a doxology (cf. Rom. ix. 5; xi. 33-36; Gal. i. 5; Eph. iii. 21; Phil. iv. 20; 1 Tim. i. 17), and now the thought of the wonderful deliverance to which he looks forward naturally prompts the exclamation, **To him be glory for ever and ever. Amen.** The wording here is identical with that of Gal. i. 5. Many editors claim that there is a difference, in that the doxology there is addressed to God, whereas the present one is addressed to Christ. But there is little or nothing in the context to bear this out, and it is safest to assume that throughout **the Lord** denotes God.

12. FINAL GREETINGS. iv. 19-22

(19) Give my regards to Prisca and Aquila, and to Onesiphorus's household. (20) Erastus stayed behind at Corinth, and I left Trophimus ill at Miletus. (21) Do your best to come before winter. Eubulus sends you his regards, as do Pudens, Linus, Claudia, and all the brothers.

(22) The Lord be with your spirit.—Grace be with you.

In this concluding section the Apostle first sends his **regards** 19 (lit. 'Greet') to certain special friends. **Prisca and Aquila** were two of his oldest and most devoted helpers. The latter was a Jew from Pontus (now part of north-east Turkey, on the Black Sea), and the former (otherwise Priscilla) was his wife; she is named before him six times in the N.T., possibly because she belonged to a noble Roman family, or because she had a more forceful personality. We first hear of them in Acts xviii. 2, when they were settled in Corinth, having been obliged to leave Rome as a result of Claudius's edict expelling the Jews. Paul brought them to Ephesus with him (*ib.* xviii. 19), and in 1 Cor. xvi. 19 we find them joining him in sending greetings to the Corinthian church. Still later they seem to have been in Rome, for in Rom. xvi. 3 f. Paul sends his regards to them, remarking that they had 'risked their necks' for his life, and that not only he, but all the Gentile churches, owed them gratitude.

The Apostle also asks to be remembered to **Onesiphorus's household.** His tone and language suggest that Onesiphorus himself was already dead: see on i. 16.

Paul next mentions, apparently as pieces of information which will be new to Timothy, that **Erastus stayed behind at** 20 **Corinth,** and that he had **left Trophimus ill at Miletus.** We hear in Rom. xvi. 23 of an Erastus who was city treasurer (Gk. *oikonomos*) at Corinth, while according to Acts xix. 22 Paul sent an Erastus along with Timothy ahead of him to Macedonia. It is, of course, impossible to be sure that either or both of these can be identified with this Erastus, but if the latter it was natural that Paul should keep Timothy up to date about an old comrade. What seems to be implied is that he had dropped out of the party when Paul was being taken under escort to Rome.

Trophimus too was an old associate. A Gentile Christian from Ephesus, he had been with Paul on the closing stages of his third missionary tour when he went to Miletus (Acts xx. 4), and shortly afterwards was seen with him in Jerusalem (*ib.* xxi. 29). Some critics have found it incredible that Paul and Trophimus could have been together at Miletus twice over, but there is nothing really surprising in it since the town lay on the main road and Trophimus was an Ephesian. The verse creates great difficulties for the 'fragments hypothesis', for its supporters would like to place Trophimus's illness in the earlier (according to them, the only authenticated) visit to Miletus, but have to confess that, on this assumption, he must have made an astonishingly rapid recovery to be in Jerusalem so soon afterwards. If the letter is genuine, it is natural to suppose that Trophimus accompanied Paul after his arrest, but fell sick on the way and dropped out of the party at Miletus. According to some, this reference provides a further argument against Timothy's being at Ephesus when the letter was written. The cities are so close that, if he had been, he was bound to know that Trophimus had not gone on to Rome, and why.

One of Paul's reasons for dwelling on the absence of these two old friends is to impress upon Timothy his need for his presence and comfort. He adds a further reason for urgency
21 with the plea, **Do your best to come before winter.** During the winter months the Adriatic could be virtually closed to shipping, and Timothy's journey might be held up indefinitely if he delayed. The final trial is going to be held before very long, and unless he comes soon he may be too late. It is thus likely that the letter was written in the late summer or autumn. For the date, see Introduction, pp. 34-36.

Of the four names listed in the following sentence, **Eubulus sends his regards, as do Pudens, Linus, Claudia, and all the brethren,** all save the first are Latin, a point which confirms the view that the letter was written from Rome. The first is completely unknown, and while legend has busied itself with the second and fourth, the only one we can identify with any degree of plausibility is **Linus.** He is almost certainly the Linus who, according to tradition (Irenaeus, *Haer.* iii. 3. 3), succeeded Peter as leader, or bishop, of the Roman church, and who in consequence is still commemorated in the canon of the Roman mass. None of the four, it appears, belonged to the Apostle's intimate circle (see on 11 above). There is no real contradiction between this verse and Paul's complaint in 16 that everyone had deserted him at his preliminary hearing. None of those mentioned here was probably of sufficient standing at the time to appear in court on his behalf; in any case it was one thing to send messages like these in a letter, and quite another to take the drastic step of standing up in court to give testimony for Paul.

The first half of the closing greeting, **The Lord** (here prob- 22
ably = Christ) **be with your spirit,** is addressed to Timothy
personally, as the singular adjective (lit. 'thy') indicates. It
closely resembles Gal. vi. 18 and Phm. 25, with the difference
that in those passages the prayer runs, 'The grace of our [or
'the'] Lord Jesus Christ be with your spirit'. The second half,
as the plural pronoun **you** (Gk. *humōn*) shows, is addressed to
the Christian community in which Timothy finds himself as a
whole: see on 1 Tim. vi. 21. If 2 Timothy is the latest in date of
the three letters, as seems highly probable, these are the last
words written by the Apostle which have survived.

THE EPISTLE TO TITUS

1. GREETINGS. i. 1-4

(1) Paul, a servant of God, and also an apostle of Jesus Christ concerned with the faith of God's elect and with their knowledge of the truth which goes with godliness, (2) for the sake of the hope of eternal life, which God, who does not lie, promised from all eternity, (3) but at his own good time has made his word manifest in the preaching with which I have been entrusted in virtue of the commission of God our Saviour: (4) To Titus, my true child in the faith we share. Grace and peace from God the Father and Christ Jesus our Saviour.

Compact and intricately constructed, this opening salutation is more elaborate and solemn than those of 1 and 2 Timothy: for parallels, cf. Rom. i. 1-7; Gal. i. 1-5. Quietly but firmly it repeats Paul's claim to be an apostle, and also defines more completely than any other N.T. passage the scope and function of apostleship, as well as glancing briefly at the nature of his message. Addressed as it is to a personal friend (for Titus's relationship with Paul, see Introduction, pp. 1 f.), many have found it strangely formal, and have suggested that it betrays the hand of an imitator, who might suppose that a vigorous assertion of Paul's apostolic status would be expected. The stress, however, is less on Paul's own claims than on the purpose of his ministry. In any case the difficulty, if difficulty it is, disappears if we remember (see on 1 Tim. i. 1; 2 Tim. i. 1) that the letter was intended for the Cretan church generally, and that these clauses were probably drafted with it in view. The fact that several turns of phrase are used which differ from those normally employed by Paul has also been advanced as an argument against authenticity. Actually this points, if anywhere, in the opposite direction; an imitator would have taken pains to reproduce the idiom of the letters he knew.

1   Paul begins by calling himself **a servant of God,** a title he
uses only here. It is hard to fathom an imitator's motive for
substituting it for the more regular 'servant of Christ Jesus'
(e.g. Rom. i. 1). In the O.T. Moses, the prophets, and non-
Israelites who accomplish God's purposes for him are designated
'servants of God'. Paul is therefore indicating, not so much his
total subservience to God (cf. the less accurate rendering, 'God's
slave'), as the fact that he is in God's service, carrying out a
task for him. This service is more precisely defined in **and also
an apostle of Jesus Christ,** where **also** is not directly represented in the Greek, but is suggested by the particle *de.*
    The words which follow, **concerned with the faith of
God's elect and their knowledge of the truth which goes
with godliness,** are to be taken with **apostle;** they define two
of the chief ends the apostolic worker has before him. Because
the Greek preposition (*kata*) opening the clause can mean
'according to', 'conformably with', some interpret Paul as implying that as an apostle he preaches in accordance with the
orthodox faith. What he says, however, is **the faith of God's
elect,** and it is strange that he should claim that his message is
in some way regulated by other people's faith. The preposition
can equally mean 'in relation to', 'concerning', as in 2 Tim. i. 1,
and if so understood it points to the sphere in which Paul exer-
cises his apostleship and the ends he hopes to achieve by it.
    First, his ministry has to do **with the faith of God's elect,**
i.e. he preaches the gospel so that those whom God has chosen
and is calling may come to, or grow in, faith (cf. RSV's 'to
further the faith . . .'). 'Faith' is not used here with the objective sense of 'the faith', but with the subjective meaning usual
in Paul. The formula **God's elect** is used only by Paul in the
N.T. (Rom. viii. 33; Col. iii. 12: but cf. Mk. xiii. 27, etc.);
according to the O.T., Israel was God's chosen people, but
under the new dispensation the Church has inherited that role.
    Secondly, his ministry is **concerned with . . . their know-
ledge of the truth** (for the phrase, see note on 1 Tim. ii. 4:
also 2 Tim. ii. 25; iii. 7), for saving faith issues in a correct grasp
of the apostolic message. Here Paul glances by anticipation at
the errors of the Cretan false teachers, who he implies are
defective in **the truth.** The same innuendo is present in the

clause **which goes with godliness,** which qualifies **the truth.**
'Godliness' (Gk. *eusebeia*: cf. 1 Tim. vi. 3 and see note on *ib.* ii.
2) stands for the basically sound religious attitude and life in
which true Christianity, as opposed to the teaching the letter
is going to criticize, finds expression.

Paul adds a third characterization of his apostleship: it is **for 2
the sake of the hope of eternal life.** The opening preposition
is *epi* (lit. 'on', 'for'), and it is not immediately clear how the
clause should be connected with what precedes. It is not easy,
grammatically or from the point of view of sense, to link it with
godliness, still less with **faith** or **knowledge,** but it reads
excellently as a further qualification of **apostle of Jesus Christ,**
especially in view of its parallelism with the *kata* clause above.
If this is correct, Paul's point is not, as some suppose (translating *epi* by 'in'), that as an apostle he is sustained by **the
hope of eternal life;** this narrows the thought unduly, as well
as missing the parallelism with the preceding clause. Rather he
is suggesting that it is his function to promote that **hope.** For
epi with the dative meaning 'with a view to', 'for the sake of',
cf. Eph. ii. 10; 1 Thess. iv. 7; 2 Tim. ii. 14. Eternal life, or life of
the world to come, sums up the blessedness to which Christians
look forward: cf. iii. 7; 1 Tim. i. 16; vi. 12; 2 Tim. i. 10).

This hope, Paul continues, is solidly grounded. In the first
place, **God, who does not lie, promised** it **from all eternity.**
If we interpret the last three words (Gk. *pro chronōn aiōniōn*: lit.
'before eternal times') as in 2 Tim. i. 9 (cf. Eph. i. 4), his meaning is that the promise formed part of God's eternal purpose
ratified before the created order existed. This is the exegesis of
most of the fathers, and is probably correct, especially as we
have precisely the same contrast between God's pre-cosmic
resolve and its disclosure in Jesus Christ in 2 Tim. i. 9 f. Many
moderns, however, prefer to translate 'ages ago' (so, e.g. RSV),
arguing that the Apostle's reference must be to the O.T. promises which, as Christians read them, are the basis of the hope
of eternal life. In either case God's promise can be trusted,
since it is made by One **who does not lie** (Gk. *apseudēs*: only
in Wis. vii. 17 in the Bible). For God's fidelity to what he has
promised, cf. Rom. iii. 4; Heb. vi. 18.

In the second place, **at his own good time** God **has made 3**

his word manifest, i.e. has demonstrated the truth of his promise by actually revealing his purpose on the plane of history. The sentence involves an anacoluthon, for we should expect a second relative clause, 'but which . . .'. Paul is forced to change his construction, at the cost of stylistic elegance, because God does not, strictly speaking, make the Christian hope **manifest.** By **his word** Paul does not in the first instance mean the pre-existent Logos, as some have assumed; this seems ruled out by the defining phrase which follows. The expression stands rather for God's purpose (i.e. to give eternal life to the elect) as declared in the gospel (cf. Col. i. 25). For **at his own good time,** which draws a deliberate contrast with **from all eternity,** cf. 1 Tim. ii. 6; vi. 15: the idea that the saving events took place at a specially opportune moment fixed by God's eternal counsel is characteristically Pauline (Gal. iv. 4; Rom. v. 6; Eph. i. 10).

God's **word** cannot be manifested in the void; it has been given concrete expression **in the preaching with which I** (the pronoun is deliberately emphatic) **have been entrusted.** By **the preaching** Paul means, not his own act of proclaiming the gospel, but, more concretely (cf. 1 Cor. i. 21), the apostolic message. In stressing that he personally has been charged with it **in virtue of the commission of God our Saviour,** he is tacitly glancing at the teaching of the Cretan errorists, which cannot claim equivalent authority. The language closely resembles that of 1 Tim. i. 1, where see note on **God our Saviour.**

At last, after his laboured but deeply significant opening, 4 Paul reaches his correspondent: **To Titus, my true child in the faith we share** (lit. 'common faith'). For the expression **true,** i.e. legitimate, **child,** see on 1 Tim. i. 2. As in that passage, Paul is recalling that his disciple is one of his own converts (see Introduction, p. 1), and is tracing their special relationship to **the faith** he has been instrumental in planting in him. Some prefer the rendering, 'the common faith', i.e. the faith which all Christians share, and compare the use of 'common salvation' in Jud. 3; but this is to destroy the intimate, personal note which the present context requires.

The greeting **Grace and peace,** in distinction from 1 Tim.

i. 2 and 2 Tim. i. 2, conforms to the usage of the acknowledged Paulines. On the other hand, **from God the Father and Christ Jesus our Saviour** is an unusual formula. We expect 'our Lord', but Paul is perhaps moved to insert **our Saviour** so as to balance the description of God as 'our Saviour' in 3. It is significant that his two other applications of the title 'Saviour' to Christ in this letter (ii. 13; iii. 6) follow closely on verses in which he has designated God by it.

2. INSTRUCTIONS ABOUT CHURCH OFFICIALS.
i. 5-9

(5) The reason why I left you in Crete was that you might put right anything that was defective and appoint elders in every place as I directed, (6) men who are above reproach, husbands of one wife, with children who are believers and not chargeable with loose living or insubordinate. (7) For as God's steward the overseer ought to be above reproach—not self-willed, nor quick-tempered, nor a heavy drinker, nor violent, nor greedy for gain, (8) but hospitable, right-minded, temperate, just, devout, self-controlled, (9) holding fast to the trustworthy word which accords with the teaching, so that he may be able both to exhort on the basis of sound doctrine and to refute objectors.

Paul proceeds at once to remind Titus of the task he is expected to carry out as his deputy in Crete. Essentially it is to organize the Christian communities in the island by setting up responsible ministers and by combating false teaching. This section deals with the former half of his assignment, and presupposes an organization broadly similar to, though somewhat less advanced than, that envisaged in 1 Timothy. First, there is a board of elders, or presbyters, who as such, we may conjecture, are not strictly ministers, but form a court of notables with general responsibility for each community. Normally, but not necessarily, elderly men would be chosen; and some sort of

definite appointment, or ordination, is implied. See on 1 Tim. v.
17. Secondly, there are executive officers known as overseers
(in small communities there might be only one) who actually
performed the ministerial and pastoral duties required. These
are selected from the ranks of the elders, so that the two titles
are virtually, though not strictly, interchangeable. For overseers, see Introduction, pp. 13-16; also notes on 1 Tim. iii. 2; v.
17. The chief difference from 1 Timothy is that there is no mention of deacons in this letter. This is evidence of a less elaborate,
perhaps less advanced, stage of church organization, since
deacons were the assistants of the overseers. See on 1 Tim.
iii. 8.

5   **The reason,** Paul begins, **why I left you in Crete was
that you might put right anything that was defective.** We
need not suppose that he is giving Titus information for the
first time, still less that he is responding to a request from the
latter. As in 1 Timothy, he is recapitulating instructions already
given in outline, partly no doubt because it was useful to have
them down in black and white, but also for the benefit of Titus's
flock, to which he expected him to communicate the letter. The
context implies that Paul himself has conducted a mission in
Crete; the verb used (Gk. *apoleipein*) conveys the idea of leaving
behind. This cannot be identified with the brief stop recorded
in Acts xxvii, and it therefore seems best to date it after the first
Roman captivity (see Introduction, pp. 7-10).

While Christianity has caught on in a number of districts,
the church in Crete is evidently in a pretty disorganized state.
Hence, among the various things that need putting right, Paul
requests Titus to **appoint elders in every town as I directed.**
Whereas the existence of elders is assumed in 1 Timothy, here
they are being set up for the first time. For Paul's practice, cf.
Acts xiv. 23. Some, impressed by the fact that Paul nowhere
mentions elders by name in his acknowledged letters, prefer to
translate 'appoint elderly people to office', the office being
explained in 7 as that of overseer. But this places a quite unnecessary strain on the various contexts where 'elder' occurs in
the Pastorals as well as on the Greek: see on 1 Tim. v. 17. We
note that the entire responsibility for choosing the elders seems
to be left with Titus, an arrangement which was probably made

necessary by the immaturity of the Cretan communities. The **I** in **as I directed** is emphatic; the clause looks forward to the following verse and impresses on Titus that his elders must be the kind of men Paul approves.

The list of qualifications, positive and negative, closely resembles that prescribed for overseers in 1 Tim. iii. 2-7. The elders must be **men who are above reproach** (the singular 6 is used in the original, the construction being 'if anyone is above reproach . . .'). That is, they should offer no loophole for criticism: see on 1 Tim. iii. 2; 7. Further, they should be **husbands of one wife,** an expression which probably means (see on *ib*. iii. 2) 'married only once', being applicable to a man who has not married again after the death or divorce of his wife.

Their children, too, provide a useful test of their suitability. They should be **believers,** sharing their father's faith in Christ, and in their daily conduct they should **not** be **chargeable with loose living** (Gk. *asōtia*: the cognate adverb is used in Lk. xv. 13 of the prodigal son's 'riotous living') **or insubordinate.** For the latter quality, cf. 1 Tim. iii. 4; a man who cannot bring up his children to be well behaved must lack the combination of sympathy and firmness called for in an elder.

Paul supplies a reason for these qualifications, and adds a further string of them—**For as God's steward** (lit. 'manager 7 of a household or family') **the overseer ought to be above reproach.** Because of the abrupt introduction of **the overseer** (Gk. *episkopos*) in the singular in a discussion about elders, and also because Paul seems to be starting his list afresh and to be using material which reappears in 1 Tim. iii. 2-7, several editors bracket 7-9 as an interpolation. They belong to a period, they argue, when the monarchical, or one-man, episcopate had become established. The MSS, however, lend no support to this view, and the connexion of the verses with what precedes is confirmed by the repetition of **above reproach** from 6. Their affinity with 1 Tim. iii. 2-7 is easily explained if we assume that in both passages Paul is borrowing from a conventional list of qualities desirable in church officials. The singular **the overseer** is probably generic: see on 1 Tim. iii. 2. Paul's sudden switch from elders in general to overseers is natural enough if,

as argued in Introduction pp. 13 f. and in the notes on 1 Tim.
iii. 2; v. 17, the latter were executive officers who were chosen
from the ranks of the former.

A Christian congregation, Paul states in 1 Tim. iii. 15, is
'God's household'; hence an overseer is **God's steward.** The
emphasis is on **God's;** it is because he represents God that he
must be **above reproach.** Five vices which an overseer should
eschew are then added. He must not be **self-willed,** i.e. obstinate or arrogant, **nor quick-tempered,** since pastoral work
requires patience, **nor a heavy drinker, nor violent** (for both
these, see on 1 Tim. iii. 3), **nor greedy of gain.** This last
weakness (see *ibid.*) was a special temptation to ministers who
had to handle the church's offerings and charitable relief. The
complaint of many moderns that the standards implied in this
list, as in 1 Tim. iii. 2-7, are altogether too worldly and down-
to-earth betrays an extraordinary lack of realism. Paul is laying
his finger on temptations to which church officials must have
been exposed, by the very nature of their responsibilities and
work, just as much in the apostolic age as later.

To counterbalance the five vices he adds seven virtues
which are even closer to those listed in 1 Tim. iii. 2 (where see
8 notes). The overseer should be **hospitable,** because the responsibility of entertaining visitors on behalf of the community
devolves on him; **right-minded** (Gk. *philagathos:* lit. 'good-
loving'), an adjective connoting devotion to all that is best;
temperate, in contrast to the disorderly traits condemned in
the previous verse; **just, devout,** i.e. exemplary in his relations
both to his fellow-men and to God (cf. 1 Thess. ii. 10 for the
same two qualities juxtaposed); and **self-controlled,** a virtue
hailed in Gal. v. 23 as one of the fruits of the Spirit.

Finally, the Christian minister must have the right doctrinal
9 equipment **so that he may be able both to exhort on the
basis of sound doctrine and to refute objectors.** It is here,
in the twofold task of building up the faithful and eliminating
error, that, as an elder who is also an overseer, he faces his chief
challenge. (For **sound doctrine,** see note on 1 Tim. i. 10.) If
he is to cope with it successfully, he must be a person who
himself holds **fast to the trustworthy word which accords
with the teaching.** In other words, he must be heart and soul

devoted to, and by implication convinced of, the truth of the apostolic message—as one might paraphrase the complex phrase literally rendered in the last eight words. That message is **trustworthy,** i.e. can be relied upon, when it agrees with **the teaching,** i.e. faithfully reflects 'the pattern of teaching' (Rom. vi. 17) which the Apostle himself had delivered. There is a critical glance here at the false teaching which will shortly be denounced. It is also noticeable that the primitive kerygma is already beginning to take shape as a fixed body of orthodox doctrine (see notes on 1 Tim. vi. 20; 2 Tim. i. 13 f.; ii. 2).

3. THE FALSE TEACHERS. i. 10-16

(10) For there are plenty of insubordinate people, futile talkers and deceivers, especially those of the circumcision. (11) Their mouths ought to be stopped, for they are upsetting whole households by teaching things they should not for the sake of sordid profit. (12) One of themselves, a prophet of their own, remarked, 'Cretans are always liars, pernicious beasts, lazy bellies'. (13) This testimony is correct. Therefore reprove them sharply, so that they may be sound in the faith, (14) paying no heed to Jewish fables or to rules imposed by men who reject the faith. (15) All things are pure for the pure; but nothing is pure for those who are polluted and unbelieving, but both their intelligence and their conscience are polluted. (16) They profess to know God, but they deny him by their actions, being detestable, disobedient, and disqualified for any good action.

The mention of **objectors** in 9 provokes Paul to launch an attack on these misguided teachers, whom he accuses of being morally corrupt as well as of sowing error and confusion among the faithful. They are evidently Cretans by birth, and while their teaching has close points of contact with that of the Ephesian errorists (1 Tim. i. 3-11; vi. 3-10; 2 Tim. ii. 14-18), it has certain specifically local features, and its Jewish character

is more strongly stressed. Vigorous action is called for at once,
for the Cretan congregations have not had time to establish
themselves and they are already being undermined.

10   In **For there are plenty of insubordinate people,** Paul
is giving the reason why the appointment of overseers of the
character and equipment he has stipulated is urgently necessary.
Those who are described in 9 as setting themselves against the
apostolic doctrine are apparently all too numerous, and the adjective **insubordinate** vividly depicts their propensity to flout
the church authorities. They are also **futile talkers** (Gk.
mataiologoi: for the cognate noun, cf. 1 Tim. i. 6), using impressive language with little or no solid content of truth, and as
a result are **deceivers,** taking in their gullible auditors.

So far Paul's diatribe is too general to tell us anything concrete about their heresy, but now he adds that his strictures
apply **especially** to **those of the circumcision.** He uses this
expression in Rom. iv. 12 of Jews, but in Gal. ii. 12 and Col. iv.
11 (cf. also Acts x. 45; xi. 2) of Jewish Christians. The latter
must be the meaning here (cf. Moffatt's 'those who have come
over from Judaism'). So we can infer that, while the rebellious
group consisted of both Gentile and Jewish Christians, the
latter formed the more active element. There is evidence
(Josephus, *Antiq.* xvii. 327; *Bell. Iud.* ii. 103; Philo, *Leg. ad
Gaium* 282) that Jews were numerous in Crete.

11   Paul is for giving the dissidents short shrift—**Their mouths
ought to be stopped.** This translation (AV, RV), which goes
back to Tyndale, preserves the vigorous metaphor of the Greek
verb *epistomazein* (hapax), which means to put a muzzle, not
simply a bridle, on an animal's mouth. This is urgently necessary, **for they are upsetting** (the verb literally means 'are
turning upside down') **whole households by teaching
things they should not.** This cryptic phrase recalls 1 Tim. v.
13 ('saying things they ought not'), where (see note) scholars
have suspected a veiled reference to magic arts. There may be
such a reference here, but it is equally possible that Paul is
thinking of the errorists' false teaching.

What is at all events clear is that these dangerous people, as
the Apostle sees them, are not moved by the desire to serve
God or their fellow-men, but are out to make a **sordid profit.**

He accuses the Ephesian dissidents, too, of having mercenary motives (1 Tim. vi. 5), but in neither case indicates whether the expected **profit** was to come from fees, gifts, or some other source. This, again, is a touch of local colour, for the Cretans had a bad name in antiquity for avariciousness (e.g. Polybius, *Hist.* vi. 46. 3).

In so behaving, Paul continues, they are merely living up to the unflattering picture of the Cretan character which **One of 12 themselves, a prophet of their own,** has drawn. He then quotes the line (it is a hexameter in the original), **Cretans are always liars, pernicious beasts, idle bellies.** He quotes similar semi-proverbial tags from Menander in 1 Cor. xv. 33 and (if Acts xvii. 28 reports him accurately) from Aratus in his speech at Athens. The poet in question here is, according to Clement of Alexandria (*Strom.* i. 59. 2), Epimenides of Cnossus, in Crete, a religious teacher and wonder-worker of the sixth century B.C. The line has at times been attributed to Callimachus (*c.* 305–*c.* 240 B.C.) because the first half occurs in his *Hymn to Zeus*, but it is probable that he was citing a phrase which was already proverbial by his time. Paul calls Epimenides **a prophet,** thus emphasizing the authority of his judgment; but it is interesting to note that Plato, Aristotle, Cicero, and others speak of him as an inspired, prophetic man.

Epimenides, it seems, stigmatized the Cretans as **always liars** because they claimed to have the tomb of Zeus on their island. This was a flagrant imposture, for Zeus was the chief of the gods and, in the view of his devotees, very much alive. The saying, however, became a popular slogan, a jibe giving expression to the shocking reputation for mendacity which the Cretans had in the ancient world. So prevalent was this that the verb 'to Cretize' (Gk. *krētizein*) was a slang word for lying or cheating. Commentators have questioned whether Paul would have written so tactlessly, not to say rudely, in a real letter intended to be read out to a Cretan audience (as iii. 15 suggests this letter was). But the Apostle is alarmed and angry at the sectaries' conduct, and in such a mood people do not always mince their words. In any case he would scarcely have expected the true Christians in the Cretan communities to suffer from nationalist touchiness.

No deep innuendoes need be read out of **pernicious beasts, idle bellies.** Without pressing details (it is, after all, a quotation), Paul regards the line as expressing, with rough and ready accuracy, the untruthfulness, boorishness, and greed of the dis-
13 sident group in Crete. **This testimony,** he adds, **is correct.** The tone of the sentence suggests that he has had bitter personal experience on the island. So Titus is to **reprove them,** i.e. the dissidents, not the Cretans generally, **sharply.** His severity, however, is not to be negative, but should aim at ensuring **that they may be sound in the faith.** For the notion, characteristic of the Pastorals, that doctrinal orthodoxy is 'healthy', while error is a form of disease, see on 1 Tim. i. 10; vi. 4.
14   In the words which follow, **paying no heed to Jewish fables or to rules imposed by men who reject the truth,** Paul at last throws some light on the content of the errorists' teaching. First, it consists of **Jewish fables** (lit. 'myths'), which are probably much the same as the 'interminable fables' attacked in 1 Tim. i. 4 (where see note), although here they are specifically designated **Jewish.** Secondly, the errorists are demanding the observance of regulations which the Apostle dismisses as **rules imposed by men.** These cannot be, as some of the fathers thought, the prescriptions of the Mosaic Law, which for Paul had a divine origin. Nor can the reference be to the 'tradition of the elders', with its distinction between clean and unclean meats, etc., since he adds that the authors of these rules are **men who reject the truth.** It is fairly certain that what he has in mind are Jewish-Gnostic ascetic requirements (e.g. the banning of marriage and proscription of certain foods) such as are implied in 1 Tim. iv. 3-6. It is noticeable that he describes the similar ascetic tendencies of the Colossian heresy as 'commandments of men' (Col ii. 21 f.).
     This interpretation is confirmed by the comment which Paul characteristically interjects in criticism of the errorists' attitude:
15 **All things are pure for the pure.** The sentence has the ring of a proverb, and the principle it embodies was enunciated by Jesus himself when dealing with Jewish food laws or Pharisaic requirements of ritual purity (cf. Mk. vii. 15; Mt. xv. 10 f.). In Rom. xiv Paul had at length expounded the view that what makes a particular article of diet 'unclean' cannot be anything

in the article itself, but solely the eater's interior attitude. So here he argues that ritual purity is at best artificial; if a man's moral condition is healthy, the distinction of 'clean' and 'unclean' should have no meaning for him. It should be observed that the Apostle is playing on the ritual and moral sense of **pure.** When modern people quote the apothegm, they usually take the word exclusively in the moral sense and deduce that the man who is himself pure need not fear contamination by anything impure. This is a dangerous half-truth, and far from Paul's meaning.

Paul then carries the attack into his adversaries' country, restating his maxim in the negative form: **nothing is pure,** in the ritual or any other sense, **for those who,** so far from being morally clean in their interior disposition, **are polluted and unbelieving.** The last words are of course aimed at the false teachers, although they have a general bearing too. The trouble is that **both their intelligence and their conscience are polluted,** and they have lost the capacity to distinguish good and evil. For this kind of corruption, cf. 1 Tim. iv. 2; vi. 5; 2 Tim. iii. 8.

Paul brings his diatribe to a close with the damning indictment, **They profess to know God, but they deny him by their actions.** As the false teaching envisaged has Gnostic traits, there is almost certainly an allusion here to the higher, more esoteric knowledge of God which the sectaries claimed. Against this it has been pointed out that it was the special boast of the Jews that, unlike the pagan world, they knew God as he had revealed himself to men (cf. Gal. iv. 8; 1 Thess. iv. 5; 2 Thess. i. 8). As the Cretan heretics were Judaizers, it is therefore possible that the Apostle is criticizing the complacent assumption that they were an élite possessing a privileged knowledge of God. These two interpretations, however, are in no way mutually contradictory, especially as it is clear that Jewish and Gnostic elements were fused in the heresy.

So far from being justified in their boast, Paul argues, **they deny him by their actions,** i.e. their conduct eloquently refutes it. Just as faith without works is dead, so the quality of a man's life is the decisive test of his knowledge of God (1 Jn. ii. 4). It is not clear whether Paul is thinking of the sectaries'

loose behaviour in general, or more specifically of ascetic practices which amounted to a denial of the goodness of God's
creation. The reference to human regulations in 14 and the
parallel in 1 Tim. iv. 4 make the latter more probable.

In fact, so far from having any special insight into God's
nature, the sectaries are **detestable, disobedient, and disqualified for any good action.** The first adjective is a strong
one, coming from a noun (Gk. *bdelugma* = 'abomination': cf.
Lk. xvi. 15) which denotes what causes horror and disgust
to God. The second recalls **insubordinate** in 10 and suggests
the sectaries' refusal to accept God's word as expounded by
Paul and his associates. As a result, while the 'man of God'
is described in 2 Tim. iii. 17 as 'completely equipped for
every good work', they are fit for nothing in the Christian
community.

4. ADVICE FOR DIFFERENT CATEGORIES
OF CHRISTIANS. ii. 1-10

**(1) As for you, what you teach should be in keeping with
sound doctrine—(2) that the older men should be sober,
dignified, circumspect, sound in faith, in love, and in
steadfastness. (3) The older women, similarly, should be
reverent in demeanour, no gossips nor enslaved to excessive wine, teaching what is good, (4) so that they may
train the younger women to be devoted to their husbands
and children, (5) circumspect, chaste, domestic, kind,
submissive to their husbands, so that God's word may
suffer no scandal. (6) Urge the younger men similarly to
exercise self-control (7) at all points, showing yourself a
model of good conduct, in your teaching showing integrity, gravity, (8) and sound speech to which no exception can be taken, so that any opponent may be put to
shame since he has nothing discreditable to say about us.
(9) Slaves are to be submissive to their masters in all
respects, and to give them satisfaction without answering
back (10) or pilfering, but displaying all-round honest**

trustworthiness, so that they may in all respects embellish the teaching of God our Saviour.

Having provided for the appointment of proper ministers and put Titus on his guard against the subversive sectaries, Paul turns to the pastoral oversight of the Cretan communities themselves. As in the corresponding passages in Col. iii. 18-iv. 1 and Eph. v. 22-vi. 9, he breaks them up into groups, although the division here is based on age, sex, and status rather than family. As elsewhere, he seems to be adapting currently accepted lists of admirable qualities. In requiring each of the groups to observe a high standard of conduct, he is concerned as much for the good reputation of the church as for the furtherance of the gospel in an environment of doubtful morality.

His opening words, **As for you** (Gk. *Su de*: lit. 'But you'), 1 are emphatic. The false teachers castigated in the previous section have been leading people astray; Titus's line must be precisely the opposite. So his teaching **should be in harmony with sound doctrine,** in contrast to the sectaries' 'fables' and man-made regulations. For **sound doctrine,** cf. i. 9: also see note on 1 Tim. i. 10. Paul's advice is going to be strictly practical, but he does not conceal his conviction that the basis of good behaviour is correct belief.

First, he deals with the senior section of the community. Titus's advice should be **that the older men should be** 2 **sober, dignified, circumspect.** There is no imperative verb in the Greek, which has an accusative and infinitive construction in 2-5. This is probably dependent on the unexpressed command implied in 'speak' or 'teach' in 1. For **sober** (Gk. *nēphalios*), see on 1 Tim. iii. 2; it refers here to general restraint in indulging desires. For **dignified** (Gk. *semnos*) and **circumspect** (Gk. *sōphrōn*), see on 1 Tim. ii. 2; iii. 8; 11 and 1 Tim. ii. 9; iii. 2; Tit. i. 8 respectively.

Even a pagan code might urge gravity of deportment and interior self-mastery on the elderly; now Paul adds a specifically Christian touch by requiring them to be **sound in faith, in love, and in steadfastness.** For the triad cf. 1 Tim. vi. 11 (where see note) and 2 Tim. iii. 10. There is nothing un-Pauline

about it, as its occurrence in 1 Thess. i. 3 proves. The Apostle
may have singled out **steadfastness** either because it was a
peculiarly suitable quality in men facing the difficulties and
discouragements of age, or, more probably, because it was
particularly necessary in churches troubled as the Cretan ones
were and it was therefore fitting that the elderly should set an
example of it. In **sound in faith** (cf. i. 13: for the opposite,
cf. 1 Tim. vi. 4 and Rom. xiv. 1—'sick in faith') he is not
referring to correctness of doctrine, **faith** being equivalent
to 'the faith', but to the old men's subjective attitude; this
is borne out by the subjective connotation of the two other
nouns.

3   Paul's advice for **the older women** in part recalls that given
for deaconesses in 1 Tim. iii. 11. They are to be **reverent in
demeanour,** where the noun denotes comportment or bearing
viewed as the expression of one's interior character or disposition, while the adjective suggests the behaviour of a good
priestess carrying out the duties of her office. The two further
requirements, **no gossips nor enslaved to excessive wine**
(cf. 1 Tim. iii. 11), fasten realistically on weaknesses to which
elderly ladies (and men) are in every age prone unless they are
careful. The critics who object that the Apostle could not have
included such qualities in his list have a rosier view of human
nature and the first-century Church than he had and should
re-read 1 Corinthians with their eyes open.

More positively, the role of these elderly women is summed
up in the adjective **teaching what is good** (Gk. *kalodidaska-
lous*). This does not envisage formal instruction (this is forbidden in 1 Tim. ii. 12, and there is no reason why Paul should
take a different line in Crete), but rather the advice and encouragement they can give privately, by word and example.
This enables Paul to make his transition to the junior section of
4 the community. The older women are to set a high standard **so
that they may train the younger women to be devoted to
their husbands and children.** . . . In antiquity, among pagans
and Jews alike, these twin virtues were regarded as the glory of
young womanhood, and are frequently mentioned on funerary
inscription. Cf. the oft-quoted epitaph, from Hadrian's time, on
a grave-stone found at Pergamum, in Mysia: 'Julius Bassus . . .

to his most sweet wife, devoted to her husband and devoted to her children'.

Further, the young wives should be encouraged to be **cir-**5 **cumspect** (in the sense of self-controlled: a quality constantly referred to in the Pastorals), **chaste, domestic, kind, submissive to their husbands.** The first two adjectives stress the propriety of their sex life. The word translated **domestic** (Gk. *oikourgos*) literally means 'working at home'. Some MSS give *oikourous*, i.e. 'home-keeping', but *oikourgos* is the rarer word, and it is also better supported; the difference of meaning is in any case slight. The ancients, both Jews and Gentiles, esteemed the stay-at-home wife, and Paul had special reasons for preferring her not to gad about (see on 1 Tim. v. 13).

Some prefer to render the original of **kind** (Gk. *agathous*) by 'good' and to treat it as an adjective qualifying the preceding word taken substantively ('good house-workers'). This, however, destroys the rhythm of the sentence, and is in any case unnecessary, since *agathos* can bear the sense of 'kindly', 'benevolent' (cf. Mt. xx. 15; Mk. x. 17 f.; 1 Pet. ii. 18). Paul's point is that, while the young housewife should be occupied with her household tasks, she should not forget the kindly sympathy she owes to her family and her domestic helps.

For Paul's views on the duty of wives to be **submissive to their husbands,** cf. 1 Cor. xiv. 35; Eph. v. 22; Col. iii. 18. As he held them consistently throughout his life and as they coincided with contemporary ideas in both the Jewish and the pagan worlds, there is no need to treat the present passage (as some editors do) as evidence for the greater freedom for their sex which, under the liberating influence of Christian teaching, women in the early Church were claiming. For such claims, see on 1 Tim. ii. 11.

Paul has a special reason for demanding a high standard in this and other respects from young women, viz. **so that God's word may suffer no scandal.** The outside world will immediately blame the gospel itself for any conduct shocking to contemporary susceptibilities on the part of the faithful. The language, like that of 1 Tim. vi. 1, echoes LXX Is. lii. 5. For the Apostle's concern for the external reputation of the Church, see on 1 Tim. iii. 7.

6   Paul's tone becomes sharper when he comes to **the younger men. Urge** them, he requests Titus, using the imperative for the first time, **to exercise self-control.** Once again we have this quality which is so much prized in the Pastorals (see on 1 Tim. ii. 9), for the verb used here (Gk. *sōphronizein*) is related to the adjective (Gk. *sōphrōn*) translated 'circumspect' in 2 and
7 5. It is not wholly clear whether the next three words, **at all points,** are to be taken with this infinitive or with the phrase which follows. Either is grammatically possible, but the former seems preferable (*a*) because they then indicate the wide scope of the **self-control** demanded, and (*b*) because **yourself** in the following clause then recovers its true emphasis.

   Paul knows that preaching by itself will be of little use; Titus will be most likely to achieve his effect if he shows himself **a model of good conduct.** The accent here, as already hinted, is strongly on **yourself;** Titus is still relatively young, and so his manner of conducting himself should carry weight with young men. For the Apostle's insistence that the Christian leader should himself set an example, see on 1 Tim. iv. 12.

   This mention of Titus as **a model of good conduct** causes Paul to digress from his main theme, viz. the advice his disciple should give to his flock, and expatiate briefly on the wider example he should himself set. Thus **in** his **teaching** he should
8 reveal **integrity, gravity, and sound speech to which no exception can be taken.** Many interpret **teaching** objectively, of the content of Titus's message; but since this is covered by **sound speech,** it is preferable to take it actively as referring to his activities as a teacher (for this use of Gk. *didaskalia,* cf. Rom. xii. 7; 1 Tim. iv. 13; 2 Tim. iii. 16). By **integrity** Paul means purity of motive, the absence of any desire for gain; while **gravity** denotes a high moral tone and serious manner: for the word, see on 1 Tim. ii. 2. The substance of his message is comprised in **sound speech to which no exception can be taken,** where **sound** bears the sense usual in the Pastorals of 'agreeable to the apostolic gospel'.

   The motive behind these prescriptions is a good, practical one, viz. **so that any opponent may be put to shame since he has nothing discreditable to say about us.** Paul's description of the adversary (lit. 'anyone on the opposite side') is

deliberately vague; it can, and no doubt does, include pagan
critics of Christianity, but its primary reference is to ill-
disposed individuals in the community itself who, Titus may
be sure, are eagerly waiting for the least opportunity to catch
him out. His best defence will be the complete integrity of his
preaching in manner as in matter.

Returning to his theme, Paul stresses that slaves, too, have a
great spiritual responsibility; they should **be submissive to** 9
their masters in all respects. His teaching resembles that
given in 1 Tim. vi. 1, where see note. Presumably he has
Christian households in view, and is not prescribing blind
obedience to orders of doubtful morality. Editors are divided
whether **in all respects** should be construed with **be submissive,** as above, or with **give them satisfaction.** Since
there is no **and** between the two phrases in the Greek, either is
grammatically possible, and both yield acceptable meanings;
the translation given perhaps makes the words balance better
with **in all respects** in 10.

Not only are slaves to be **submissive,** i.e. obedient, to their
masters, but they should also **give them satisfaction without** 10
answering back or pilfering. They should carry out their
duties with a positive desire to please, thinking of their status
as Christians rather than slaves. The verb rendered 'pilfer' (Gk.
nosphizesthai) literally means 'to separate', or 'to lay on one
side', and so becomes a euphemism for petty theft or the
quiet misappropriation of 'perks'. So far from descending to
that level, the Christian slave should strive to exhibit **all-round
honest trustworthiness.**

At the end Paul gives the profoundly Christian reason why
slaves should maintain this high standard of conduct. It is a
reason which shows that they share, equally with their masters,
in the supreme task of honouring God in their lives to which
the whole Church is dedicated—**so that they may in all
respects embellish the teaching of God our Saviour.** In
other words, their dutiful behaviour will help to make the
Christian message appear attractive and noble, and so will com-
mend it to the outside world. For **God our Saviour** (characteristic of the Pastorals), see note on 1 Tim. i. 1.

5. THE MOTIVE FOR CHRISTIAN LIVING.
ii. 11-15

(11) For the grace of God has been manifested for the salvation of all men, (12) training us to renounce irreligion and worldly desires, and to live soberly, uprightly and religiously in the present age, (13) while we look forward to our blessed hope and the manifestation of the glory of the great God and our Saviour Christ Jesus, (14) who gave himself for us to ransom us from all iniquity and to purify for himself a people of his own, zealous for good works. (15) These are the things you should teach; exhort and reprove with full authority. No one must underrate you.

The previous paragraph has been a challenge to the several groups in the Cretan churches to accept the specifically Christian pattern of behaviour. Its prescriptions may at first sight seem prosaically humdrum and conventional, but Paul now eloquently reminds Titus that they have their basis in the gospel itself. It was precisely in order to raise men to a higher quality of life that God intervened in history in the incarnation.

11   The opening particle **For** indicates that he is about to state the theological ground of the advice just given. This is that **the grace of God has been manifested for the salvation of all men.** As normally in Paul, **grace** stands for God's free favour, the spontaneous goodness by which he intervenes to help and deliver men. God's **grace** is something of which, apart from revelation, men could never have formed any notion; but now it **has been manifested.** The underlying metaphor is that of the sudden breaking out of light, as at the dawn. The reference (cf. iii. 4; 2 Tim. i. 10) is, not simply to the nativity, but to the whole earthly career of Jesus Christ, including his death and resurrection. In this we have a marvellous disclosure of the divine love and favour. And this disclosure has been made **for the salvation of all men.** Again, as in 1 Tim. ii. 4 (where see note), we have the thought of the universality of salvation, but it is possible that the Apostle is also implying that God's grace

244

extends to all classes of mankind, including the slaves mentioned above.

The main emphasis of the sentence falls on the next clause, **training us to renounce irreligion and worldly desires,** 12 **and to live soberly, uprightly and religiously in the present age.** Paul is stressing what we may call the educative or disciplinary aspect of God's saving activity. Negatively, Christians under the guidance of grace (it is almost personified) have made a clean break with false conceptions of God (**irreligion**), and also with purely this-world inclinations. The decisiveness of this rupture with the past is brought out in the original by the word rendered **renounce,** which is in the aorist participle indicating a once-for-all act. It is not far-fetched to see in it a reference to their baptism, when they turned their back on their pagan life and accepted Christ.

More positively, they have the opportunity of learning, under the influence of divine grace, to conduct their lives in a fully Christian fashion. The three adverbs Paul uses pin-point successively the Christian's relation to himself, to his fellow-men, and to God. As so often in the Pastorals, the language and imagery reflect those of contemporary Hellenistic moral idealism, and this comes out particularly in the conception of the educative function of grace, which some find akin to the Greek notion of *paideia* and so reject as un-Pauline. It is dangerous, however, to notice only the resemblances and not the differences. Whereas in Greek ethics the driving force was the individual's reason and will, here it is God's free grace. Further, it is not true that for Paul in his acknowledged letters grace consists exclusively 'in a single overwhelming gift which is received in a moment in the act of faith' (E. F. Scott). In numerous passages (e.g. Rom. vi. 14-24) he indicates his belief that God's helping hand is with the Christian after his conversion bringing the qualities of the new life in Christ to flower.

Paul is speaking of life **in the present age.** For the expression cf. 1 Tim. vi. 17: also Rom. xii. 2; 1 Cor. ii. 6; 2 Cor. iv. 4. It enshrines the Jewish-Christian belief that the present order is under the dominion of evil powers, which will be overthrown when God establishes his kingdom. Hence, while we live in the world, we Christians **look forward to our blessed hope and** 13

the manifestation of the glory of the great God and our Saviour Christ Jesus. The sentence (it is perhaps an excerpt from a Christian hymn or liturgical formula) contains a glowing expression of the eschatological expectation of the primitive Church, which impatiently awaited the Lord's second coming at the right hand of God. For the writer this expectation is still vivid and real, and this confirms the early date of the letter.

As so often in Paul (Rom. viii. 24; Gal. v. 5; Col. i. 5), **hope** stands for the object hoped for. Despite the particle **and,** the phrase which follows stands virtually in apposition to it and defines in what the Christian hope consists (for the construction, cf., e.g., Acts xxiii. 6). This is nothing less than the **manifestation,** or supernatural revelation (for the term, see on 1 Tim. vi, 14), of Christ on the last day, when, according to the prophecy in Mt. xvi. 27, 'the Son of Man will come in the glory of his Father with his angels'. In that passage as in this **glory** denotes the awful radiance in which God dwells.

It is extremely difficult to decide whether the second half of the verse should be translated (*a*) as above, or (*b*) as '. . . our great God and Saviour, Christ Jesus'. The following are points in favour of the latter (RV, RSV, NEB): (i) the absence in the Greek of the definite article before **Saviour**; (ii) the fact that it has the support of the Greek fathers; (iii) the lack of parallels elsewhere in the N.T. to the description of God as 'great' and to an 'appearing' of God; (iv) the frequent occurrence in pagan texts of 'God and Saviour' as a formula applicable to a single personage. If the last point is accepted, the words may be an affirmation of the Christian claim for Christ as against the imperial cult.

Some of these considerations are less weighty than others. For example, the absence of the article cannot count as decisive, for 'Saviour' tended to be anarthrous (cf. 1 Tim. i. 1), and in any case the correct use of the article was breaking down in late Greek. The fathers, again, were influenced in part by theological motives in choosing (*b*); and as against them the early versions, which are older, support (*a*). If (*a*) is accepted, we need not suppose that Paul is speaking of two distinct 'manifestations', one of God and one of Christ; **the glory of the great God** describes the divine radiance with which Christ is invested at his coming. The considerations which, in the present editor's view, swing the balance in favour of (*a*) are (i) that Paul nowhere else, either in these or in his other letters, explicitly describes Christ as God (Rom. ix. 5 may be an exception); (ii) while he regularly speaks of 'God' and 'Christ' side by side (e.g. 1 Tim. i. 1; v. 21; vi. 13; 2 Tim. i. 1; iv. 1; Tit. i. 4; iii. 4-6), they are invariably distinguished as two persons; (iii) the Christology of the Pastorals seems to suggest that Christ's relation to God is one of dependence, and their stress on the uniqueness of God (e.g. 1 Tim. vi. 16) also militates against (*b*).

Having hailed Christ as **our Saviour,** Paul proceeds to define his work: **who gave himself for us to ransom us from all 14 iniquity and to purify for himself a people of his own, zealous for good works.** The opening words recall Gal. i. 4; 1 Tim. ii. 6 (where see note). The interpretation of Christ's work in terms of ransom goes back to his own statement in Mk. x. 45. The language used is reminiscent of LXX Ps. cxxix. 8 ('for he will ransom Israel from all his iniquities').

As the Lord had promised in Ezek. xxxvii. 23, deliverance from sin is followed by cleansing, and so Paul passes to this aspect of Christ's saving work. The basic idea is the O.T. one of the cleansing of the people by Moses with the blood of the covenant (Ex. xxiv. 8), and the suggestion is that Christ's blood cleanses his people from sin (cf. 1 Jn. i. 7). The result is that Christians become Christ's own people, his peculiar possession. The words translated **a people of his own** (Gk. *laos periousios*) are used in LXX Ex. xix. 5; xxiii. 22; Dt. vii. 6; xiv. 2; xxvi. 18, where they denote the people whom God has redeemed and who are therefore 'peculiar' to him. For the conception of the Church as the new Israel, cf. Gal. vi. 16; Phil. iii. 3; 1 Pet. ii. 9 f. Because they have been thus set apart, it is fitting that Christians should be **zealous for good works.** For the interest in practical Christianity in the Pastorals, see on 1 Tim. ii. 10.

The closing words, **These are the things you should 15 teach,** look back to ii. 1, using the same imperative verb; the practical advice Titus is going to give should be set in its proper doctrinal framework. He is not only to declare this message, but is to **exhort** people to accept it and **reprove** them for any slackness in doing so. He can act **with full authority,** for his message is the authentic apostolic one and his commission comes from God. **No one** is to **underrate** him. Paul gives almost exactly the same advice to Timothy in 1 Tim. iv. 12, making special reference to his youth. In this case, as Calvin acutely observes, the remark is intended more for the Cretan churches than for Titus himself. Paul desires to impress on them the authority of his delegate.

6. THE SOCIAL CHALLENGE TO CHRISTIANS.
iii. 1-11

(1) Remind them to be submissive to rulers and authorities, to show them obedience, to be ready for any honourable task, (2) to speak evil of no one, not to be quarrelsome but conciliatory, showing perfect gentleness towards all men. (3) For we ourselves were at one time foolish, disobedient, misguided, enslaved to all sorts of lusts and pleasures, passing the time in malice and envy, detestable and loathing one another. (4) But when the goodness and generosity of God our Saviour was manifested, (5) he saved us, not in recognition of any deeds we had ourselves accomplished in righteousness, but in virtue of his own compassion, by means of the washing of rebirth and renewal through the Holy Spirit, (6) which he poured out on us richly through Jesus Christ our Saviour, (7) so that, having been justified by his grace, we might in hope become heirs of eternal life. (8) This is a trustworthy saying, and I wish you to insist on these things, so that those who have believed in God may be careful to busy themselves with good works. These are admirable truths and useful for people. (9) But keep clear of foolish speculations, genealogies, dissension, and controversies about the law; for they are profitless and futile. (10) As for a separatist, have nothing to do with him after giving him a first and second warning, (11) for you can rest assured that a man like that is perverted and self-condemned in his sin.

So far Paul has been concerned with the internal arrangements of the Cretan churches and the duties of their members
to one another. Now he comments briefly on their relationship
to the civil power and their pagan environment generally. The
point he makes is that they should be models of good citizenship
precisely because the new, supernatural life of the Spirit bestowed by baptism finds expression in such an attitude.

Titus is to **Remind** his flock (the imperative is in the present, 1
suggesting that this is to be a regular practice) **to be submissive
to rulers and authorities, to show them obedience.** Paul
is possibly glancing at the notoriously turbulent character of
the Cretans, of which Polybius tells us (*Hist.* vi. 46. 9), but the
maxim exactly reflects the teaching he gives elsewhere (1 Tim.
ii. 1 f., and esp. Rom. xiii. 1-7) about the respect Christians owe
to the civil power. He believed that its authority ultimately
stems from God, but he was also concerned, like other N.T.
writers, for the good name of the Church in society.

The Cretans are also **to be ready for any honourable task**
(lit. 'for every good work'). The reference is not, it seems, to
specifically Christian works of charity, as in ii. 14 and elsewhere
in the Pastorals, but to the activities of whatever kind which go
with good citizenship. Christians should be to the fore, as far
as possible, in showing public spirit in their district.

In harmony with this they should make it their aim **to speak 2
evil of no one, not to be quarrelsome but conciliatory,
showing perfect gentleness towards all men.** While the
verse recalls Paul's advice to the Romans (Rom. xii. 18-21) to
live peaceably with all their neighbours, leaving it to God to
avenge injuries, it seeks to draw a more positive picture of the
proper attitude of Christians to the pagan society in which they
are placed. The key to this should be **gentleness** or 'courteous
consideration' (Gk. *praütēs*: AV 'meekness'), a quality which
is often attributed in the N.T. to our Lord (Mt. xi. 29; xxi. 5;
2 Cor. x. 1). He himself praised it in the Beatitudes (Mt. v. 5),
and Paul reckoned it one of the fruits of the Spirit (Gal. v. 23).
The insistence on **all men** (for exactly the same emphasis, cf.
Rom. xii. 17; Gal. vi. 10; Phil. iv. 5) is deliberate. This gentle
courtesy which is so essential a trait of the Christian character
must be exhibited to the world in general, including those who

are most hostile or whom one likes least, and not just to one's fellow-Christians or personal friends.

3 The Cretans, Paul now suggests, have a powerful motive for behaving in a considerate, conciliatory manner to their pagan neighbours, inasmuch as **we ourselves** (with characteristic humility he brackets himself with them: cf. 1 Cor. xv. 9) **were at one time,** i.e. before our conversion, fully as bad as they are now. The Apostle frequently draws a similarly highly coloured contrast between his converts' present position and past experience (Rom. vi. 17 f.; 1 Cor. vi. 9-11; Eph. ii. 2 ff.; Col. iii. 7 f.), and some would argue either that the present passage is modelled on those in the acknowledged letters or that the theme had become conventional in hortatory contexts of this sort. It should be noted, however, as a small pointer to authenticity, that he normally addresses his correspondents directly, whereas here he includes himself in the contrast.

In their unregenerate state, he claims, the Cretans, and Titus and himself no less, had been **foolish,** in the sense of blind to the reality of God and his law; **disobedient,** i.e. contemptuous of God's will, but also probably, in view of 1 above, impatient of authority; **misguided,** a word which suggests that they had left the right track and were the dupes of false guides; **enslaved to all sorts of lusts and pleasures,** in other words, given over to carnal and material things; and as a consequence **passing the time in malice and envy,** i.e. in a thoroughly anti-social manner. Little wonder that they had ended up **detestable** to other people and **loathing one another.**

Paul paints the picture in dark, exaggeratedly self-accusing colours, but it accurately reflects the sincere revulsion which, as a Christian, he felt as he looked back on the kind of life in which he, and other converted Christians like Titus and the Cretans, had previously been involved. It was nothing they had been able to accomplish themselves, but only the divine inter-

4 vention, **when the goodness and generosity of God our Saviour was manifested,** that had been able to extricate them from it.

This verse is parallel to ii. 11 above, and, as there, **was manifested** (the same verb, *epephanē*) signifies the earthly appearance, or incarnate life, of Jesus Christ: see notes on ii. 11;

2 Tim. i. 10. In him the compassionate love of **God our Saviour** (see note on 1 Tim. i. 1) has been suddenly made visible; it has shone out like a new dawn. The noun translated **goodness** (Gk. *chrēstotēs*) is confined to Paul in the N.T. As applied to men it stands for one of the fruits of the Spirit (Gal. v. 22); used of God, it connotes his kindness and pitying concern (Rom. ii. 4; xi. 22; Eph. ii. 7). It is often found coupled, in Greek and Jewish writings (including the LXX), with **generosity** (Gk. *philanthrōpia*: lit. 'affection for men'), and Paul seems here to be echoing a current cliché. The latter term connotes regard or respect for men, humanity, or benevolence. While **generosity** was sometimes attributed to God, inscriptions show that in the Hellenistic age it was the most prized of the stock virtues acclaimed in rulers. This makes it probable that, here as elsewhere in these letters, the Apostle is deliberately modelling his language on that of the contemporary ruler-cults in order to assert the more impressively the claims of Christianity.

It was then, Paul proceeds to explain, when God's loving purpose had been revealed in the incarnation, that **he saved us.** 5 The aorist tense of the verb indicates that it was a once-for-all act; and this salvation, he characteristically adds, was not bestowed **in recognition of any deeds we had ourselves accomplished in righteousness, but in virtue of his own compassion.** For the insistence on the gratuitousness of grace, cf. 2 Tim. i. 9: also Rom. iii. 24; etc. The contrast between **we . . . ourselves** and **his own** is emphatic and intentional. In spite of the fact that the Cretan churches included many converts from Judaism, Paul is probably not thinking so much of the scrupulous observance of the Mosaic law as of upright moral conduct in general (for this sense of righteousness, cf. 1 Tim. vi. 11; 2 Tim. ii. 22; iii. 16). Some detect here a discrepancy with the teaching of the acknowledged letters, arguing that the righteousness of which Paul speaks in them is the righteousness of the law. Even in Romans, however, he makes it clear (cf. ix. 11) that his polemic against works extends beyond the law to good deeds of whatever sort by which men might suppose themselves to acquire merit with God.

This salvation God has mediated to us **by means of the**

washing of rebirth and renewal through the Holy Spirit.
The reference is clearly to baptism, which is also described as a
washing (Gk. *loutron*: lit. 'bath') in Eph. v. 26 (cf. also 1 Cor.
vi. 11). From the grammatical point of view it would be equally
possible to take **renewal** as dependent on the preposition **by
means of** (Gk. *dia*: lit. 'through') and parallel to **washing.**
On this exegesis Paul would be distinguishing two processes, the
washing of baptism proper, and the subsequent restoration
effected by the Holy Spirit. The translation adopted, however,
which takes the **renewal** in close conjunction with the **washing,** preserves the balance of the sentence better; and the fact
that Pauline, and early Christian thought generally, connect the
Spirit closely with baptism is decisive in its favour.

On this interpretation the effect of baptism is first defined in
terms of regeneration (Gk. *paliggenesia*), or **rebirth.** The Stoics
used this word to denote the periodic restorations of the world,
and in Mt. xix. 28 (its only other occurrence in the N.T.) it is
used eschatologically of the new birth of the whole creation in
the messianic age. In the mystery religions it denoted the
mystical rebirth experienced by initiates. Although Paul does
not employ it elsewhere, the conception of baptism as a new
birth was taught explicitly by other N.T. writers (cf. Jn. iii. 3-8;
1 Pet. i. 3; 23), and he himself speaks of Christians dying and
rising to life again with Christ in baptism (Rom. vi. 4) and
henceforth being sons of God (*ib.* viii. 14).

In this way early Christianity interpreted baptism in the
light of current eschatological ideas about the restoration of the
world in the coming messianic age, now believed to have
dawned. This thought is elaborated in Paul's further description
of baptism as a **renewal** (Gk. *anakainisis*: for the word and the
idea, cf. Rom. xii. 2). By this he means the complete trans-
formation, or elevation to a new order of being, which the
Christian undergoes in baptism. He becomes, according to 2
Cor. v. 17, 'a new creation' through his union with Christ,
'freed from the law of sin and death' (Rom. viii. 2). The teaching here is thus thoroughly in harmony with the baptismal
theology of Paul's earlier letters, and the objection that it represents a further 'step towards sacramental religion' than he could
ever have taken is strangely misconceived. The accent of the

passage is wholly on God's mercy and grace, and if faith is not explicitly mentioned this is because (as in 1 Cor. vi. 11, where it is not mentioned either) Paul is concerned with the results of baptism rather than its conditions.

This re-creation is effected **through the Holy Spirit** (the genitive in the original is causative), **which he,** i.e. God the 6 Father, **poured out on us richly through Jesus Christ our Saviour.** The figure of pouring out, applied to the bestowal of the Spirit, is used in Acts ii. 17 (recalling Joel ii. 28); ii. 33. For Paul's belief that the Spirit was imparted in baptism, cf. 1 Cor. vi. 11; xii. 13; 2 Cor. i. 22; Gal. iv. 6; Eph. i. 13. The importance of this idea in the primitive Church is well illustrated by the story of our Lord's baptism, which was regarded as the prototype of the Christian sacrament, and in which the descent of the Spirit figured prominently. It is naturally through Christ (for **our Saviour,** see on 2 Tim. i. 10), as a result of their faith-union with him, that the Spirit is mediated to Christians (cf. Acts ii. 33). Though not explicitly stated elsewhere by Paul, this is implicit in his teaching. The triadic scheme, with its underlying assumption of the cooperation of Father, Son, and Spirit, is also of a kind very familiar in his other letters.

The final purpose of the bestowal of the Spirit is now defined as, **so that having been justified by his grace we might in** 7 **hope become heirs of eternal life.** Paul's point is that, having been justified and their justification having been ratified in baptism, Christians have not only entered upon the new life of the Spirit, but they can confidently look forward to the last day, since their sins have been blotted out by Christ's death and they can therefore anticipate a favourable verdict. As adopted sons, they are **heirs of eternal life** (Rom. viii. 17; Gal. iv. 7); but since their inheritance, or more correctly the full possession of it, lies in the future, they are strictly described as heirs **in hope** (Rom. viii. 24 f.; Eph. i. 13 f.).

So paraphrased, the thought of the passage seems as thoroughly Pauline as the language. Many object that, whereas for Paul justification is the sole necessary condition of becoming **heirs of eternal life,** this is here represented as the result of the pouring of the Spirit upon us in baptism. The argument rests, however, on a misconception of Pauline theology and a false antithesis between justification and baptism. For Paul, as 1 Cor. vi. 11 shows, the two were inseparable aspects of one process. The sacrament was the outward and visible expression of the act of faith by which the Christian accepted Christ, and thus inaugurated the restored relationship with God which justification connotes.

Paul concludes his glowing statement with the formula so familiar in the Pastorals (1 Tim. i. 15; iii. 1; iv. 9; 2 Tim. ii. 11), 8 **This is a trustworthy saying.** Here, as in 1 Tim. iv. 9, though this time without any doubt, it looks back rather than forward. This supports the widely accepted view that all or part of 3-7 is a quotation, probably from some hymn or liturgical piece connected with baptism. In favour of this are (*a*) the rhythm and heightened tone of the passage, and (*b*) the awkward placing of **saved** in the original and the lack of an expressed subject, which both suggest that something may have been bodily inserted. If this is correct, 3 should be excluded from the citation as too akin, in style and content, to what precedes. So too, probably, should 4, since both **was manifested** and **God our Saviour** are in the idiom of the Pastorals. Since both 5a and 7 have a strongly Pauline tang, the extract may well be limited to 5b-6, i.e. the specifically baptismal section. It is perhaps hazardous, however, to try to identify the **trustworthy saying** exactly, for Paul has clearly interwoven thought of his own with whatever traditional or liturgical material he has borrowed.

This brings him back to the theme with which this section of the letter opened, viz. the social duties of Christians. He wants Titus **to insist on these things,** i.e. the truth just expounded about God's free grace and our rebirth in baptism through the Spirit, **so that those who believe in God,** i.e. Christians, **may be careful to busy themselves with good works.** In other words, as a result of his teaching they will have a special incentive to put in practice the principles sketched in 1 f. above. The verb in the infinitive (Gk. *proistasthai*) has the technical meaning 'to practise a profession', and so many (e.g. RVm, RSVm, NEB) prefer the rendering 'be careful to engage in honourable occupations'. This introduces, however, a completely fresh and not strictly relevant theme. The translation adopted, while preserving the underlying metaphor, seems to agree rather better with the context (cf. iii. 1) as well as with the emphasis on deeds of charity in the Pastorals generally.

The advice he has just given Titus, to concentrate on the wonderful truths of the gospel, reminds Paul by contrast of the sectaries and their teaching, and so he embarks on a brief digression aimed at them. **These are admirable truths,** he remarks, referring to the message he has been commending to Titus, **and useful for people.** For this stress on usefulness, cf. 1 Tim. iv. 8; 2 Tim. iii. 16. He should occupy himself with them and **keep clear of foolish speculations, genealogies,** 9 **dissensions, and controversies about the law,** which, so far from being of any value to anyone, **are profitless and futile.** The former adjective looks back to **useful** in 8; for the latter, cf. 1 Tim. i. 6 ('futile verbiage') and Tit. i. 10 ('futile talkers').

The verse gives us a few more, though all too meagre, details to supplement the tantalizingly vague picture of the heresy sketched in i. 10-16. Evidently it was broadly similar to the one which troubled the Ephesian church, and Paul characterizes it in similar terms. For **speculations,** see on 1 Tim. i. 4: cf. also 1 Tim. vi. 4; 2 Tim. ii. 23. For **genealogies,** see on 1 Tim. i. 4; they are probably the same as the Jewish fables mentioned in i. 14. As in 1 Tim. vi. 4 and 2 Tim. ii. 23, concern for these things only results in **dissension** (some MSS give the plural). The Jewish colouring of the heresy is again brought out in **controversies about the law:** for these, see on 1 Tim. i. 8 f.

What is perhaps the chief reason for Paul's anxiety emerges in the next piece of advice, **As for a separatist, have nothing** 10 **to do with him after giving him a first and second warning.** The word translated **separatist** (Gk. *hairetikos*) occurs only here in the Bible. The cognate noun *hairesis* (lit. 'heresy'), however, is used in Acts with the neutral sense of 'party' or 'school of thought' (in v. 17 of the Sadducees; in xv. 5 of the Pharisees; in xxiv. 5 of the Christians), but by Paul with the pejorative meaning of 'partisan cliques' in 1 Cor. xi. 19 and Gal. v. 20. In the second century (e.g. 2 Pet. ii. 1; Ignatius, *Eph.* vi. 2; *Trall.* vi. 1) it came to connote false theological doctrine, and *hairetikos* the holder of such doctrine, i.e. 'heretic' in the modern sense. There is, however, no sound reason for giving *hairetikos* this later meaning in the present context. The sense of **separatist** or 'sectary' fits the passage admirably, and is in full accord with the Apostle's use of *hairesis*. What is disturbing him in Crete is the tendency of the false teachers to form dissident groups, thus dividing the body of Christ.

He therefore counsels Titus to **have nothing to do with** anyone showing signs of separatist inclinations. A close parallel is provided by Rom. xvi. 17, where he bids his correspondents avoid contact with 'those who cause divisions and offences contrary to the teaching you have learned'. Titus is not to be precipitate, however, but before taking action should give the dissident member **a first and second warning.** It is not clear whether public or private admonition is intended, but the principle seems modelled on Christ's advice for dealing with erring brethren (Mt. xviii. 15-17). But if these warnings produce no satisfactory response, Titus need have no hesitation in shunning
11 **a man like that,** for he **can rest assured that** he **is perverted and stands self-condemned in his sin** (lit. 'sins self-condemned'). Paul's point is that, since he has been solemnly warned by the church authorities, he must know that he is doing wrong and his own better judgment must therefore condemn him. Nothing can be done with a man who wilfully persists in dividing the church's unity.

7. PERSONAL MESSAGES AND FAREWELLS.
iii. 12-15

(12) When I send Artemas to you, or Tychicus, do your best to come to me at Nicopolis, for I have decided to winter there. (13) Do your best to help the lawyer Zenas and Apollos on their way; see they lack for nothing. (14) Our people, too, must learn to busy themselves with good works in cases of urgent need; otherwise they will be good for nothing.

(15) All my companions send their regards to you. Give my regards to those who love us in the faith. May grace be with you all.

Like other Paulines, the letter ends with some personal messages and greetings, in this case much briefer than those in 2 Timothy. Supporters of the non-Pauline hypothesis are sometimes prepared to regard them, in whole or in part, as fragments of an authentic letter. Yet it is worth pointing out that the only sentence of a more or less general character (14) takes up the theme of good works which is recurrent in the letter. Those who treat the whole passage as fiction have to face such special difficulties as (*a*) the reference to people, and also a place, nowhere mentioned in Acts or the acknowledged letters, and (*b*) the extraordinarily lifelike touch in 12, suggesting that Paul has not yet decided which of his two associates he is going to send.

The sentence, **When I send Artemas to you, or Tychicus,** 12 **do your best to come to me at Nicopolis,** probably implies that the person dispatched (Paul has evidently not yet made up his mind which it will be) is to take over Titus's responsibilities in Crete. Nothing more is known about **Artemas** (his name may be a shortened form of Artemidorus), although late tradition makes him one of the Seventy-two (Lk. x. 1 ff.) and the first bishop of Lystra. For Paul's old friend **Tychicus,** see on 2 Tim. iv. 12. He clearly regarded him as possessed of the ability and character for leadership, for, whatever the decision now, he probably sent him later to Ephesus to deputize for Timothy.

Several cities in the ancient world were called **Nicopolis,** a name (lit. 'Victory-town') usually given to commemorate a feat of arms. The one intended here is probably Nicopolis in Epirus, on the Greek mainland south of Corfu close to the modern Pereza. Within easy reach of the Adriatic, on the Ambracian Gulf, it had been founded by Octavian (later Augustus Caesar) in 31 B.C. to signalize his triumph over Antony and Cleopatra at Actium. There is nowhere else any report of Paul's having stayed there, but it is much better situated than any of the rival claimants, e.g. Nicopolis in Cilicia, for winter residence. In 1 Tim. iii. 14 Paul says he is hoping to come shortly to Ephesus; his present resolve **to spend the winter** (he is clearly not there yet) at Nicopolis may indicate a change of plan. The notice in 2 Tim. iv. 10 (where see note) that Titus had moved to Dalmatia (i.e. Yugoslavia) fits well enough with Paul's being at Nicopolis when he joined the Apostle.

13   Nothing is known, apart from the present passage, of **the
lawyer Zenas.** His name is Greek (an abbreviation of Zeno-
dorus, lit. 'gift of Zeus'), and, in view of the bias against the
Jewish law shown in the letter, the conjecture that **lawyer** (Gk.
nomikos) implies that he was a convert from Judaism seems
highly unlikely. He was a jurist, and his profession is probably
introduced in order to distinguish him from some other Zenas.
Apollos is almost certainly the well-educated, eloquent Alex-
andrian Jew who received fuller instruction in the faith from
Priscilla and Aquila at Ephesus (Acts xviii. 24), and later
preached at Corinth (1 Cor. i. 12; etc.). The two have evidently
left Paul and are travelling via Crete to an unknown destination;
they are almost certainly the bearers of the letter. The request
to **help** them **on their way** and **see they lack for nothing**
conveys a vivid impression of the generous hospitality shown in
the apostolic age by the little Christian communities to brethren
journeying from one church to another.

His request to Titus, and his certainty that it will be acted
upon, prompt Paul to a renewed insistence on the need for
14   practical Christianity generally. **Our people, too,** he exclaims,
meaning Christians of his and Titus's way of thinking in Crete,
as opposed to the false teachers, **must learn to busy themselves with good works in cases of urgent need.** Unless
they do so, they will be in danger of proving **good for nothing**
(lit. 'unfruitful'). The expression **busy themselves,** etc., consciously re-echoes that used in 8 above (where see note). Many
prefer the translation, 'take up honourable occupations', but
this introduces a theme which has no connexion with the context. Throughout the letter Paul is clearly concerned to stimu-
late **good works** among the Cretans (in harmony with his
teaching in the Pastorals generally, where **good works** connote,
not deeds by which men hope to acquire merit, but deeds of
charity in the fully Christian sense). The theme is naturally
suggested again to his mind by the picture of the help Titus is
going to give Zenas and Apollos. This probably gives the clue
to the meaning of **too.** Paul is in effect saying, 'And not only
you, but our people in general must set an example in the
exercise of charity'. Others interpret the adverb as implying
that Paul wants **Our people,** i.e. the Christians, to show them-

selves even more hospitable than their non-Christian neighbours, the Jews of the dispersion in particular being renowned
for this virtue. But there is no hint of this in the context.

In his final greeting, **All my companions send their** 15
regards to you (lit. 'greet you'), Paul characteristically joins
his associates with himself, although here (as, e.g., in 2 Cor.
xiii. 12) he mentions no names. The request, **Give my regards
to those who love us in the faith,** i.e. those who are true
friends and true Christians, probably conveys the hint that he
does not include the false teachers and separatists in his affectionate greetings. It is impossible to determine whether the words
translated **in the faith** (Gk. *en pistei*) means 'in the Christian
faith', defining the sphere in which their mutual love is exercised (cf. 'in the faith we share' in i. 4), or is simply equivalent
(as the absence of the definite article in the Greek might
suggest) to 'in faith', i.e. loyally. On the whole the former
seems the more likely.

The closing prayer, **May grace be with you all,** where **you**
(Gk. *humōn*) is in the plural, includes the whole community.
As in 1 Tim. vi. 21 and 2 Tim. iv. 22, the plural betrays that
the letter was expected to be read out publicly.

INDEX

Abiram, 186
Actium, 257
Acts of Paul and Thecla, 169, 185
Adam, 59, 63, 68, 179
Aeons, 11, 44, 63
Alexander, 10, 56, 58, 211, 216 f.
Ananias and Sapphira, 58
Angels, 86, 91 f., 122, 127
Antioch, Pisidian, 197, 199
Antitheses, Marcion's, 12, 151
Apocryphal writings, 5, 126
Apollos, 7, 256, 258
Apologists, 22, 24
Apostasy, apostate, 93 f., 169, 180,
    181, 186, 193
Apostleship, Paul's claim to, 39 f.,
    59, 64 f., 153, 158, 164, 225, 226 f.
Apostolic Constitutions, 77, 84, 115,
    117, 128
Apostolic Fathers, 22, 24
Aquila, 43, 220, 221, 258
Aratus, 235
Aristotle, 235
Artemas, 256, 257
Artemis, 43
Ascension of Isaiah, 91
Asceticism, 11, 12, 48, 75 f., 93-97,
    99-101, 148, 185, 236, 238
Asia Minor, 14, 15, 35, 36, 43, 168,
    169
Athletics, illustrations from, 99-102,
    108, 141, 171, 174, 175 f., 208 f.

Baptism, 47, 142-144, 159, 173,
    179 f., 185, 245, 252 f., 254
Barnabas, 57, 80, 106, 123
Bate, H. N., 84
Beatitudes, 249
Bernard, J. H., 91, 141
Beroea, 43
Bishop, monarchical, 14, 73, 74, 108
Bishops. *See* Overseers
Body, Greek view of, 185
Book of Common Prayer, 78
Brindisi, 215

Caesarea, 7, 8, 43, 217
Callimachus, 235
Calvin, J., 248

Caria, 169
Carpus, 211, 215
Catacombs, Roman, 66, 171
Chester Beatty Papyrus, 4
Child-bearing, salvation through,
    59, 69 f.
Christ, death and resurrection of,
    180, 184 f.; essence of Christian
    mystery, 89 f.; faith union with,
    18, 20, 53 f., 153 f., 172, 178, 180,
    200, 252; giver of life, 154; incarna-
    tion of, 90, 145 f., 158, 163, 205,
    244, 250 f.; judge, 205; mediator,
    18, 59, 63; pre-existence of, 90,
    163; saving work of, 63 f., 247;
    Saviour, 155, 163 f., 225, 229, 244,
    246 f., 253; second Adam, 63;
    second coming of, 94, 119, 145 f.,
    163, 193, 210-212, 244, 246;
    spiritual bridegroom, 117
Church, doctrine of, 17, 86-88, 247
Church organization, 4, 13-16, 28,
    30, 70-85, 111-128, 229-233
Cicero, 47, 235
Claudia, 220, 222
Claudius, Edict of, 221
Clement of Alexandria, 4, 85, 235
Clement of Rome, 3, 10, 167 f., 174
Colossian heresy, 12, 45, 236
Conscience, 41, 46 f., 56, 57, 71,
    82, 94, 154, 155
Corinth, Corinthian church, 1, 2, 6,
    7, 35, 77, 94, 95, 140 f., 185, 221,
    258
Corpus Hermeticum, 85
Credal (catechetical) formulae, 17,
    19, 54, 162, 177, 205
Creed, Apostles', 143; baptismal,
    142, 143, 144, 205
Crescens, 211, 213
Crete, Cretan church, 2, 7, 10, 11, 13,
    35, 77, 78, 122, 225-259 *passim*
Cynics, 100, 136
Cyprian, 128
Cyril of Jerusalem, 144

Dalmatia, 211, 213, 257
Damascus, 52
Damascus Document, 74

INDEX

Dathan, 186
Daube, D., 108
Deaconess, 13, 15, 71, 83 f.
Deacons, 13-17, 70, 71 f., 75, 77, 80-85, 115, 124 f., 174, 175, 230, 240
Decalogue, 50, 112 f.
Demas, 8, 210, 212 f.
Demetrius, 58
Devil (Satan), 56, 58, 70, 79, 80, 94, 119 f., 188, 191 f.
Diana, 43
Dibelius, M., 53, 86, 90
Didache, 5, 72
Didascalia, 84, 115
Diogenes Laertius, 137
Doxology, 55 f., 146, 147, 220
Dress, female, 59, 66 f.
Dualism, 11, 95, 96

Easton, B. S., 114, 138, 154, 167, 173
Elders (presbyters), 13-16, 71 f., 75, 104, 107 f., 110, 115, 121-130, 159, 229, 230 f.
Elect, the, 178, 226
Elymas, 58
Emperor worship, 20, 40, 43, 146, 246, 251
Ephesus, Ephesian church, 2, 3, 6, 7, 8, 10, 13, 15, 16, 39-223 passim, 233, 235, 255, 258
Epimenides of Cnossus, 235
Epiphanius, 213
Epirus, 35, 257
Epistle of Aristeas, 139
Erastus, 7, 220, 221
Essenes, 95
Eternal life, 16, 52, 55, 101, 139, 141 f., 149, 153, 161, 225, 227, 228, 248, 253 f.
Eubulus, 220, 222
Eunice, 154, 157
Eusebius, 9, 10, 35, 128, 213
Evangelist, 207
Eve, 59, 68 f.
Excommunication, 58, 184, 216 f.

Fables (myths), 11, 12, 41, 44 f., 48, 97, 99, 233, 236
Faith, 17, 18, 20, 40 f., 46, 47, 51, 53 f., 56, 57 f., 59, 65, 69, 70, 82, 85, 97, 99, 102, 104, 132, 138, 139, 140 f., 154, 157, 167, 197, 198, 225, 226, 239 f., 254
Fall, 179

False teaching, teachers, 2, 3, 10-12, 19, 30, 43, 44-49, 60, 65, 87 f., 93-97, 102, 132-138, 148, 150-152, 181-188, 189, 195-197, 198 f., 200 f., 206 f., 228, 229, 233-238, 239, 255 f., 258, 259
Felix, 217
Festus, 9
Food, abstinence from, 11, 93, 95 f., 236 f.
'Fragments hypothesis', 5, 8, 19, 28-30, 32, 210, 211, 212, 217, 221

Galatia, 213
Gamaliel, 48
Gaul, 211, 213
Gealy, F. D., 32, 53, 54, 103, 140, 158
Genealogies, 11, 41, 44 f., 248, 255
Glory, the divine, 86, 91 f., 146 f., 178 f., 244, 246 f.
Gnōsis, 11, 12, 151 f.
Gnostics, Gnosticism, 4, 11, 12, 28, 44 f., 60, 63, 70, 95, 150, 151, 164, 185, 236, 237
God, conception of, 18, 20, 42, 51, 87, 93, 96, 139, 146 f., 198, 202 f., 225, 227 f., 244, 246 f., 248, 251. See 'God our Saviour'
'Godliness', etc. (Gk. eusebeia), 17, 22, 59, 61, 86, 89, 97, 99 f., 111, 113, 132, 134, 135, 139, 140, 192, 195, 225, 226 f.
'God our Saviour', 20, 39, 40, 59, 62, 102, 162, 163, 225, 228, 239, 243, 248 f., 250, 254
Good works, 17, 18, 20, 59, 67, 111, 116 f., 147, 148, 181, 188, 238, 244, 247, 248, 249, 254, 258
Gospel of Truth, 4
Grace, 18, 39, 41, 51, 53, 54, 102, 106, 141, 149, 152, 158, 161, 162 f., 171, 172, 210, 225, 228, 244 f., 251, 253, 254, 256, 259
Grace at meals, 96 f.
'Gravity' (Gk. semnotēs), 17, 59, 61, 70, 78, 238, 242
Greetings, formulae of, 2, 21, 36, 39-41, 152, 153 f., 220-223, 225-229, 257-259
Guthrie, D., 54, 102

Haggadah, 44
Hair, women's, 59, 66 f.
Harnack, A. von, 34

Harrison, P. N., 22, 24, 28 f.
Hermetic literature, 139
Hermas, 117, 136, 139
Hermogenes, 168, 169
Hippocrates, 129
Hippolytus, 105
Holy Spirit, 18, 19, 28, 46, 47, 48, 57, 90, 93, 94, 101, 105, 106, 107, 158, 159, 167 f., 203, 248, 252-254
Hope, 97, 102, 225, 227, 244, 246, 248, 253
Hymenaeus, 10, 56, 58, 186, 184, 188
Hymns, excerpts from, 89-93, 161 f., 179-181, 246, 254

Iconium, 169, 199
Ignatius of Antioch, 2, 14, 28, 80, 83, 112, 125, 143, 177, 201, 255
Irenaeus, 4, 27, 44, 45, 104, 185, 201, 222

Jambres, 192, 196 f., 200
James, M. R., 169
Jannes, 192, 196 f., 200
Jeremias, J., 45, 56, 92 f., 122, 170
Jerome, 4
Jerusalem, 1, 6, 7, 80, 123, 214, 221
Jesus, words of, 94, 133 f.
John Chrysostom, 98, 179, 183
Josephus, 95, 196, 201, 203, 234
Joshua, 106
Jubilees, Book of, 44
Judaism, 12, 45, 61, 74, 96, 112, 113, 114, 123, 196, 201, 202
Judaizers, 11, 45, 48, 65
Justification, 16, 248, 253 f.
Justin, 143

Kingdom, Christ's, 204, 205; God's, 211, 220
'Knowledge of the truth', 17, 59, 62, 188, 190, 192, 196, 225, 226
Koinē, 25, 27, 48, 54, 61, 62, 67, 192, 202, 204
Korah, 186

Last days, disasters of, 93 f., 192-197, 206
Law, Jewish, 11, 12, 18, 20, 41 f., 44, 48-51, 126 f., 156, 236, 248, 251, 255
Laying on of hands, 13, 98, 106-108, 128, 158, 159
Lectra, 169

Lietzmann, H., 34
Linus, 220, 222
Lock, W., 180
Lois, 154, 157
Love, 41, 46, 51, 53 f., 57, 97, 104, 139, 140 f., 158, 160, 238, 239
Luke, 15, 104, 123, 126, 211, 213 f.
Lydia, 169
Lystra, 1, 197, 199, 257

Macedonia, 2, 6, 29, 35, 36, 41, 42, 43, 215
Magic, 11, 196, 200, 234
Malta, 7
'Manifestation' (Gk. epiphaneia), 18, 22, 40, 90, 139, 145 f., 158, 163, 204, 246 f., 248, 250 f., 254
Manual of Discipline, 74
Marcion, Marcionism, 4, 12, 27, 28, 151 f.
Mark, 7, 180, 211, 214
Marriage, 11, 17, 75 f., 84, 95, 116, 119, 236
Mary, Blessed Virgin, 69
Mediator, 18, 59, 63
Menander (comic poet), 235
Menander (Gnostic), 185
Miletus, 7, 8, 9, 35, 123, 156, 220, 221 f.
Military metaphors, 50, 57, 171, 174 f.
Ministry. See Church organization; Deacons; Elders; Overseers
Money, 70, 77, 81 f., 132, 137 f., 140, 182, 194
Moses, 18, 48, 49, 63, 106, 140, 147, 186, 192, 196, 197, 226, 247
Muratorian Canon, 4, 10
Musonius, 137
Mysia, 169
Mystery, 70, 82, 86, 88-90
Mystery religions, 252
Myths. See Fables (myths)

Nero, 9, 34, 35, 177, 219
Nicopolis, 2, 7, 29, 35, 213, 257

Octavian, 257
Old Testament, 12, 40, 44 f., 46, 48, 49, 112-114, 148, 163, 189, 196, 201-204, 216, 226, 227, 247
Olympic Games, 176
Onesiphorus, 168, 169-171, 221
Ophites, 45

INDEX

Orantes, 66

Ordination, 98, 106-108, 127 f.; Timothy's, 141 f., 144, 159, 172, 173

Orphans, 116 f.

Orthodoxy, 17, 19, 44, 134, 150, 172, 183, 233

Overseers (Bishops), 13-16, 70-80, 81, 83, 84, 85, 108, 115, 117, 124 f., 174, 175, 190, 191, 229, 230-233, 234

Parchments, 211, 215 f.

Parousia (Second coming), 94, 119, 145 f., 163, 193, 210-212, 244, 246

Pastorals, authorship of, 4 f., 6-34; date of, 34-36; early attestation of, 2 f.; language of, 21-27, 31; mutual relations of, 2, 34-36; style of, 4, 21-27, 31, 48, 51, 54, 61, 62, 155, 160

Paul, Caesarean imprisonment of, 7, 8; conversion of, 40, 52, 53; death of, 8, 9, 10, 34 f., 205, 208; journey to Spain of, 10, 35, 36; Roman imprisonments of, 1, 2 f., 6, 7, 9, 10, 33 f., 36, 78, 156, 161, 177, 212, 214 f., 217-220

Pausanias, 176

Pergamum, 240

Personalia, 29, 31, 32 f., 36, 157 f., 220-223, 256-259

Peter, 222

Pharisees, 255

Philetus, 181, 184, 188

Philippi, 35, 43

Philo, 47, 51, 136, 137, 139, 193, 196, 201, 203, 234

Phoebe, 84, 117

Phrygia, 169

Phygelos, 168, 169

Plato, 45, 66, 110, 235

Pliny the Younger, 84

Plutarch, 129

Pneumatics, 13, 14, 71, 106

Polycarp of Smyrna, 3, 27, 112

Polybius, 104, 235, 249

Pontius Pilate, 139, 143 f.

Pontus, 221

Prayer, 56, 59, 60-62, 65 f., 96 f., 114, 156, 170 f., 189; prayer for the dead, 170 f.

Presbyter. *See* Elder

Prisca, Priscilla, 43, 220, 221, 258

Prophets, prophecy, 14, 15, 56, 57, 71, 98, 106

Pseudonymity, 5 f., 31 f., 33, 99, 103, 152, 157, 168, 174, 199

Pseudo-Philo, 44

Pudens, 222

Qumran sect, 49, 53, 73, 94, 196

Ransom, 59, 63 f., 244, 247

Rebirth (of baptism), 252

Resurrection, 11, 58, 151, 164, 177, 180, 181, 184 f.

Rome, Roman church, 2, 7, 8, 9, 10, 29, 35, 156, 168-170, 212-218, 221

'Rule of faith', 150

Sadducees, 255

Salvation, 59, 67, 69, 164, 172, 178 f., 198, 201 f., 220, 244. *See* Saviour

Sanhedrin, 217

Satan. *See* Devil (Satan)

Saviour (of God), 20, 39, 40, 59, 62, 97, 102, 158, 162, 163, 225, 228, 239, 243, 248, 250, 254; (of Christ), 40, 158, 163, 244, 246 f., 248, 253

Scandal, avoidance of, 70, 79 f., 130, 131, 138, 241

Scott, E. F., 54, 58, 82, 157, 245

Scripture, 105, 121, 126, 198, 201-204. *See* Old Testament

Second Coming. *See* Parousia

'Secretary hypothesis', 25-27, 31, 155

Seneca, 47, 136

Seven, The, 81, 83

Simon Magus, 185

Slaves, slavery, 17, 130-132, 238 f., 243

'Sober', 'self-disciplined' (Gk. *sōphrōn*, etc.), 17, 59, 66, 76, 158, 160, 229, 232, 238, 239, 241, 242, 244, 245

Soul, 185

'Sound'. *See* 'Wholesome' (or 'Sound')

Spain, 10, 35, 36

Spicq, C., 126, 193

State, attitude to, 17, 59, 60 f., 248, 249

Stephanas, household of, 72

Stephen, 81

Stipends, ministerial, 13, 121, 124-126, 135, 176

Stoics, Stoicism, 46, 53, 109, 136, 137, 138, 252

Suffering, 17, 158, 161 f., 164, 165, 176 f., 178, 180, 197, 199, 200
Teaching, teachers, 17, 44, 50, 70, 76, 97, 105, 121, 124, 229, 232 f., 238, 242; 'sound teaching', 17, 42, 50, 132, 134, 204, 206, 229, 232 f., 238, 239
Teetotalism, 11, 95, 129
Tertius, 25
Tertullian, 4, 28, 44, 105, 112
Theodore of Mopsuestia, 213
Theodoret, 213
Thessalonica, 1, 43, 213
'The truth', 59, 62, 93, 96, 135, 188, 190, 192, 196, 225, 226
Timothy, 1-3, 6, 7, 10, 13, 14, 27, 28, 31, 32, 39-223 *passim*, 248, 257
Titus, 1 f., 7, 10, 13, 14, 28, 29, 31, 122, 213, 225-259 *passim*
Tradition, apostolic, 17, 19, 76, 167, 172-4
Troas, 7, 35, 215, 216
Trophimus, 7, 221, 222
'Trust' (Gk. *parathēkē*), 149, 150, 158, 165-167

'Trustworthy saying', 22, 51, 54, 70, 72 f., 97, 101, 172, 179, 248, 254
Turner, C. H., 84
Tychicus, 211, 214, 256, 257

Valentinus, 4, 11, 44
Vices, catalogues of, 49 f., 194 f., 232
Vienne, 213

'Wholesome' (*or* 'sound'), 17, 42, 50, 132, 133 f., 158, 166, 204, 206, 229, 232, 233, 236, 238, 239, 240, 242
Widows, 16, 111-121
Wine (drink), 11, 70, 76 f., 81, 84, 122, 128 f., 238, 240
Women, 192, 195, 196, 238, 240, 241; women deacons, 71, 83 f.; women's dress, 59, 66 f.; place in church, 66, 67-70
World rulers, 12
Worship, 59-62, 71, 105

Zenas, 258
Zeus, 176, 235